Other Avon Discus Books by
The Western Writers of America

WATER TRAILS WEST

THE WOMEN WHO MADE THE WEST

The Western Writers of America

 A DISCUS BOOK/PUBLISHED BY AVON BOOKS

AVON BOOKS
A division of
The Hearst Corportion
959 Eighth Avenue
New York, New York 10019

The Doubleday & Company, Inc. edition contains the
following Library of Congress Cataloging in Publication
Data:

Western Writers of America.
The Women Who Made the West.

Bibliography.
Includes Index.
1. Women—The West—Bibliography.
2. Fronteer and pioneer life—The West.
3. The West—Social Conditions.
I. Title.
HQ1438.A17W47 1980   305.4'0978

First Discus Printing, November, 1981

ACKNOWLEDGMENTS

Western Writers of America is a nonprofit organization of professional authors and screenwriters whose purpose is to perpetuate and disseminate the history and ideals of the American West. Since 1953 they have put together thirty-five collections of the best short stories, novelettes and factual articles written by their members that have been published in the United States; many of them have also appeared in British editions and have been translated into Spanish, Portuguese, Norwegian, German and other foreign languages.

The Women Who Made the West, our thirty-sixth volume, is a unique fraternal writing effort, each chapter carefully researched, written and contributed by a woman member of WWA. In March 1978, when we advised a few members that Doubleday had approved the concept of a book about little-known but noteworthy nineteenth-century women who had contributed to our Western heritage, there was enthusiastic response, suggestions of subjects and offers to write a chapter. During the WWA annual convention at El Paso in June 1978, we held a planning conference attended by the women members and our Doubleday editor, Jim Menick, and appointed Nellie Snyder Yost as the WWA editor, to be assisted by regional editors Judy Alter, Roberta Cheney and Valerie Mathes.

Over the next six months, by mail and phone, these ladies contacted other women members, solicited brief biographies of women who might be included, arranged for several sample chapters to be written, and then selected and assigned the eighteen chapters listed on the contents page. It was a tremendous task, magnificently accomplished.

Western Writers of America thank all of the contributors for the text of their chapters and the illustrations they supplied, and we particularly thank Nellie Snyder Yost, Judy Alter, Roberta Cheney and Valerie Mathes for putting this book together.

We also wish to thank:

Harold Kuebler for his encouragement from inception of the project to his announcement at our Boulder, Colorado convention in June 1979, that Doubleday was offering a contract for its publication; *Jim Menick,* our Doubleday editor, for his advice and helpful direction; *Donald Duke* for his assistance at the El Paso planning conference.

And we owe special thanks to the many members who generously responded to our editors' requests for suggestions, researched and supplied capsule biographies, and some of whom speculatively wrote chapters from which the final selection was made:

Jean M. Burroughs	Dorothy M. Johnson	Jane Pattie
Doris Cerveri	Kay L. McDonald	D. Parker Skold
Alice Cramie	Darlis Miller	Agnes Wright Spring
Margaret Elly Felt	Hazel Emery Mills	Starley Talpot
Maurine S. Fletcher	James W. Montgomery	Lela Waltrip
Kay Graber	Annie Stillion	Katherine Wright
Edith Thompson Hall		

We also thank the following institutions and individuals who granted permission to use photographs they supplied:

Mrs. J. D. Clark	Black Range Museum
Mrs. Esper Clary	The *Denver Post*
Patty Eaton	Eastern Washington State Historical Society
Paul Frison	Utah State Historical Society

We hope that we have not missed anyone who helped create *The Women Who Made the West*—if so, thanks to you, too—with apologies!

September 1979

August Lenniger, Anthologies
Western Writers of America

Contents

CONTENTS

Introduction

Women were scarce in the American West as it expanded from the Mississippi River to the Pacific Ocean during the nineteenth century. In all this vast region, the census of 1870 listed 172,000 women over twenty years of age as compared to 385,000 men.

In 1869 Wyoming became the first territory to pass a suffrage law. Utah soon followed as Brigham Young hoped that woman suffrage would quell Eastern critics of Mormon society. Colorado, Idaho, Washington and California capitulated next. These were political rather than chivalrous acts, designed to entice enough women into the territories to bring the population up to statehood status. As late as 1914, only New Mexico and Nebraska still withheld the vote from women. With the passage of the Nineteenth Amendment in 1920, universal suffrage became the law of the United States.

In the Eastern states, women had to fight even harder to win this privilege. Instrumental in winning suffrage for all women were the crusaders Susan B. Anthony and Carrie Chapman Catt, well known and much written about in the East. Paralleling them in the West was Abigail Scott Duniway, who in 1871 set up a woman's suffrage newspaper, *The New Northwest* in Lafayette, Oregon to promote the cause. She wrote: "Half the women were overworked, the other half frivolous; all were expected to keep their place." Accordingly, the 1870 census listed no women doctors or lawyers and did not include housewives and prostitutes. There were, however, 21,000 gainfully and reputably employed women in the West. 11,000 of them were domestic servants who were paid very little; the rest were teachers, laundresses, seamstresses and milliners.

Except for California, all the universities then opening in the West were coeducational; California shortly followed suit. With the bars let down, the 1890 census could report 29 woman lawyers, 37 college professors, 85 journalists, and a fair number of physicians, all practicing in the West.

For over a century before they achieved liberation, many women longed to follow careers traditionally reserved for men. As proven in this book, some women attained their goals very early and performed well—even brilliantly. From their stories we gain a vivid picture of the tightly structured, constrained status of women's position of the nineteenth century and can appreciate something of the struggle that won them the freedom to be themselves.

In her "Great Western" chapter, Nancy Hamilton writes: "When it comes to pioneer women of the West, the stereotype is a tiny lady in calico dress and sunbonnet, perhaps holding a rifle, surrounded by a flock of children." There were some of course, but also many who contributed richly to the development of the American West in capacities other than those of wife, mother and homemaker. As such adventurous ladies as Sacajawea, Elizabeth Custer, Carry Nation, Cattle Kate and Calamity Jane have been dealt with in numerous books and articles, our chapters cover eighteen carefully selected women, most of them little known outside their own localities, whose achievements either helped liberate women from their traditional place in the social scheme or elevated their status in general.

In the following chapters you will find women who went West as brides, typical ranch women including some two-gun girls, the colorful careers of women miners, stagecoach drivers, hotel owners, practical nurses and doctors, journalists, missionaries and crusaders for women's rights. They all helped to shape the West.

On behalf of Western Writers of America, the editors and authors of this "all-woman" book take pride in presenting it for the entertainment and information of its readers. We believe it authentically and graphically portrays the struggles and endeavors of women to be themselves, to live their lives as they wished or as they had to, without censure or condemnation. In a very true sense, they led the way for the liberation of all women and made possible the freedom women enjoy today.

Nellie Snyder Yost
September 1979

THE WOMEN WHO MADE THE WEST

1

Angel of the Pecos

by EVE BALL

During the pioneering years, many young women headed into the unknown, entrusting their futures not only to new husbands but to a new country reportedly filled with danger and hardship. Barbara Jones, reared in the mountains of Virginia and a bride at sixteen, had never known wealth or ease; but what she lacked in school-book education, she more than made up for in sound common sense and an alert, inquiring mind. Her considerable contributions to her part of the West as nurse, doctor, teacher and influence for good earned her the respected title of "Angel of the Pecos."

N.S.Y.

Barbara Jones sat up in bed and listened intently. In the absence of her husband, Heiskell, she was always more alert to unusual situations. And there was, she knew, someone or something outside. An Apache would have called to her; she would have heard a cowboy's horse. The dogs hadn't barked. It was not her imagination—there *was* something outside.

She arose, drew on a robe and went into the huge room that served the Jones family for living, dining, cooking quarters and trading post. By the glow of the fireplace, she took her Winchester from the antlers above the mantel and thrust it through the narrow slit in the thick adobe wall. That opening served as both ventilation and porthole. In the bright moonlight, she could see nobody;

then suddenly a movement in the chaparral attracted her attention. Without calling her sons, Barbara Jones opened the door and drew a bead on the bushes. "Come out of it, and come with your hands up!" she ordered.

A slight, thin boy arose slowly, lifted his arms, stumbled, and came painfully toward her. Barbara leaned her rifle against the door and ran to help him into the house. She put him into a chair in front of the fireplace and added wood to the embers, then turned to him and saw that he was struggling to remove a boot. She knelt and carefully drew it from his foot—a blistered, bleeding foot. Without a word, she pulled off his other boot. His feet had not got into that condition on a horse. He had walked, and he had walked a long way.

As she lifted a kettle of water to the crane above the fire, the lad offered an explanation: "Went down the bank of Rocky Arroyo to fill my canteen. Apaches jumped my mount and pack horse; left me afoot. Hid till dark and walked all night." Barbara nodded, then filled a wooden basin with warm water, slipped a piece of lye soap into it and told him to soak his feet As he obeyed, she asked when he had last eaten.

"Yesterday mornin'. I was gettin' ready to make a fire and needed fresh water."

The woman filled a tin cup with warm milk and offered it. The lad shook his head and said he didn't like milk: "You may have some food after you've drunk this. By breakfast time you'll feel better." When he again refused she asked, "Do you want me to hold your nose and pour it down you?" He shook his head, took the cup and gulped greedily.

"Slow, sip it slow," Barbara commanded. "You'll make yourself sick."

When he had obeyed and returned the cup, she handed him a coarse towel. Then, carrying his boots and a lighted candle, she led the way across the storeroom and opened a door. By the flickering light, he could see a bed in each corner of the room. Barbara set the candle down on a keg, turned back the blankets on a bed and said, "Sammie's alone. Get in with him. My other boys sleep here, too. See you at breakfast."

John, the eldest son, brought the stranger to the long table. His face was not so pale and drawn as it had been in the night and, except for his protruding teeth, he was a nice-looking lad. Then her eyes fell to the six-shooters at his belt. Two! Well, every man carried one; and, if on horseback, a saddle gun, also. He had probably lost his short rifle with his horses.

"I see you've met John," Barbara said.

"Yes, ma'am. And my name is Billy—Billy Bonney."

"Nice lad," she thought. "Has good manners even if he doesn't like milk." It was not until a year or so later that he was called Billy the Kid.

Back in Virginia, Barbara, at sixteen, had agreed to marry Heiskell Jones—but not until she had exacted a promise from him that he would never fight a duel or take the life of a human being. That was the period when a man's word was as good as his bond, and neither had known that a war was brewing between the North and the South, or that he might have to fight in that war.

They lived in the mountains, and many of their good neighbors were Northern sympathizers. To avoid having to take sides, or perhaps having to fight against their beloved Virginia, they packed as many of their belongings as they could into their wagon. With Barbara driving and Heiskell herding their few cattle and horses behind the wagon, they left for Iowa.

The severe winters there encouraged them to seek a milder climate near Denver. But killings there were so frequent that they were impelled to search for a home where their two sons and their daughter, Minnie, might be reared in an atmosphere of friendliness rather than violence. They headed south and on the third day out overtook an itinerant newspaper reporter, on foot and carrying a carpetbag. He introduced himself as Ash (Ashman) Upson and, at their invitation, joined them. He said he had made an earlier trip to Lincoln County, New Mexico, and advised them to settle there. The winters were mild, the people friendly. Mostly Mexicans, except for the soldiers at Fort Stanton, they were kind and hospitable. There were Apaches but, unless mistreated, they molested no one.

Barbara had read reports to the contrary, but she reflected her mother's philosophy: if one takes a good neighbor with him he finds good neighbors wherever he goes.

Because the feet of the two milk cows and the oxen became sore from traveling, the Joneses made frequent stops, especially after reaching the Pecos. Upson explained that the water was alkaline and laxative, but it was *water,* and all travel was along the river. Moreover, there was good grass and plenty of wood. The wood was mostly mesquite roots, which had to be grubbed from the earth, so the Joneses burned buffalo chips, which made a good fire. There were antelope on the plains, channel catfish in the river, and the climate was delightful and healthy.

The little party arrived at what is now the site of Roswell, New Mexico, on July 4, 1866, and camped on the Hondo. Both Barbara and Heiskell liked the country so much that they decided to remain there. Ash Upson, whose destination was Lincoln, the county seat of almost one fourth of New Mexico Territory, stayed with them long enough to help construct a primitive house of the type the Mexicans used. Their *chosa,* built on the bank of the little stream, consisted of one large room with a fireplace. The only opening, facing the river, was covered by a cowhide. Then, upon the arrival of a wagon train coming upriver from Horsehead Crossing, Upson left for Lincoln.

The Joneses met their first Apache a little later when John came in to tell his mother there were buzzards circling over the Pecos not far away. That meant that something was wounded. Had it been dead, the birds would already have alighted to feed upon it. Hoping it might be a buffalo, Barbara and her son saddled John's horse and hurried to the spot beneath the circling birds. They found a young Apache with a broken leg. Pointing to tracks in the sand, he indicated that his horse had run away toward the mountains.

Kneeling beside the young Indian, Barbara examined his leg, broken above the knee and with the lower section extended at an oblique angle. She knew that setting it would be very painful. The Apache was watching her closely, and when she pointed to a clump of sprouts on the riverbank, and then to the knife at his belt, he nodded and handed it to her, hilt first. He watched as John cut and peeled the sprouts. Meantime Barbara had slipped behind a bush to remove one of her petticoats, which she tore into strips.

"This is going to hurt terribly," she told her son, "and we don't want to have to do it but once. You get hold of his foot, and when I give the word, pull his leg straight. No matter what he does, you hold it straight while I wrap it and tie the sticks to it so the ends of the bones can't separate."

To their great relief, the Apache braced himself on his elbows, gritted his teeth, pushed himself back and made no sound. When the operation was done, all three relaxed. John then used his hat to carry water to the Indian. Then they lifted him onto his one good leg, boosted him onto John's horse, face down, and began the three-mile walk back to the *chosa,* where Heiskell helped them carry him to a pallet in front of the fireplace.

For three weeks they nursed and cared for Magoosh, the Apache. When he indicated by signs that he was ready to return to his tribe, they began to debate ways of getting him there. "I see no way but for us to lend him a horse," Barbara said.

"And never see it again," replied Heiskell.

"He can take mine," John said. "He'll turn it loose, and it will come home."

Heiskell doubted this, but Barbara packed food for their guest and John saddled his horse. The Indian rode away. Four days later, the horse returned with the saddle and bridle—and a beautiful bow and quiver of arrows tied to its mane. That took care of the Apaches as far as the Jones family was concerned.

Shortly after Magoosh left, Tom Jones was born. He was the first Anglo child to be born on the Pecos in the part of old Lincoln County that is now Chavez. Before the end of their second year on the Hondo, the family moved to Picacho, a tiny Mexican settlement farther up the river. Their new home was an empty adobe house of two large rooms. Its builder had abandoned it three years previously, and no one knew where he was. The family received a warm welcome from their Mexican neighbors, some of whom spoke a few words of English.

When one of them killed deer or cattle, he brought meat. A woman donated a mortar and pestle and taught Barbara to grind corn into meal. She also brought her garden seeds: squash, pumpkin, *frijoles* (pinto beans) and a vegetable new to the Joneses—chili pepper—and taught them how to use it. It became one of their favorite foods.

Barbara had neither flour, sugar, coffee nor soda, and she needed fabric for replacing their worn-out clothing. There was a trading post at Fort Stanton, only two days distant by wagon, but the family had no money, and as yet nothing to barter or exchange. The neighbors wore buckskin garments, but Barbara had no skins, nor did she know how to tan them. Again the neighbors came to her rescue, until a corn crop enabled the Joneses to trade with the Apaches for buckskin. It was not long before Barbara not only supplied her family, but was making fringed trousers and shirts for men going through the country. After she added gauntlets to her stock, she had a constant market for them.

After a time, Heiskell and Jim were offered work at Fort Stanton, which necessitated a move closer to the post. There had been no surveying done in the area and, if land were sold, the purchaser could obtain only a quitclaim deed, conveying simply the seller's interest. So, desiring to retain possession of the farm on the Hondo, the family decided to leave John, almost seventeen and dependable, to care for their cattle and horses while the rest moved to the mouth of Eagle Creek, a tributary of the Ruidoso. John would be alone on the Hondo, but would be only 35 miles from them. They could visit him occasionally.

On the new site they found another abandoned adobe, good water, wood and grass. The men worked only two days each week. Each Thursday evening they rode the 10 miles up Devil's Canyon to the fort. Friday morning they butchered a week's allowance of beef for the Apaches and cut it into portions according to the sizes of the families. Saturdays were Issue Days, and the building from which the beef was distributed was the Issue House.

The Apaches lined up alphabetically, filed past a table and were given their supply of meat. Few spoke any English, but Jim quickly learned some of their highly inflected language, especially the nouns. So friendly were the Indians that Heiskell sometimes took one of his younger sons along and let him spend the night with an Apache family.

When the Indians learned that Barbara Jones was a "medicine woman," they would occasionally take their sick children to her for treatment. Though she feared the results, should a patient die, she never refused to do what she could to give relief. Providentially, all recovered.

After some trouble with the officers, the agent, Frederick Godfroy, moved his headquarters to Mescalero. That meant a 30-mile trip for the Jones men and, once again, the family moved—to Dowlin's Mill on the Ruidoso. The men still had to ride 20 miles to their work, but the Dowlins offered Barbara the use of a *chosa* and a small salary for managing a trading post they maintained there, close by their sawmill.

Dowlin's Mill was a busy place. Many people came for lumber and other supplies: whiskey, tobacco, ammunition and food, in that order. Often the customers and travelers stayed at the mill for three or four days at a time. While there, they heard Barbara's children say "Yes, ma'am," or "No, ma'am," as was the custom in Virginia. Soon everyone was addressing her as "Ma'am Jones."

Two more sons were born to Barbara at Dowlin's Mill. Busy though she was, she taught all her children to cook and do housework, thus freeing herself to attend to the trading post and to make buckskin garments for sale. There was constant need, too, for her services in caring for the ill or wounded; the surgeon at Fort Stanton was seldom available to minister to civilians, especially Apaches and Mexicans.

One morning Ma'am Jones decided to ride down to the Hondo to take food and clothing to John. Marion Turner, who had spent the night at Dowlin's, asked to accompany her and the children. With her baby in her arms and five-year-old Sammie astride the pack mule, they rode down the Ruidoso. When they heard a wild turkey gobbling on the mountain, Turner found and killed it.

"I'll roast it for supper," Ma'am said. "With corn bread and onion stuffing, it's John's favorite food."

John was not about when they arrived at the *chosa,* but his mother knew he would come in from his work at suppertime, so she went ahead preparing the bird for the spit in the fireplace. Shortly before sunset, a rough-looking, unkempt man came to the door, and asked for John. Ma'am told him, "He hasn't come in yet, but he should soon. Get down and have supper with us."

But when John came in, instead of his customary hearty welcome, he seemed unhappy at finding Ma'am and the children there and greeted the stranger with a curt "Howdy, Riley." The meal was eaten in almost total silence. Even Turner seemed remote and disapproving. The meal finished, the stranger said, "I've come to settle that business, John."

"Suits me," John replied, then turned to Turner and said, "Take Ma'am and the children down to the river." Turner nodded, picked the baby from the bed, took Ma'am's arm, steered her out the door and down the steep bank of the Hondo.

Sixty years later, Sam Jones said, "I reckon they forgot me; anyway, I stayed and seen the show. John and the other fellow walked out the door, with John in front, and stood back to back.

They must 'a' planned it previous. They began countin', slow-like, and at each count they took a long step forward. When they got to ten, they whirled and fired. Riley fell and John bent over him. I ran to John. I heard Riley gasp and say, 'Oh, John, I forced this on you.' Then he lay still.

"Next thing I knowed, Ma'am came. She bent over Riley and said he was dead. She asked Turner if he knew who the man's friends were. Turner said he reckoned he did, if he had any, and Ma'am asked him to go get them and have them bring a wagon to get him. Turner nodded, and then Ma'am said, 'And ask them to come unarmed. Tell them I said so.' Then she turned to John and he explained the trouble.

" 'Riley ordered me to get off this land,' he said. 'Said he was goin' to take it. I told him over my dead body. He wanted to shoot it out then, but I owed the Romeros some work and wanted to pay them first. So he said he'd come today.' "

At once Ma'am sent John to round up the cattle, horses and pack mules from the Hondo land, while she gathered and stacked the contents of the house. Packing the mules as quickly as they could, they set out for Dowlin's Mill. There they packed all they could into their two wagons and turned their backs on New Mexico. With Ma'am driving the four-mule team and Heiskell on the near side of the wheelers of the six-ox team, they headed out. The older boys, on horseback, followed with the cattle and the remuda.

Ma'am Jones hadn't left the violence of Denver years ago just to see her sons embroiled in a New Mexico feud. When they had crossed Apache Pass, she pointed her wagon tongue West and headed for Arizona. Heiskell had offered no opposition because of the promise he had made before marrying, and anyway, he was as loath as she to have John mixed up in gun trouble.

Two years later (1877), the Jones family returned to the Pecos country. Arizona had been a disappointment and they had gone on from there to the grasslands near the fort that was the forerunner of San Angelo, Texas. But nowhere had they found country that suited them as well as the one they had left, so they returned to the Pecos, forded it at Horsehead Crossing and followed it north.

At the confluence of Seven Rivers and the Pecos, they were

amazed to find a large vacant adobe building. Its thirty-inch walls and roof parapet indicated its construction as a fort; its counters and shelves, a trading post. That night Ash Upson, the foot traveler they had picked up south of Denver some years before, came to their camp. He was surveying land and told them that people who made a first filing on any tract had homestead rights. If they beat all others to the Las Cruces Land Office, the land was theirs. Since the big adobe building near which they were camped had been abandoned three years earlier, Heiskell had only to file on the site and take possession.

"But we have a place on the Hondo," Heiskell reminded him.

"Not anymore," Ash said. "Someone has already beat you to it."

So they stayed at Seven Rivers; it was fortunate that Upson had happened along when he did.

One of their new neighbors was Hugh Beckwith, the younger son of a titled English family who was ranching along the river. He had married the daughter of a wealthy Spaniard, the sheep king of the Estancia Valley, and had built a great adobe hacienda surrounded by high walls that formed one outside wall of the house and extended around a rectangular plot of two acres, with stables opposite the house.

When the Jones family opened their new trading post, men from the Beckwith ranch occasionally came for supplies. Although courteous, they were by no means friendly. It was Ma'am's first experience with such lack of acceptance, and she found it incomprehensible. As her son Sam expressed it, "I wouldn't say we didn't ever look *down* on nobody, but we shore as hell didn't look *up* to nobody."

There was much traffic up and down the Pecos, and among the Pilgrims—as the Jones boys called them—were undoubtedly many fugitives from justice. At that time, the postmaster at Lincoln had "bills for over five thousand wanted men." There were not that many voters in Lincoln County, but there were certainly many outlaws.

When Billy the Kid was on the Ruidoso, he usually stayed with George Coe; when he was on the Pecos, he was a welcome guest in the Jones home. From their first meeting with him, the family had accepted Billy without reservation and regarded him as a worthy friend. Heiskell Jones once said, "I never knew Ma'am to be fooled on a hoss, and never but once on a man—that was when she married me." Apaches, too, came occasionally, but never when the Joneses had other guests. Except for stealing horses once in a while, they made little trouble.

Ma'am was determined to have her family conform to her standards of conduct and held religious services in her home every Sunday morning. Since she considered the odor of sanctity closely related to that of soap, she sent her men to the Pecos to bathe every Saturday night—and they obeyed, even though they sometimes had to break the ice to do so. She and Minnie used a tub in Ma'am's room. That done, the family lined up before Ma'am, who took The Book, at that time the only one in the house, and read a chapter. They then repeated the Lord's Prayer, asked questions and held discussions. No liquor was sold during these services, nor during dances held at the trading post.

Ma'am was equally determined to give her children as much education as she could. She taught them to read from the Bible and, primitive as her equipment was, her boys acquired enough knowledge of the three R's to enable them to calculate mentally, within ten pounds, the weight of a steer and what it would bring at $3\frac{1}{2}$ cents a pound—the going rate.

As neighbors moved into the area they asked permission to send their children to Ma'am's school. She took them in but refused compensation. The girls helped prepare the noon meal, provided free by the Joneses, and washed the dishes; the boys kept the wood box and water buckets full. When Ma'am mentioned to a neighbor that their last month's grocery bill had been $17.00, she was surprised at the response. Her students began bringing antelope, beef and fish; those who raised corn or *frijoles* sent along abundant quantities.

Eventually Ma'am prevailed upon the men of the community to build an adobe schoolroom on the bank of the Pecos. A Captain Shattuck, a former Confederate officer who had been injured and could do little physical work, became the teacher and worked without pay, as Ma'am had, except for the unsolicited contributions.

As more people moved in, other trading posts were established. Les Dow built and operated a saloon. Cowboys came for miles to get drunk and shoot up the town. Pilgrims joined them, of course, and times were often lively. Ma'am had officiated at weddings, births, illnesses and deaths. But the new situation became increasingly complicated as the violence increased. Surgery was often required, and she did what she could. The surgeon at Fort Stanton recognized her amateur skills and presented her with a "doctor book." That and her Bible now constituted her whole library.

On one occasion a man was shot and Ma'am was called. She boiled a white silk bandana and probed for the bullet with a knitting needle. Miraculously, most of the wounded men recovered. Those who didn't were buried in what was known as the Jones Boot Hill on a bluff on the Pecos. Crude homemade coffins, lined with white calico, enclosed the remains, and Ma'am or Captain Shattuck read a chapter from The Book and said the Lord's Prayer.

Firmly convinced that entertainment and recreation were beneficial, Ma'am opened the trading post for frequent dances. There was no admission fee; at midnight a supper was served, with the women of the community furnishing everything except the meat and coffee. Almost any cowboy could saw out a tune on a fiddle, or pick a "gittar"; a few played harps (harmonicas), and Pa Jones played a homemade drum. The dances lasted all night, and breakfast was served before the guests left.

Long before the settlers realized that the rivalry for beef contracts between John Chisum and Major Murphy would culminate in the Lincoln County War, Ma'am sensed and feared that possibility. Determined to prevent her sons' participation, she did her best to keep them neutral. Despite her caution, however, there was a near confrontation between John and a Murphy man who came to one of the dances. As the man was telling John "so long," Ma'am walked out the door just as he uttered an oath. John whipped out his pistol and ordered the offender to get on his knees, crawl to his mother and apologize. When he had done so, the bewildered fellow turned to John and said, "You don't call *that* cussin', do you?"

"My mother does" was the reply.

Ma'am's problem was especially difficult because her son Jim was Chisum's trail boss. At that time when a cowboy worked for a man he became the defender of his employer, his family and his cattle. If necessary, he died for him. However, the Jones boys maintained their neutrality until Marion Turner, now an officer of the law, rode out from Lincoln to deputize John, Jim, and thirteen-year-old Bill to take part in what turned out to be the four-day siege of the McSween house in Lincoln. The next morning she saw them ride away with Turner and several other men he had deputized.

For a short time after they left, Ma'am walked the floor and prayed; then it occurred to her that *working* and praying would be more effective. As she cleaned her house, she reflected that she had reared her nine sons as best she could, strictly according to the wisdom of King Solomon which, in her judgment, was the best method known to mankind.

For all of that long week, she awaited word from Lincoln; at its end, all who had ridden away returned except Robert Beckwith. He had been buried on the banks of the Bonito. John had a slight wound—only a scratch, he said. When Ma'am had welcomed her sons and heard their report, she sent Sam to saddle her horse. When he brought it to the door, she reached for her bonnet.

"Where are you going?" John asked.

"To Mrs. Beckwith."

"After the way they have treated us!"

"She's a mother who has just lost a son, her firstborn. I must go."

La Señora admitted her, and the two women fell into each other's arms.

Not until after her death did Ma'am Jones become known as "The Angel of the Pecos." She would have been embarrassed and distressed by the appellation had she known of it. In her own estimation, she was merely one of the many women on the frontier who, although possessing little academic training or schooling, had simply done the best she could. Though poor, she was unaware of it and, like the others, she gave unselfishly of what she had as she reared her family and knitted it into a solid unit. She taught by example and by the Bible. Once, when John and Jim had a disagreement, she put a twig into John's hand and told him to break it. He did so with ease; but when she gave him a bundle of *nine*, he could not break the bundle. There was no need for talk.

Her ambition for her sons was that they be good citizens; for her daughter Minnie that she be chaste, marry a good man and rear a fine family. For Ma'am there was little deviation from the straight and narrow path, even though it might mean the death of one of her menfolk.

So—let this be a toast to the Ma'am Jones women. They have too long been "unwept, unhonored and unsung." It is time that they be recognized and their memory respected.

———————

For centuries, the academic point of view had been that if an occurrence was not recorded, it did not happen. Eve Ball pioneered in the field of oral history, and for years had difficulty in having her books published.

To her, history is much like an iceberg, only a small part of which is visible. Exploring and recording the hidden facts intrigued her. Now, to her great delight, oral history is part of the curriculum in many universities. Her books are not only accepted, they are used as texts in the United States and in England. They include In the Days of Victorio *and* My Girlhood Among Outlaws.

BIBLIOGRAPHY

BOOKS

Burns, Walter Noble. *The Saga of Billy the Kid*. New York: Doubleday, Page, 1926.

Coe, George. *The Frontier Fighter*. Boston: Houghton Mifflin, 1935.

Keleher, William A. *The Fabulous Frontier*. Albuquerque: University of New Mexico Press, 1966.

Sonnichsen, C. L. *The Mescalero Apaches*. Norman: University of Oklahoma Press, 1958.

INTERVIEWS

Big Mouth, Mescalero Apache scout; he knew the Jones family.

Blazer, Paul; grandson of Dr. Blazer.

Clark, Opal (Mrs. L. D.), daughter of Sam Jones.

Coe, Mrs. Frank, wife of Frank.

Johnson, William (Bill), grandson of Hugh Beckwith; stepson of Wallace Olinger.

Jones, Sam, Frank, Bill and Nib.
Shattuck, Judge Edward (Ned), son of Captain Shattuck.
Slaughter, Miss Fannie, daughter of Charlie Slaughter.
Ward, William (Bill), neighbor of Jones family.

RECORDS

Jones family Bible; it had lists of births, deaths and marriages.
Lincoln County Court records.
Mescalero Apache Reservation records.

2

A Bride Who Went West

by BARBARA KETCHAM

Nannie Alderson, who came from a wealthy family in West Virginia, was used to luxuries and servants. Nevertheless, she unhesitatingly married the cowboy who captured her affections, and in 1883 set out with him on the 1,800-mile journey to her new Montana home, a tumbledown shack shared with her husband's cowboys.

N.S.Y.

INDIANS HAVE BURNED YOUR HOUSE. COME IMMEDIATELY WITH SHERIFF AND POSSE.

Nannie Alderson, still weak from childbirth, looked first at her infant daughter and then at the landlady who had just read the telegram to her.

"I thought it was congratulations from Mr. Alderson's brother-in-law in Kansas." Her voice shook.

It was March 20, 1884 in Miles City, Montana. The Yellowstone River had flooded the city, leaving huge chunks of ice on the dirt streets and mud on the wooden sidewalks. With no telephones in Miles City and telegrams delivered by horse, it had taken two days for word to arrive about the fire at the Alderson ranch, 100 miles away.

"They burned the house the day our baby was born," Nannie thought as a messenger went to find her husband.

Walt Alderson returned to his wife's bedside along with the old Kentucky doctor who had delivered their baby. "Your husband has been deputized, and it is necessary that he go and see about this," he told her. "But if you are going to worry yourself sick, he won't go."

Nannie gave her consent, but soon tired of the repeated warnings of the bad effect that worry would have on the baby. She must think of the loss as one only of material things, she told herself, but the next few days gave her time to ponder what had happened.

Since Nannie and Walt had come to Montana as newlyweds the year before, they had lived close to the Indians. Their ranch was located near Lame Deer Creek 60 miles above the meeting of the Rosebud and the Yellowstone rivers. General George Crook had fought the Indians on the Rosebud only six years before. Custer had marched up it, crossed over the divide, and met his death at the Battle of the Little Big Horn. Nannie had read about these happenings when she was a young girl, never dreaming she would live so close to the Indians herself. Little did she know the part Indians would play in her life.

The West itself had taken some getting used to for petite Nannie Tiffany Alderson, who stood barely five feet tall. Born to a wealthy family in Union, West Virginia, Nannie had been used to luxuries and servants. The West seemed far away until at age sixteen she visited an aunt in Atchison, Kansas, which was "Far West" at that time. Nannie fell in love with Kansas and became a frequent visitor to her aunt's home.

During one of her visits to Atchison, the Baptist minister had taken ill, and Nannie and her aunt took turns looking after the old gentleman. One night Nannie looked up to see a nearly six-foot-tall blue-eyed cowboy. "I'm Walter," he said.

"I know," she said, recognizing the minister's oldest son.

The next few nights, Nannie and Walt talked while sitting by the minister's bedside. Walt told her how he had run away to Texas when he was thirteen and, being good with horses, later joined other cowboys on the trail to Kansas. As the evenings passed, Walt told Nannie of his dream to start a cattle ranch in Montana, and shyly asked, "Would you be afraid to share that kind of life with me?"

How romantic it seemed to her. She would be a helpmate to her man in a new country. They became engaged shortly after his father's death.

While Nannie made plans for the wedding, Walt returned to Montana to find a site for their ranch. He was in partnership with Johnny Zook, who provided the capital while he supplied the experience.

Nannie was eternally grateful to her aunt in Kansas who had taught her to sew. During the year of their engagement, Nannie made her wedding dress of white embroidered mull and earned the money to buy her wedding veil by sewing for others.

Nannie and Walt were married at 10 A.M. on April 4, 1883 in her home in Union, West Virginia. She was twenty-three and he was twenty-eight. That afternoon they crossed the mountains by stage to Alderson, West Virginia, where they were entertained by Walt's relatives before leaving for Montana.

The newlyweds took the train as far as Miles City, which was the end of the line for the Northern Pacific Railroad. From here, Nannie was to go to Bozeman to stay with friends while Walt went to the ranch to finish the house.

But Nannie had other ideas. "Mr. Alderson, I want to go with you to the ranch," Nannie told her husband.

"The house isn't finished yet."

"I don't care. I want to be with you."

"Okay, Partner." He was easily persuaded.

Coming from the South, where only servants were called by their first names, Nannie had called her husband "Mr. Alderson," and he called her "Mrs. Alderson." The West changed that, and "Partner" became a special name for each, later shortened to "Pardsy."

Nannie would remember every part of the journey from Miles City to their ranch. They left on April 17 in a spring wagon, which was similar to a buckboard but more comfortable. Their 100-mile journey would take two days.

The first stop was at noon at Piper Dan's, a road ranch 35 miles out of Miles City. For dinner, they had buffalo steak cut from one of the last buffalo in that part of Montana. That night they stayed at another road ranch on the Tongue River.

One of Nannie's first lessons as a Western wife was the importance of rivers and divides, and that the location of every tiny creek might be a matter of life and death to men and animals.

The second day of their trip, they crossed over the divide to the Rosebud and went on down a long gulch to Lame Deer. All that day, they had passed low, drab, log shacks, daubed with mud and weeds growing on the dirt roofs. At first she thought these primitive huts surely belonged to Indians or to animals. Her heart sank lower as she saw them.

"Is ours as bad as that?" Nannie finally asked her husband.

"Worse," he told her. Then he explained that their house was really a maverick shack thrown together as a shelter for men working in the Wolf Mountains as tie cutters years before.

Her first glimpse of her home was anything but reassuring. Their dirt-roofed cabin was so low that it was hardly taller than a man, and the cabin had only one window. An immense pair of elk antlers hung over the door, one prong supporting a human skull perforated by bullet holes. Nannie later learned that the skull had been picked up on the battleground of Lame Deer, and most of the bullet holes had been put there by the "boys'" target practice. The "boys," who were to share the next few years with them, were Johnny Zook, Old Uncle, Baltimore Bill and Brown Taliaferro.

The men had worked hard to prepare the cabin for Nannie. A bright fire burned in the stove fireplace, and the dirt floor had been covered with a clean wagon sheet of white canvas. Over the canvas were several tanned skins from buffalo, mountain lion, wolf, coyotes and two red fox pelts. Much to her surprise, there was a white bedspread for the couch. A grey army blanket hung across an opening in the logs separating the bedroom and kitchen.

While Nannie rested from the journey, the men prepared the evening meal. She felt homesick until she sat down to eat one of the best suppers of her life: hot biscuits, venison, bacon, potato chips, dried fruit and coffee. She was surprised that men in Montana could cook so well, and most of what she learned her first years as a housewife she learned from them.

The table was a let-down lid of a chuck box like those used on roundup wagons. This along with the stove and some homemade three-legged stools were the sole furnishings of the kitchen. The next day, "Uncle" built a table and benches. Adding her own touch, Nannie covered the table with some white oilcloth and bright red doilies. On the table she proudly placed her grandmother's silver, an old-fashioned lazy susan with vinegar, salt, pepper and mustard bottles, and two delicate china cups and saucers. She felt she was making a real stride toward homemaking.

Evenings were spent singing to the accompaniment of her guitar. Her first lesson of making the best of things came when, upon unpacking the guitar, she found it broken across the neck. With strips of surgical tape which they kept handy in case of accidents, Walt and Johnny taped it together.

While Nannie had been prepared to "rough it," one thing had bothered her all the way to Montana: would the ranch be equipped with an outside toilet? She had heard that men living alone in the West didn't bother with such conveniences. Much to her relief, not only did the ranch have one, but it surely was the best of outhouses. It was made of boards which Uncle and Baltimore Bill had whipsawed out by hand, and because Uncle couldn't bear to have a foot of his precious lumber wasted, he refused to trim off the ends of the boards in the outhouse. They couldn't put a roof on the building, so all summer and fall it was open to the sky.

Nannie missed having another woman to talk to, but she thoroughly enjoyed visiting with the boys and other cowboys who stopped by. They always shared a meal with visitors no matter who it was—white man or Indian.

Living close to the Indians was a new experience to her, but not a frightening one. Hardly a day passed that the Indians didn't visit them to beg for food. Since the buffalo had gone, the Indians often roamed, visiting members of their tribes. Some days the shack would turn dark, and Nannie would look up to see an Indian blocking the window.

A steady visitor of the Alderson's was an old chief, Two Moon, who had played a leading part in the Custer battle. Nannie wasn't afraid of the chief and often thought how absurd he looked in his white man's clothing. He usually wore his cotton shirt inside out, and his pants more like a pair of leggings. As the Aldersons found out, Two Moon had quite a sense of humor in spite of his limited vocabulary. The chief would ask in sign language how much Walt would take for Nannie. One time Walt held up one finger, and the chief laughed long and loud. Another time, when Walt began opening and shutting both hands very rapidly, Two Moon counted up to fifty and then said disgustedly, "God damn, too many." It was the most he ever said in English.

While Nannie and Walter were partners in a new adventure, it was more of a challenge for her. In that first year she put up with rattlesnakes, washed in hard water (and discovered that clothes would never be white again after the first washing), took care of meat after it was butchered, made preserves, and raised a garden in hard, difficult land. In spite of hardships, Nannie didn't complain, but marveled at the freedom of the people and the beauty of this new land.

The new house was finished in August, and what a house it was. "There was no house like it anywhere in eastern Montana outside of Miles City," Nannie wrote afterwards. It had four rooms and was built of hewn logs seven inches square, so closely fitted together that it looked like a frame house, and it had *windows*. The kitchen had a built-in cupboard with drawers and bins for flour and sugar underneath to take the place of the old chuckwagon box which was her first kitchen cabinet. The house had board floors, built double for warmth.

Of the four rooms, one was a bunk room for the boys, and another was Johnny Zook's room. Across the hall were the kitchen and Walt and Nannie's bedroom, which again served as the living room. As a present from Johnny Zook, the Aldersons received walnut furniture from St. Joe, Missouri, along with bright carpets and curtains. On the walls, lined with muslin and then covered with a flowered paper, Nannie hung two etchings and old-fashioned oval portraits of Walt's parents. Her grandmother's silver candlesticks stood on the stone mantel of the huge fireplace, where they burned logs five feet long.

Nannie never regretted sharing their home with their own cowboys. In an age when cowboys were often treated as tramps, Nannie had a great deal of respect for them.

What a joy the new house was for her. However, it would be a short-lived joy; it would last only seven months, from August to March. Another Indian chief, Black Wolf, would be responsible for the destruction of her Montana home.

When the Aldersons left for Miles City to await the birth of their first child, the "boys" stayed on the ranch. On that particular day in March 1884, Black Wolf, who lived across the divide from them, came to the ranch, begging for food and tobacco. The boys fed the chief and afterwards watched him smoke his pipe.

"I bet I can put a hole in the old chief's hat without touching his head," said Hal Toliver, who had been with the Aldersons for several months. A $5.00 bet was made, and Hal drew his six-shooter and fired. The shot just nicked Black Wolf's scalp, but the Indian was furious and was convinced the men meant to kill him.

Realizing what they had done, the men rode 10 miles to Young's store for help, and returned with three cowboys. But they were too late. Indians from Black Wolf's lodge had already moved in, with the women and children sitting in a semicircle while the men carried out the bureau drawers and emptied their contents. Hal realized the Indians were going to burn the house. He bravely rode up as close as he could and promised the Indians beef, coffee, ponies and tobacco. When they started shooting at him, he left. The Indians camped by the house from Tuesday, March 18, until Saturday, March 21. During this time, they ate a year's supply of groceries, including ten deer hams that Nannie was curing, and all their chickens. Then they burned the corral posts and poles and cut up the saddles. From the top of the hill, the ranch hands watched the house roar into flames.

When the sheriff and deputies arrived on the scene on Sunday morning, they arrested two Indians who admitted setting fire to the house. These Indians were later sent to the penitentiary. That wasn't all; Hal Toliver was wanted not only by the civil authorities, but by the Indian Bureau. How he escaped was another story:

Riding Walt's best cutting horse, and assisted by the Youngs, he blackened his light hair and mustache, and got away, even riding some miles with a stock inspector who was trying to find him. Later, friends told the Aldersons that Hal had wanted to come to Miles City to see Nannie and the baby, but his friends persuaded him to leave. Hal eventually wound up in Kansas, where he married and became a prosperous farmer. Nannie wondered if Hal ever realized how she and Walt had been hurt by his $5.00 bet.

Nannie and the baby stayed in Miles City from March to August while another house was being built. While the new house was adequate, it was not the house the Indians had burned, and they could never again recover the family treasures that had been lost. After the fire, the ranch hands sifted the ashes, looking for Nannie's silver, but they couldn't find it. Years later, Nannie's son met an Indian who told of getting some silver from his mother's house, but the Aldersons never got to see it.

Built on the Tongue River, 30 miles east across the divide from their old house, the new house was also close to Black Wolf's lodge; so it was no surprise when, one morning shortly after breakfast, Black Wolf came to their ranch. He said his papoose was sick and needed milk. Walt invited him to sit down and have some coffee while Nannie got the milk. There was a piece of steak on the platter in front of Black Wolf, and when Nannie set his coffee down, he pointed first to the steak and then to the stove as a sign that he wanted her to cook it more. Knowing how often he ate raw meat, she said, "You can eat it that way or not at all." Although he didn't understand English, he got the drift and proceeded to eat the steak as it was.

Of the two braves in Black Wolf's lodge who admitted setting fire to the Alderson home, one of them died in prison; the other was later pardoned. As soon as he reached home, the Indian walked the 10 miles to spend the day with the Aldersons, believing they would be glad to see him. They wouldn't have known him from any other Indian except that he told them in sign language that he had set fire to their tepee, had his hands tied together, and had gone on a long ride on the train (choo-choo) and that his comrade had gone to sleep and that he himself had now come home to stay.

Not all experiences with the Indians were bad. The Aldersons hired an Indian lady, Rattlesnake, to do their washing, and her daughter, Bob-Tailed Horse, to look after the baby. Because the young girl disliked her name, Nannie called her Minnehaha, which was later shortened to Minnie. The young girl was a good and faithful nurse for the baby and often carried her on her back, as she would a papoose. When the baby, Mabel, started to walk, Minnie made her some moccasins.

From the fall of 1884 to the spring of 1886, when she took the baby and went home to visit her mother and grandmother, Nannie never left the ranch or saw civilization. The trip East proved an interesting experience for Mabel, who had seen only Indian women and played only with Indian children. While shopping in St. Paul, Minnesota, with a friend, Nannie laughed when Mabel ran up to women in the stores and called them "Pretty Mammas."

Their second daughter was born while Nannie was in West Virginia, and they named her Fay Sue. While Nannie enjoyed the luxuries of West Virginia and the company of other women, her heart longed for Walt and the boys. When Walt arrived for Thanksgiving, he told her that the harsh winter was wiping out huge herds of cattle in Montana and Wyoming. With this on his mind, Walt returned to Montana, while Nannie and the girls stayed behind until the spring of 1887.

Like so many other ranchers who were affected by the harsh winter, the loss of cattle to the Aldersons had been great, and Walt and Johnny Zook decided to end their partnership. Zook took the house and all the furnishings, and Walt took his interest in cattle. For the third time in four years, the Aldersons moved.

This time, the new ranch was near the head of Muddy Creek on the Rosebud, 10 miles from their first home. And, with the move, another Indian, Little Wolf, came into their lives.

As a Cheyenne chief, Little Wolf had been a great leader. With Dull Knife, an older chief, he commanded the great march of his people in 1878, when they defied the orders of the government, left their reservation in Indian territory and went north, back to their old home in Montana. Until his surrender at the end of that journey, Little Wolf had been regarded as one of the most dangerous of hostile Indians. A leader in keeping the peace, he was made chief of the Indian police by the military authorities at Fort Keogh. However, when he killed another Indian he was trying to arrest, he lost his standing with his people and had no voice in their councils.

A pathetic figure of a deposed chief, Little Wolf maintained his dignity. He felt that the Indians should be friendly with the white people, and that after a while they would get to be one big people. He told the Aldersons this in sign language, and Nannie remembered the beautiful, sweeping gestures of his arms.

Little Wolf brought one of his two wives to do the washing for Nannie. While the women were busy, the chief took the children for walks, always checking for snakes. He patiently helped them find pretty rocks for their playhouses, and sometimes gathered *kinnikinnic,* a bark which the Indians used in place of tobacco.

Nannie trusted Little Wolf, but his wife was not always so trustworthy. Sometimes she would take the Aldersons' towels home with her, and the chief would bring them back, saying, "Squaw *hypersiba* (no good)."

The years spent at Muddy Creek passed quickly, with the arrival of another baby girl, Patty, and later a son, Walter, Jr., nicknamed Bud. Nannie hadn't realized how excited the girls were about having a brother until they printed a note to their friends on Tongue River, which said, "Dear Albert and Joe: We have a little brother. His name is Walter. He is a boy."

When the Aldersons moved to Miles City in 1893, Little Wolf begged them not to go. "Your papooses will get sick, maybe die, and I will not see you anymore," he said, tears rolling down his cheeks. Nannie and Walt were touched by the affection the Indian showed.

There were many reasons for going to Miles City. First of all, Mabel was ten years old and had not had any schooling except what the Montgomery Ward catalog had given her. Also, the panic of 1893 had swallowed up the Stockgrowers National Bank in Miles City, and Walt's $6,000 life insurance policy was lost (the larger of two he carried). Low prices on cattle and horses made it harder to make ends meet.

Miles City proved a delight to Nannie and the children, but it was a disappointment to Walt, who first unsuccessfully grubstaked two men to open a mine, and later took a job as a deputy assessor.

On March 12, 1895, Nannie saw her husband pull up with his team of horses. She went on with her work, figuring he would be in after taking care of the horses. Later, the living-room door opened, and the doctor looked in and left. Something was wrong!

As Nannie hurried to the back porch, a friend came to meet her. "Walt's been badly hurt," he said. "We think he was kicked in the head by one of the horses." Wanting to spare the children from seeing their father in that condition, Nannie took them to a neighbor's and then helped the men carry Walt inside the house.

For six days Walt lay unconscious, with Nannie by his side. Two doctors and the surgeon from Fort Keogh did everything they could, but Walt died on March 18, 1895—Mabel's eleventh birthday.

Nannie thought afterwards about life's ironies. To Miles City she had come as a bride, and at Miles City she had her first child and heard the news that their house was burned by Indians. Now, in Miles City, her husband had died. She had come full circle.

After Walt's death, Nannie built a house across the street from the Episcopal church in Miles City. She was a good cook and took in boarders. Later she moved the family to Birney, Montana, where she opened a store and was in charge of the post office.

Freight teams from Sheridan, Wyoming, stopped regularly for food and for her pleasant company.

A frequent visitor was Little Wolf, who was now very old and nearly blind. He and his squaw (the one who had taken their towels) would make the 30-mile trip to see Nannie and the children. Nannie again was touched with the devotion of Little Wolf and his squaw, who walked the 30 miles leading his horse.

After five years in Birney, Nannie moved farther up Tongue River to Youngs Creek, where she lived until 1919.

With all her family married except Fay, who was teaching school, Nannie went to live with her daughter Patty Eaton, at Eaton's Ranch, one of the oldest and best-known dude ranches, located outside of Sheridan, Wyoming. Here she was close to her children, grandchildren, and later great-grandchildren.

While Nannie never complained about the hardships in her early years, her years at Eaton's were enjoyable ones, spent traveling with the Eatons and spending the winters in Kansas with her cousin.

Nannie's first grandchild, Dexter Cutter, called her "Domo" because he couldn't say "Grandma," and the nickname took hold. She was affectionately known by this name to the many dudes at Eaton's for the next twenty-eight years.

Dude children loved Nannie and used to ride down to her cabin to visit her. She fed them countless cookies, cupcakes, and lemonade or "swizzle," her own recipe for soft drink. The parents, realizing what a strain her hospitality would impose on her slender resources, insisted that she make a small charge. At the end of the first summer, she had cleared $230 and told Patty, "I hope all that money doesn't spoil me."

It wasn't just children who came to see her. Grown, sophisticated men and women came to visit and linger. One of her admirers was General George C. Marshall who, even in the middle of masterminding World War II, never forgot her birthday.

The hordes of young who came to visit her did not come for her swizzle alone, they came because "Domo" was fun. She did not tear a man down, but had a way of making the shyest person relax and the smallest stand tall.

On her eightieth birthday, Nannie was honored by a party at the Sheridan Inn, attended by 400 people. Invitations were printed on replicas of Sheridan's first newspaper, published in 1887. By that date, Nannie had already been in the West for over four years. Guests wore old-fashioned or Western clothes. Nannie was beautiful and delicate as a cameo in a dress of white silk organdy with a tiered, ruffled skirt edged in black lace. A bonnet was tied neatly under her chin with black velvet ribbons. The Frontier Cowboys quartet furnished the music; Nannie led the grand march and danced the first quadrille.

Friend of the great and the near great who came to Eaton's ranch in those early days of dude ranching, Nannie was still loyal to her friends of pioneering days. She had come full circle from the gracious Southern home, through roughing it on the frontier, and now to association with the wealthy people who came to Eaton's for a taste of the West. Her story was written by Helena Huntington Smith in *A Bride Goes West,* published in 1941.

Consideration of other people was always Nannie's main concern, even in her last days. The late author Emmie Mygatt, who also had spent many summers at Eaton's, recalled the last time she saw "Domo": "Domo must have been eighty-six years old and couldn't have weighed more than eighty-six pounds." It was time for Emmie's family to leave the ranch to return East, and they had come to say good-bye to Nannie, who was in bed and looking "very white and tinier than ever." Nannie seemed upset that they had found her in bed, and apologized to them. After a few lively words and a cheery farewell, they left, knowing it was probably the last time they would ever see their friend. The next morning, however, as Emmie's family approached Nannie's cabin, they saw her tiny figure standing on the footbridge which spanned the small stream in front of her cabin. Immaculate as always, she wore a lacy lavender shawl against the morning chill. Emmie said her family got out of the car and ran towards Nannie, and noticed that her face was set, and her hands trembled on the rail. "I always want you to remember me standing up," she said, then she waved and walked slowly away. There was something in her bearing that made them realize that she had given all she had.

Those nine words to Emmie would become a legacy for the indomitable Western woman who had come from Southern luxury to dirt floors, Indian attacks, hardships and tragedy. She had met them as she met her final farewells, "standing up."

On September 12, 1947, two days before her eighty-seventh birthday, Nannie Alderson died and was buried in Sheridan. Considerate of others to the end, she told her family, "I don't want any of you to feel badly; I've lived a long and full life."

WWA Associate member Barbara Ketcham is the mother of five teenagers, and lives in Sheridan, Wyoming, with her husband, Garey, and family. She works full time as a secretary to a local architect, and does free-lance writing in her spare time.

Her articles have been published in The Rotarian, Woman's Day, Farm Wife News, The Western Horseman, Empire Magazine, Montana Magazine, The Exceptional Parent Magazine, Bits and Pieces, *and* The Western *(a Norwegian magazine). Her work has also been included in five anthologies.*

Ketcham was a charter member of Wyoming Writers and has held every office in the organization. She finished her term as president during June 1979.

BIBLIOGRAPHY

BOOKS

Alderson, Nannie T. and Smith, Helena Huntington. *A Bride Goes West.* Lincoln, Neb.: University of Nebraska Press, 1969.
Brown, Mark K. and Felton, W. R. *Before Barbed Wire.* New York: Bramhall House, 1964.
Johnson, Dorothy. *Some Went West.* New York: Dodd, Mead & Co., 1965.

NEWSPAPERS

Sheridan Post, September 1887, January 24, 1889, February 7, 1889, March 21, 1889, April 17, 1889
Sheridan Press, August 27, 1941, September 13, 1947

PERSONAL INTERVIEWS

Mrs. William Eaton (Patty)
Mrs. John Duncan (Dorothy)
Elsa Spear Byron

3

A Transplanted Britisher

by PEGGY SIMPSON CURRY

Welsh-born, twenty-two-year-old Martha James visited Wyoming Territory in 1882; as lady-in-waiting to the bride of wealthy Sir William Armstrong, she expected to return to England with them. But she met a cowboy—and became the first white woman settler in the Big Horn Basin, then peddler, retail store manager, and postmistress. Her story illustrates the transition of a transplanted Englishwoman who became as Western as her adopted land.

N.S.Y.

On a brilliant October day in 1882, Martha James rode a rocking stagecoach into vast Wyoming Territory. She was twenty-two years old, a lady-in-waiting to the bride of Sir William Armstrong. They were traveling toward Moreton Frewen's "castle" at the 76 Ranch near the Powder River. After a summer in Cheyenne, Martha looked forward to this last adventure before returning to England with the Armstrongs.

Petite, attractive and vivacious, she had no way of knowing she would never return to England, nor to her birthplace in Wales. She was destined to become the first white woman in Wyoming's long and lonely Big Horn Basin. Many of her neighbors would be outlaws, Indians and prostitutes. She would meet Buffalo Bill Cody, members of the Hole-in-the-Wall Gang, and a challenging minister, soon to be murdered. She would survive tragedy, poverty, exhausting physical labor and devastating winters. And she would achieve the unique distinction of becoming a liberated and successful businesswoman in a man's world.

Frewen's so-called castle was a pleasant surprise. Located at his headquarters of three ranches, the house was large and elegant, built of logs. A huge hall reached clear to the roof with fireplaces at each end. Walls were decorated with buffalo hides, Indian trophies, mounted heads of buffalo, elk and deer. The dining room could seat twenty people. There was a big kitchen, an office, a library and a long walnut staircase leading to the second floor, where sleeping quarters were as fine as any Martha James had ever seen. Between the long hallway and the bedrooms was another kind of room: an open space with potted plants and vines climbing up from the main floor below. Moreton Frewen classified it as the musicians' gallery.

Martha James looked him over carefully. He was twenty-nine, only seven years older than herself and it was rumored he was a snob. But look what he had done with his life while she was tending the ladies! He presided over acres of rangeland, three ranches. This very year Frewen had raised $1.5 million and organized the Powder River Cattle Company Limited. Besides all this he had a telephone and his stagecoaches brought not only people but also flowers to this remote place. No wonder parties went on all summer and during the fall hunting season. Only one thing was missing.

"You don't have a garden," Martha said. "No fresh vegetables."

Always one who enjoyed talking and expressing honest opinion, she was startled by his reaction. He let her know he wouldn't tolerate gardens. They would attract trash, upstarts, people who would build fences, drill wells, ruin the wild and free country.

Something stirred deep inside the little lady-in-waiting. "Why should homesteaders be upstarts? Haven't they the same rights as you?"

"Never! We risk our money and open up this country. They come in and ruin it."

She soon forgot their difference of opinion. There was music, dancing and card playing. Anyone who didn't want to hunt could enjoy the library. The food prepared by the male cook was excellent and Martha was flattered by the attention of cowboys, ranch hands and male visitors. Women were scarce in Wyoming Territory.

As fall moved toward winter, Martha scarcely noticed the snows and the winds. She was falling in love with Frank Bull, the head wrangler. Handsome, with a warm personality, he was fascinated by horses and was expert in caring for them. Besides, he had ambition. He intended to file on his own homestead land and raise his own horses. With Martha as his wife, they would become landed gentry on a par with Moreton Frewen.

Only one visitor attempted to discourage Martha. Frank Gireaud was part Indian, a former scout for the United States Army. "You shouldn't stay here," he said. "This is squaw country. You're a real lady. Go back to England where you belong."

Martha could see no faults in Frank Bull. He did like to drink whiskey, but she was sure he would never be like the men who gathered in Buffalo, the nearest small town. There ranch hands held regular celebrations where "all hell broke loose," with drinking, shouting, shooting and fist fights.

In May of 1883, when the snows had melted in lower country and the green was coming on, Martha James and Frank Bull were married in Buffalo. After prolonged farewells, they left Frewen's castle.

There was joy in Martha's heart as they traveled north in their heavily laden wagon that held the precious trunk she had brought from England. In it were her beautiful clothes, pictures and mementos from Wales and England. She looked at the sunlit hills, the flower-covered valleys, the shining mountains and told herself she could handle whatever lay ahead even though she knew nothing about cooking or cleaning a house.

She continued to believe she could cope with any difficulties as they slept on the ground and she helped her husband cook over campfires. She tried to forget her hands were becoming rough and red. After three long days of travel, they arrived in a beautiful valley near a river. Frank told her they had come home. They began unloading the wagon.

Suddenly a dozen Indians rode up. They climbed on the wagon and tried to open Martha's trunk. Terrified, she watched while Frank offered them tobacco and talked to them. Soon they rode away. Frank assured his trembling bride that tobacco gifts always prevented Indian trouble. And tomorrow—tomorrow he would start cutting logs to build their house.

Days later, a group of soldiers stopped by. A white man had murdered an Indian girl, and the Indians were on the warpath. Frank and Martha must hurry to Buffalo. The soldiers rode quickly away.

To Martha it was all unreal—Frank quickly packing, taking down their tent, hitching up the team. They drove all night, following the river. At daylight Frank found a place to ford the high spring water. As the horses tried to climb the opposite bank, the wagon tilted and water rushed in. Moments later, Martha's precious trunk was gone, tumbling downstream in the roaring waters. Martha burst into tears. A short time later, soldiers again rode out of the willows. They had come back to see if Martha and Frank were unharmed. They tried to find the lost trunk, but it was never recovered.

Three days later, a shaken Martha and her husband reached Buffalo. Her dreams had been destroyed. What did the future hold in this cruel country? Moreton Frewen came to the rescue. He and his stockholders had invested in new land across the Big Horn Mountains in a remote area known as the Big Horn Basin. This was the Bar X Ranch. A fine house would be built for summer guests south of Ten Sleep Valley on Canyon Creek. Martha and Frank could be caretakers.

In October Martha and Frank crossed the Big Horn Mountains, following a rough, narrow road that had once been an old Indian trail. After two days of traveling, they came down into fenceless country. Miles of golden-brown grass bowed in the wind. High crimson rock walls stood to the west and massive limestone cliffs lay north, opening toward mountain crests.

Frank set up their tent in a spot where they would spend the night. Soon Martha discovered a band of Shoshone Indians camped near them. She didn't sleep much. The next day they reached a cow camp owned by the Two Bar Cattle Company. Martha was treated like royalty, for there was no other white woman in the vast and lonely country. The men moved out of their cabin and turned it over to the visitors. In the morning they traveled on toward the home ranch of the Bar X on Canyon Creek, where Frewen had promised them a fine house.

Again Martha faced disappointment. Rooms had been started,

but were only four and five logs high. The weary travelers drove on to another cow camp owned by the Two Bar Company. There they were offered a crude, unfinished cabin to live in while they waited for the Bar X house to be completed.

Martha Bull stared at the dirt floor and the rough log walls that hadn't yet been chinked. Cold wind blew through the open spaces. With darkness, rats moved in. Something had to be done, she told herself. Then came a morning when the hillside near the cabin was covered with elk. Frank and one of the Two Bar men killed ten head. Martha helped harness a team, and the elk were hauled to the cabin. As soon as possible, Martha began making hide coverings for the floor, walls and ceiling of the cabin.

Her hands sore, her back aching, the former lady-in-waiting became sick. Frank worried. "I've got to get to a ranch and find some medicine. I hate to leave you but I've got to."

Terrified and alone, Martha lay in the darkness waiting for Frank's return. The cold wind swept over her. Rats ran across the bed. She thought of the Indians who were hunting elk and camped near the cabin. Staggering out of bed, she blocked the door with everything she could find and tried hard to sleep, but the rats kept running over her.

It was a long time before Frank came home. He had only a few pills, but he had talked with an old Indian who advised him to make sage tea. "I boil the sagebrush leaves, and you must drink the water," he told his wife.

Soon she began to feel better. A few days later, the man who was building Frewen's house arrived. He needed help to bring cut logs off the mountain and offered Frank a sorrel horse in payment. Frank could start his own horse herd. Horses were hard to find in the lonely expanse of Big Horn Basin.

Martha's determination overcame her disappointment and weakness. "I'll help," she said. And so it was that she spent her first Christmas in married life in a tent on a mountain. A small stove helped keep out the cold. Frank built a shelter near the tent to protect the horses. That afternoon he hung a freshly killed deer between the tent and the horses.

Christmas night was bright and cold with moonlight glittering on the snow. Then a blood-chilling scream split the air. A big mountain lion was moving toward the deer while the horses reared, jerking their ropes, squealing in fear. Frank fired a shot.

The lion fled, but all through the rest of Christmas night his screams and roars echoed over the mountain. He stayed in the vicinity for a week.

After hauling logs off the mountain, the horses had to be kept close to the cabin. The government allowed Indians to hunt the Big Horn Basin: Shoshones in winter and Arapahoes in summer and fall. One night all the horses disappeared, and Frank went out to look for them.

Forty Indians showed up at the primitive cabin. A squaw carrying an armful of long red socks came in and tried to talk to Martha. Soon the cabin was filled with Indians, poking fingers in food, touching everything. Martha's temper flared. She grabbed a butcher knife. "Get out!" she screamed. The Indians ran from the cabin. Meanwhile Frank found the horses. Later an Indian chief came with a gift of beaded elkskin moccasins. His people meant no harm. They only hoped to trade socks for coffee.

By March the fine house Frewen had promised was built. Martha and Frank moved in. At last she had a comfortable place to live, but she was uneasy. The Indians had quit coming to visit. They thought the big house was ruining their hunting.

The Bulls' first child, a girl, was born in July of 1884. While Martha had a good bed and a nice house, there was no doctor, nurse, nor other woman to share the struggles of childbirth. Martha delivered her baby, an experience that would be repeated with her other children. For the first time since the homestead dream crumbled and her trunk was washed away, her joy overcame disappointment and bitterness.

Soon another happy event took place. A Nebraska family with children arrived, and plans for the first school began. By August a young man from New York became the first schoolteacher in the vast valley dominated by the Wind River that became the Big Horn River as a result of an Indian ceremony, the Wedding of the Waters.

Other changes were in the making across the mountains at Frewen's ranching kingdom. Frewen's wife, sister of Lady Randolph Churchill, became the aunt of a baby boy christened Winston Churchill. This happy event was offset by the death of Irish remittance man Gilbert E. Leigh, a close friend of Frewen. On a hunting trip in Ten Sleep country, not far from the Bar X Ranch, Leigh fell over a cliff into Ten Sleep Canyon. In a series of interviews granted in her later years, Martha stated that Leigh's body was kept on a table in the dining room at the ranch for months. The odor became unbearable, and the body was finally taken to Buffalo. Although she was noted as a woman of honesty and integrity, a newspaper report of the time contradicts her story. Was another body kept in the house? Was Leigh's body there only a short time? Is the newspaper report in error? Perhaps one day historians may agree on an answer. A stone monument shipped to Wyoming by Leigh's family commemorates the disaster on the wall of Ten Sleep Canyon and is visible from the highway.

In the midst of these events, problems had arisen in the Powder River Cattle Company Limited. It was to become Frewen's last season in Wyoming. Soon the company would be dissolved. The English interests would sell out and take their money home to England.

Martha found the rumored decline of the company unbelievable, and with good reason. In May of 1883, when she married Frank Bull, historical records indicate the 76 brand marked from 45,000 to 80,000 head of cattle. Twenty-seven roundup wagons and 400 cowboys were on the job.

While Frewen's world was ending, Martha had been saving her money. She had a woman's dream of one day owning a sealskin coat and a gold watch. She had accumulated $200. Then along came a man with thirty head of horses, including a Clydesdale stallion:

"If we had the horses, we could start our own place, have our own business," Frank said.

One dream gave way to another. Martha's money was used to buy the horses. Frank homesteaded a few miles down Canyon Creek from the Bar X and began building their first owned home. It was a rough cabin, more a dugout than a room, but life there became a series of interesting experiences and tragedies. On the interesting side, Martha began to have many visitors, mostly men. The Shoshones and Arapahoes became friendly, often stopping to visit. Then there were the drifting men who were always glad to find food cooked by a woman. Some confessed to be members of the Hole-in-the-Wall Gang, but no one of them claimed to be the already famous Butch Cassidy. There were also honest settlers and the familiar cowboys.

One day the horse herd belonging to Martha and Frank disappeared. Shortly after the horses were missing three strangers came to the door of the dugout-cabin. They claimed they had lost their horses and must borrow the three remaining saddle horses in the pasture. Martha faced them, holding her baby girl in her arms. Frank told them to take the three horses.

"We hadn't any choice," he told Martha later. "They're thieves, and God knows what they might do to us."

Martha was angry and bitter. All her hard-earned money put into a horse herd to be stolen by thieves! The next day the three men returned not only the three saddle horses, but also the herd that was missing. Then they handed Martha a twenty-dollar bill. "For the little kid," they said. Even thieves were motivated to gestures of kindness by the sight of a small child in what was still a sparsely populated area.

In October of 1885 Martha's second child, a boy, was born. Again she delivered him herself. He was a sickly baby. Ten months later, in the dry, hot summer of 1886, he died in Martha's arms. Now the landscape became a symbol of Martha's emotions. Tears no longer fell, and rains didn't come to ease the burned-up rangelands.

By autumn there was no feed for cattle. Thousands came into the Big Horn Basin, and many herds trailed past the Bulls' dugout home. They were thin cattle, mostly skin and bones. Men were advised to build dugouts and get ready for a long, hard winter. Martha was numb to all the trailing herds and the talk of the cattlemen. And she was carrying her third child.

By December the severe winter of 1886–87 gripped the land. Temperatures hovered at forty and fifty degrees below zero, and four feet of snow covered the ground. Martha's third child, a girl, was born in the same primitive manner as the other two, with no help. Not yet recovered from the death of her second child, the young woman who had once known the luxury of Frewen's castle on the Powder River now faced more worry. The little girl was not well.

And there were other problems. In the blizzard cold of January, Martha and Frank worried about a stallion and a mare they kept in their barn at night. Martha made blankets out of extra bed quilts to cover the two animals. A severe blizzard struck two days after she had made the blankets. Starving cattle crowded around the cabin, breaking the windows. Could she keep her children warm, especially the sick baby?

Frank insisted there was something unusual she must see. He carried her to the barn through the blowing snow. There she stared in disbelief. The cattle had eaten the quilt blankets from the backs of the stallion and the mare. Willow pegs driven into logs to hold the saddles and harness were chewed up.

Temperatures remained at forty and fifty degrees below zero for weeks. Thousands of cattle died. Late summer was welcome after the melting snows. But in September the sick baby became worse. The closest doctor was in Buffalo, across the Big Horn Mountains.

They started for Buffalo early that September morning. On top of the Big Horn Mountains a blizzard met them. Snow grew deeper and deeper. Frank had to stop, tie the team to a tree and unroll bedding to the bottom of the wagon where Martha, her daughter Gwendolyn and the sick baby huddled under a tarp. Leaving them, Frank set out to find a cabin he thought was somewhere close.

It was dark when he returned but he had found the cabin. After driving a short distance through deepening snow they reached the limited shelter. The roof had fallen in, except for a few poles that covered a place where a fire could be built. Martha's heart sank when she saw it.

After clearing snow from the floor and placing bedding close to the fire, they found food in the grub box. Then Martha put Gwendolyn to bed and held the sick baby in her arms. Frank brought the horses into the shelter.

Tired, cold and hungry, Martha and Frank sat up all night. He kept the fire going. She held the sick child, desperately wishing for a doctor. By morning the weather cleared and the sun came out. Moving slowly through the snow, the family rode the creaking wagon toward Buffalo. As they finally neared the town and a doctor, the sick baby grew very quiet. She had died in Martha's arms. It was the worst of all experiences in the cruel land that Martha had come to hate.

During the next few years, life seemed to improve. The horse herd grew. By 1893 the family had grown to four healthy, living children: Gwendolyn, Frankie, James and Bessie. A fifth child was expected in the near future. Hard work and responsibility eased sad memories of the two babies who had died. And there were the summers when the family camped out in the Big Horn Mountains near Ten Sleep Meadows in search of rich range grass for the horses. There a stream, Bull Creek, was named for them.

Then, in 1894, an event occurred that was destined to change Martha's life. Frank sold a team of horses to a settler a distance away on the other side of Big Horn Basin. While he was taking the horses to the new owner, Martha made plans to use the money. She would buy clothes for herself and the children. There would be an end to jackets made from tanned rabbit skins and pants and shirts created from discarded clothes of the cowboys. And she would fashion curtains for the window of the dugout-cabin.

Days passed. Frank didn't come home. Three long weeks went by before he returned, riding bareback on an Indian pony. Where was the team, their wagon? Frank confessed he had lost everything they owned drinking and gambling.

Martha thought of their children and the future. What little security she had known was now gone. Desperate and angry, she told her husband to leave and never come back. She could no longer stand living with him. Frank took his guns and rode away.

The future looked bleaker than ever before. What did a lone woman do with a family and no income? Winter was coming. What did she have? Only a few clothes, poor shelter, no wood and very little food. Then a good neighbor, Robert Waln, came to the dugout door. He paid her $50 he owed for work Frank had done for him. Martha spent $10 for food and gave another $10 to a neighbor woman to buy cloth in the town of Casper, many miles away in the center of the state. Later she discovered a horse that hadn't been gambled away. She traded it for firewood.

The winter was long, cold and lonely. The woman who had once shared the world of English nobility now thought she and her family were living like animals. When spring came, neighbor Waln plowed a garden patch for her. With seed she had saved and some offered by neighbors, she planted a garden. During the summer she took what little money she had left and paid to have a room built onto the dugout-cabin. Once again neighbor Waln tried to help. He brought her a window for the new dirt-floored room. Her spirits lifted. She felt as though she now lived in a castle.

Another difficult winter was approaching. Martha's conscience began to trouble her. Christmas had been almost ignored the year before, and she vowed never again would her children lack presents. As the holiday season approached, she polished the window in the new room, made a curtain from a flour sack and carefully cleaned the dirt floor. She made dolls with rags, corncobs, potatoes and black beans. A Christmas tree was set up, and the children helped with decorations made from rabbit skins they had saved. Bright red rose hips were fastened on strips of fur from the rabbit bellies. These were hung on the tree limbs and swung back and forth when a breeze struck them.

In the spring Martha was appointed the first postmistress in the Spring Creek area and given a small salary. She named the post office Cedar, Wyoming, because cedar trees covered the hill near the building. Later that spring, two men were running a peddler's wagon up and down the Big Horn Basin, selling things the cowboys needed, mostly clothes and tobacco. One of the peddlers offered to "grubstake" Martha for an order of goods.

"You won't have to leave the post office," he said. "People will come to you."

Martha was against going in debt. The peddler assured her she wasn't really going in debt. She could pay him off as she sold the items. Agreeing to this, she found herself selling without taking to the road. That summer she made a profit.

Late autumn brought complications. Frank came to the door, pleading to be taken back. "I'll never drink again," he promised.

Martha had made up her mind never to live with him again. She refused to talk to him. Frank began to cry and walked away among the cedar trees. Suddenly she could stand it no longer. She ran after him, calling, "Frank, come back!"

A happy family reunion took place. Martha agreed to give up her job and go with him to the small town of Lovell, where he assured her there were unlimited opportunities for business success. When they reached Lovell, Martha traded $200 in cash and some tobacco stock for four acres of land. They built a two-room house on the property. People were kind and friendly. From the front window, they could watch Mormon caravans go by to settle in Wyoming. Life seemed to be happy at last.

Then one day Frank had a new idea. He must show her a place on a river named Stinking Creek. A man could light a match, and the air would burn natural gas. Near the river was bottomland, the best land for a farm, a great place to raise cattle, chickens, pigs and have a garden.

Accompanied by their five children, they went to Stinking Creek. As they were eating lunch, three men drove up in a buggy. One man was a surveyor and another a man to become famous in Western history, Buffalo Bill Cody. The third man, carrying a bottle, invited Frank to walk along the river with him. The surveyor looked over the land while Buffalo Bill gave the youngsters a box of cookies and visited with Martha.

It was some time before Frank returned. He was drunk. Angry and disillusioned again, Martha drove the team back to Lovell. As soon as he sobered up, Frank promised to reform. Then one night he came home late, scarcely able to walk. Martha never went to bed. She started packing and by morning was headed back to Ten Sleep country with the children. She drove to a cabin on the Two Bar Ranch and asked a man there to sell her Lovell property. He recovered her $200. She ordered medicines, Arbuckle's coffee, pins, needles, thread and tobacco. Then she loaded her wagon and started peddling merchandise around the Big Horn Basin.

For two years she covered the area, keeping her headquarters at the original homestead on Canyon Creek. Many times the children accompanied her. They took along two beds and a grub box and camped at convenient places. In bad weather neighbors kept the children while Martha took to the road, often driving in storms. She was making money, saving it, determined to improve life for herself and her children.

Was she ever afraid during the time she peddled? Never, although she never carried a gun and there was never a lock on the door of the improved dugout-cabin, only a latchstring. She did carry an axe to cut wood. She drove through country still occupied by thieves and other fugitives from justice. And wild times still dominated Cheever's Flats not far from her homestead. There prostitution and gambling flourished. Her only challenge was a so-called minister who had a larger stock than hers and also made the rounds in Big Horn Basin. But one day he disappeared. "Rubbed out," the neighbors said. Three years later, his rig was found along a river bank after a cloudburst. Many questionable characters disappeared during Martha's early years in Basin country.

After she had saved money from peddling, Martha Bull moved

to the small town of Ten Sleep and leased some state school land. Later she accepted a job with Watkins Medicine Company and covered the territory around Buffalo, Wyoming. She ran the Watkins wagon for a year. Once again settled in Ten Sleep, she managed a small retail store and the post office for several years. During those years, she was active as a doctor and nurse in the area. Many children were brought into the world with her assistance.

Later on, Martha sold the retail store and bought a small ranch near the mouth of Ten Sleep River. As was her custom, she paid cash for the ranch. Her children were growing up, and life held security and peace. Her husband, Frank Bull, had suffered an early death from alcoholism.

In 1907, when Martha Bull was forty-seven years old, romance again entered her world. Robert Waln, the faithful neighbor she had known since 1886, had become a widower. Martha sold her ranch and married him. He built a beautiful home for her in the small town of Hyattville. She became as devoted a mother to her stepchildren as to her own family. Agnes Wright Spring, Wyoming historian, states, "She gave to posterity law-abiding, substantial young men and women, all of whom were fine citizens."

After Robert Waln's death, Martha returned to the small town of Ten Sleep, the closest settlement to the ranching areas where she had lived. It was also the place where she had known the good years of store management and served as postmistress. The name of the town held a peculiar fascination for Martha. Derived from the Indian method of recording time, the name represented "ten sleeps," or ten days of travel from various areas in Wyoming and Montana. Perhaps to Martha Bull Waln it represented "many sleeps" from England and Wales.

When she was seventy-five, still attractive and petite, Martha granted her only known series of interviews to Paul Frison, who later published a collection of her statements in his book *First White Woman in the Big Horn Basin*. She summed up her life as one that had missed the great operas and art galleries of the world. But, she concluded, she had found the art and music she needed in the world of nature. She had never felt she needed to make an outward display of religious feelings. For her, religion was a private matter and came from within. She believed in praying while she cut wood or in times of happiness, when her children were well.

When Martha Bull Waln was eighty years old, in 1940, the county commissioners of Washakie County, Wyoming, waived her taxes, acknowledging her to be the first white woman in the Big Horn Basin. She died in 1944 at the age of eighty-four. The record of her life indicates, as she once stated, that she "carried her end of the ropes through good and bad."

Peggy Simpson Curry has published poetry, fiction and articles in a wide range of national magazines. Her work has been printed in The New York Times, The Saturday Evening Post, Today's Poets, Ladies' Home Journal, Audubon, The Living Wilderness, Collier's, Christian Science Monitor, Toronto Star, Good Housekeeping, Boys' Life *and other publications.*

She is the author of three adult novels: Fire in the Water, So Far from Spring *and* The Oil Patch. *A juvenile novel,* A Shield of Clover, *was published in 1970. She has published a book of poetry,* Red Wind of Wyoming, *and a textbook for writers,* Creating Fiction from Experience. *Two of her short stories, published in 1957 and in 1970, won the Golden Spur Award given by Western Writers of America for distinguished short fiction about the American West.*

BIBLIOGRAPHY

BOOKS

Bragg, Bill. *Wyoming's Wealth.* Basin, Wyoming: Big Horn Book Company, 1976.

Burt, Struthers. *Powder River.* New York: Farrar and Rinehart, 1938.

Frink, Maurice. *Cow Country Cavalcade.* Boulder, Colorado: Johnson Publishing Company, 1954.

Frison, Paul. *First White Woman in the Big Horn Basin.* Worland, Wyoming: Worland Press, 1969.

Larson, T. A. *Wyoming History.* New York: W. W. Norton & Company, Inc., 1977.

Smith, Helena Huntington. *The War on Powder River.* New York: McGraw-Hill Book Co., 1966.

NEWSPAPERS

Big Horn *Sentinel,* 1884
Big Horn *Sentinel,* 1885

PAGE SUMMARY

Spring, Agnes Wright. Martha James Bull Waln (1860–1944)

INTERVIEWS AND DISCUSSIONS

Bragg, Bill
Larson, T. A.

4

Three Wishes

by NELLIE SNYDER YOST

Many ranch wives had other compelling interests in their lives besides home, family and cattle. An avocation made it possible to endure the loneliness of a life where they might not see another woman for weeks at a time. Grace McCance Snyder, pioneer child of the prairie, found her avocation very early, and stayed with it until it won for her the title of "Queen of the Quilters," "one of the most extraordinary quilt artists America has ever produced," according to "Quilt Fair '78." Of all the pioneer women included in these pages, Grace, the lady of "Three Wishes," now in her ninety-eighth year, is the only one still living.

N.S.Y.

Grace Snyder was enjoying one of the most satisfactory experiences of her life as she pressed her forehead against the airplane window and looked down on a small cottony cloud, floating lazily in the vast blue California sky. For more than half a century she had longed to see the top side of a cloud—and now she was seeing it! That it looked much the same as the bottom side didn't matter. That she had seen it from the top did.

She was disappointed that the day was so clear that there were few clouds to be seen, even over the Rockies, but she was loving it all. Her two weeks in California with her brothers and sisters had been most pleasant, but now she was eager to be at home again on her Sandhills ranch, and back at work sewing thousands of tiny pieces together into the beautiful flower-basket pattern of her newest quilt.

As a child growing up on the high plains of central Nebraska, Grace McCance had dreamed three dreams and wished three wishes. She wished that she might one day make the most beautiful quilts in the world, marry a cowboy, and look down on the tops of the high white clouds that drifted daily above her wide, treeless prairies. At that time it had seemed impossible that any of her dreams would ever come true.

She was only three when, in 1885, her family moved from Cass County, Missouri, to the Nebraska homestead. The move was a drastic change for all of them. Her mother, Margaret McCance, only twenty-four that spring, was already the mother of three little girls. A slender, black-haired lass, she never in her life, except during her nine pregnancies, weighed as much as 100 pounds. She and her husband, Charles, had gone to school together in Missouri. After their marriage, they had lived on a rented farm in the old, well-settled, timbered country where they had grown up.

Like so many young men of his time, Charles contracted "land fever." In central Nebraska, he had learned, a man could homestead a quarter section (160 acres of land), live on it five years, then "prove up" and receive a deed to it. Eager to take advantage of such an opportunity, he made the trip west in the fall of 1884, filed on a quarter section 12 miles northwest of Cozad, a village on the Union Pacific Railroad, and the following spring took possession of the land.

To finance the move, he sold the family milk cow, then rented a railway boxcar and loaded into it his big mule team, wagon, farm machinery and household goods. He rode all the long way in the rough, dirty little car with his possessions, unloaded at Cozad, hitched the mules to the wagon, loaded the other things and drove through the rolling hills to his homestead. There he hurriedly built a 12 × 14 foot, one-room sod house and a small barn. Sod buildings cost almost nothing and were a boon to the prairie settlers, for most of them had very little money. A house like Grace's first Nebraska home could be built for about $10. With a good tar-paper roof, two or three windows, a door and a wooden floor, such as the McCances had, they cost slightly more.

Grace, her mother and her two sisters, five-year-old Florry, and six-month-old Stella, came out on the train in May. Her father was there with the wagon to meet them and take them to their new home. The vast, grassy prairies, without a tree or a stream anywhere, were so different from the fields and trees and big white farmhouses they had always known. It all seemed so raw and new and bare.

The two older girls adjusted quickly and soon came to love their prairie home. But for the young mother, used to pretty things and a gentle way of living, the everlasting winds that blew across the shadeless prairie, and the tiny, crowded sod house were a sore trial. They had no milk cow either, or chickens, and they had to haul water for household use. And there were almost no neighbors near enough to visit.

With fierce determination, however, she set about to make do with what little she had. She planted a fine garden on the patch of ground that had yielded up the sod for the walls of her dwelling. She carried rainwater from the nearby pond where her husband watered his mules until the hot summer winds sucked it dry, and used it to do her laundry on a scrub board, with lye soap she made herself; she baked delicious, crusty loaves of bread from her homemade yeast.

To banish the drabness of her prairie home, she planted four-o'clocks by the doorway and watered them during dry spells with the water left from Saturday baths in the tin washtub. Indoors, she prettied her one room by making curtains out of bleached flour sacks, embroidered with flying red birds, for its three little windows. From cigar boxes she made little shelves, brackets and comb cases and hung them from pegs driven into the earthen walls. On one peg she hung their big gilt-framed marriage certificate. A handsome document, decorated with colored scrolls, flowers, doves and cupids, it gave quite an elegant touch to the little room.

By early summer, the McCances' small supply of cash was gone, but at a point 30 miles south of Cozad, at the present site of the little town of Eustis, a new railroad, the Burlington, Chicago & Quincy Highline, was building westward, and men and horses were in demand. The wages were good, as much as $2.00 a day for a man and team, so the family put a camping outfit together and moved to the end-of-track for the rest of the summer. There they lived in a tent while Charles, with his big mule team and a "scraper," helped throw up the high grade that would later carry the shining rails on to Colorado.

The camp, made up of many families and numerous single men, was large and noisy, but by summer's end Charles had earned the money he needed to buy a milk cow and some chickens, and to lay in the necessities to see his family through the long winter ahead.

After returning to the homestead, Charles set about adding a second sod room to the house and digging a cellar cave into a nearby bank. Food stored in the cave was protected from freezing by the thick earthen walls, and there Margaret tucked away her garden's root vegetables and the tomatoes and beans she canned in tins, with lids made airtight with hot sealing wax. Her flour sacks of dried sweet corn hung from pegs in the soddy kitchen. Cut from the cobs as soon as she was settled on the homestead again, and spread on sheets on the flat roof, the sun-dried corn made toothsome winter eating.

Like other prairie pioneer children, the McCance girls had only homemade toys. Their favorites were the corncob dolls they made by the dozens after winter closed in and they could no longer play on their beloved prairie. Their mother helped them dress the lady and girl dolls in scraps of old silks and satins from her piece bag; the papa dolls, made from cobs the mules had stepped on and split part way up, had two legs to put trousers on. The babies—and all the cob families had lots of babies—they made from the tiniest "nubbin" cobs. Grace and Florry spent hours at the corn pile, hunting the finest and longest corn silks for hair for their lady dolls, whose fancy hats were made of dried sunflower heads trimmed with barred and speckled chicken feathers.

By this time the family had acquired a milk cow and chickens, and by the next year they had a well of their own. Then other families came, settling on nearby quarter sections, and before long there was a schoolhouse, Sunday school and community socializing.

By the second spring, Margaret owned a few turkey hens—her "money crop"—and Grace and Florry were given the chore of trailing the birds to the nests they insisted on hiding far from home. For plain outright aggravation, the girls learned, there are few jobs to match that of trailing turkey hens to their nests. Guided by a stubborn wild instinct, the hens strayed afar to lay in hidden places where snakes and skunks ate their eggs and coyotes sometimes snared them from the nests. The girls had to follow the hens, find the nests and bring the eggs home, until the hens were ready to "nest," when their mother installed them and their eggs in barrels and boxes near the chicken house.

The hens often strolled the prairie for hours before slipping, like the shadow of a cloud, into the clump of tall grass selected for their nests—usually at the very instant the girls were not watching. The task wasn't so demanding that first year or two, but when the flock came to number twenty or thirty hens, the girls had their hands full. The reward came in the late fall, when the barrels of dressed turkeys were shipped to Omaha. The check that came back provided winter clothing for the family, and bright wool stocking caps and mittens for the faithful herders.

By the third spring, Grace's father had accumulated several head of cows; too many to picket on the prairie as he had the milk cow. From now on, the cattle would have to be herded, and six-year-old Grace was elected to do the herding. Always a lover of the out-of-doors and of animals and nature, Grace gloried in her new occupation: keeping the cows out of their own and the neighbors' little unfenced corn and wheat fields. There was one drawback—loneliness—no one to talk to or play with during the long days on the prairie, and nothing to do with her hands.

One evening, after the longest, lonesomest day she had ever known, Grace watched her mother setting tiny, quick stitches into the diamond-shaped calico scraps she was sewing into a Lone Star pattern quilt top. And right then Grace knew what she wanted to do while herding. But when she asked for pieces to sew while she sat with the cattle, her mother told her she was too young to piece quilts. There were never enough leftover scraps from the clothing she made her family for Margaret to keep up with the ever-growing need for winter quilts, and her reluctance to share with Grace was understandable.

But Grace *knew* she wasn't too young, and she coaxed so hard that her mother finally cut her enough pieces for a doll-sized four-patch quilt. "You'll have to do neat work, match your corners and fasten the threads so the ends don't show," she cautioned. "I can't afford to waste thread and pieces on you if you don't." Grace followed instructions, matched her corners, took tiny, even stitches and fastened her threads properly. After that, when the sun had warmed the air enough that she could take off her mittens, she took her cigar-box workbasket and sewed the pieces together in the pattern, and began to learn and perfect the skill that was one day to make her first dream come true.

Herding came to an end when winter snows covered the grass and the cattle had to be corraled and fed. Savage snowstorms filled the canyons and covered the wide valleys. March winds melted the great drifts, then blew for days on end, turning the land brown and dry, ready for the dread scourge of prairie fires. The first to threaten the McCances came early one morning—a smoke billow, riding a high wind and climbing the sky above the far hills.

Grace's father left at once, a barrel of water and a pile of old gunny sacks in his wagon, to find and help fight the fire. For hours the family anxiously watched the smoke thicken to a haze that finally hid the sun. Then, before their terrorized gaze, the leaping flames boiled over a high hill northwest of the house. The cattle in the corral began to bawl and mill in fear. Grace and Florry were on the point of running to turn them out, then flee with their mother and sisters to the middle of the plowed field, where they would all be safe. But fire burns slower downhill, and when the licking flames reached the fireguard, plowed months before, they halted, blazed up for a moment and flickered out.

In early May, as the pastures greened again, Grace took up her daily task of herding. On the first day, before she took the cows out, her mother had a little talk with her. The cows would be finding little calves now, she said, and Grace would have to watch carefully to keep the herd together. If a cow started to stray off by herself, Grace must head her right back into the bunch; else she would hide and the coyotes might get the new calf. Grace asked where they would find the calves. Her mother said, "Most likely in the tall grass at the upper ends of the draws."

As soon as Grace had the cows out on the prairie they began to scatter all over the valley. "They were only hunting the best of the new green grass," Grace said, long years later, "but I thought they were hunting little calves. Every time one headed toward the head of a draw, I ran as hard as I could to get ahead of her and search through the tall dead grass. I wanted so much to find the calf before the cow did, but, though I ran myself to a frazzle that spring, I never found a single baby calf. The cows all seemed to find them in the corral at night, and I was so disappointed."

Later that summer a wind of almost tornadic force ripped the roof off the soddy. The heavy rain that rode on its heels made a sorry mess of the dwelling's humble furnishings. All the little shelves, brackets, pictures and curtains were either gone or a part of the sodden muddy jumble left on the floor; most of the kitchen supply of food was soaked and ruined. Out on the prairie a few days later, the McCances found a half portion of the marriage certificate, but no part of the frame or glass that had enclosed it.

The McCances had lived on the homestead for five years before Grace had her first opportunity to go to town with her father. She flew around that morning, helping pack the balls of fresh butter which had hardened in the cool depths of the well, and the extra eggs, bedded in pails of oats, for the long, hot, jolting drive to Cozad. She was almost dizzy with excitement by the time her father stopped the team at the hitch rail in front of the store and she could help him carry their trading stock into its dim interior.

She never forgot the good smells of that old-time general store: smells from its fine mixture of dried fruits, vinegar, strong cheese, coffee, leather, smoked hams, dill pickles in open barrels, new cloth, molasses, rope, overshoes, fresh-cut plug tobacco, and a hundred other things. Nor the treasure feast for her eyes in the glass showcases: foot-long fancy-headed hatpins, glittering jet belt buckles, laces, ribbons, cubes of colored glass-headed pins.

At noon Grace and her father sat in the shade of the wagon and ate store cheese, crackers and gingersnaps, washed down by long swigs of cold water from the sack-wrapped jug they carried in the wagon. The day was almost gone before they pulled in at home again, but it had been a day she would always remember.

By the time Grace was ten, she had five sisters. The family had lately moved from the homestead to a farm just across a deep, twisting ditch from the district school. Still her father's herder, she grazed the cattle from early morning until first recess, coraled them, changed her dress and dashed across the ditch (dry most of the year) to school. At last recess she reversed the process, took the cattle out to pasture and herded until dark.

And that was the spring Grace began to dream her second dream. With no scraps for quilts most of the time, she spent long hours lying on her back on the warm ground, watching the whipped-cream cloud puffs sailing across the endless blue skies. Her fascination with the ever-changing cloud shapes led to her

longing to look down on a cloud from *above;* her longing to fly
above the clouds was strong enough to hurt, as her longing for a
"boughten" doll with real hair, or for a sidesaddle of her own
sometimes hurt. But, like the doll she was almost too old for, or
the saddle she couldn't have because it cost too much, she knew
she would never get above the clouds, either.

The big rain that flooded old Stump Ditch, the deep water-
course that lay between the McCances and the schoolhouse, came
that September. The day was bright and warm when Grace corraled the cows and hurried across the ditch to school. Toward two
o'clock in the afternoon heavy black clouds suddenly rolled up
from the northeast, blotting out sun and sky. Within a few minutes
it was too dark to see to study, and the teacher told the children
they'd better hurry home ahead of the impending storm. But, before they could leave the schoolyard, lightning ripped the skies
apart, thunder rolled and crashed and the rain came down in tor-
rents.

For the next hour, wind and rain shook and pounded the
schoolhouse, lightning crackled in bright green flashes, the air
smelled of sulphur and the thunder roared without letup. Then the
storm stopped as suddenly as it had begun, and the children and
their teacher hurried outside, where they heard a deep, ugly growl
—old Stump Ditch was in flood. They all ran down to the crossing.
On the far side, toward home, a wide, shallow flood poured down
the draw toward the ditch. Already half full, the water in it was
rising by the minute, dirty, tumbling and foam-topped. The ditch
was soon brim full, with heavy froth topping the bucking waves
and big splashes leaping over its rim at the elbow turn below the
crossing that had been bone dry two hours earlier.

The children sat on the schoolhouse porch and watched the
water roaring by on both sides of them. Soon trash began coming
down the ditch: boards, tin cans, broken kegs, an old rocking
chair, tossing and turning in the rushing water. With all the raging
fury of the ditch between them and their homes, the children from
the far side knew they would not get home that night. With no
light, no supper and no beds, the pupils and their teacher dreaded
to see night come down on the valley.

Then they saw one of the farmers from up the draw coming
across the flat, the water almost up to his wagon box and his team
leaning hard into the sweep of the current. He had come to take

the children from his side of the ditch home and to bring supper to the others who would have to spend the night in the schoolhouse.

With a lantern, several quilts, bread and a pail of hard-boiled eggs and a big pot of black coffee, things seemed better. Grace and her two sisters felt pleasantly wicked about the coffee; their parents would never let them drink it at home. They finished off the bread and eggs for breakfast the next morning. By recess time that afternoon the ditch was passable, and Grace went home to tend to her herding.

That fall Charlie McCance built a double granary: two cribs with a driveway between and a shingle roof covering the whole. Now he was able to store his wheat crop over the winter; and in the spring, when the price was much better, he sold it and brought home a brand-new carryall, or spring wagon. A two-seated vehicle, it was large enough to carry the whole family; the parents and the two littlest girls in the front seat, the other four in the back seat. Its padded black-patent-leather seats were soft as air, and the long buggy box rode like a breeze above its elliptic springs. The new carriage was by no means the Cadillac of its day, but it was a far cry from the hard-riding springless farm wagon that preceded it.

In the spring of her eleventh year, Grace dreamed her third dream. She was herding cattle, on foot as usual, and the new dream had to do with a cowboy and a horse and saddle. In her geography book at school there was a picture of a cowboy on horseback, watching a big herd of grazing cattle. She had never seen a genuine live cowboy; for in Roten Valley there were only farm boys, riding heavy-footed work horses. In her dream the cowboy, riding a fine tall horse and leading another, always came galloping up to her. She would then step gracefully into the new sidesaddle on the led horse's back and ride off with him to help look after the cattle herds on his big ranch. At that time there was no romance in the dream; the important part was the horse and the new sidesaddle.

The fall of '93 was very dry. Pastures failed and there was little feed. The milk cows dried up early, and there was no butter to trade for groceries in town. The winter was cold and dry, and very little rain fell in the spring. The terrible statewide "Drouth of '94" was upon the land. By planting time the fields were hard and cracked, the pastures barely tinged with green. Gardens withered and died in the scorching heat of the long summer. Starving pigs, too small to butcher, had to be killed; the cattle grew lean and bawled with hunger. There was no market for them, for no one had any money. In town the stores closed their doors upon bare shelves, for their owners, too, had no money to settle their accounts or buy new stock.

In July a destructive, scorching wind sent the McCance family running for their lives to the cellar cave behind the house. When the danger was past and the refugees came above ground again, they found the fine new granary, with the driveway that had sheltered the new carriage, was gone; the chicken house was torn apart, and most of the hens were dead. The carriage, left outside that afternoon, stood unharmed.

The drouth dragged on. There was no harvest that fall. Homesteaders who could afford to go left the country; the rest stayed on, facing starvation. Then supplies of food, clothing, seed and livestock feed, hauled free by the railroads, began to arrive from the East—voluntary people-to-people welfare that saved the desperate settlers. A few, like the McCances, had relatives in the more fortunate states who sent what was needed, leaving the welfare supplies for the others.

And that autumn of '94, by far the most difficult the McCances had endured on the plains, the seventh baby arrived. The first boy in the family, he was a joy to them all, even though he was the only baby his father could not pay for when the doctor made the long trip out to the farm. Years later, after Charles McCance had been laid to rest in Walnut Grove cemetery, his family found the $10 promissory note he gave the doctor the day the baby was born. The payments, scratched on the back, fifty cents or a dollar at a time, covered most of the next two years.

After a mild winter, the rains came again and the prairies blossomed once more. Bountiful crops grew and the people prospered. New buildings went up, fences went in and the open range north of Cozad was a thing of the past.

In 1898 another baby, the seventh daughter, was born; and that winter the mother and all the children had the measles. The McCances now lived in a two-story house, with most of the bedrooms upstairs. The weather had turned intensely cold, and there was no heat on the upper floor. As the family sickened, one by one and two by two, Charles moved the beds down to the living room. Not only were all the children and their mother very ill, but there was the ever-present dread of pneumonia and other complications.

Their worst fears were realized when the only son, four years old and apparently recovering from the disease, had a "back-set" and became gravely ill with pneumonia. For days his life hung in the balance, and only excellent nursing and fervent prayers finally pulled him through. After nearly two months from the onset of the first case, the family was on its feet again.

January of the following year was abnormally cold, with temperatures seldom above zero, and often far below, for days at a time. Toward the end of the month, a week-long revival meeting was held at the nearby Walnut Grove church. Grace, with her father and Florry, drove over each night for the services. On the final Friday evening, the two sisters went forward in response to the invitation, gave their lives to Christ and requested baptism. Several others had done the same thing during the week and the minister announced that baptismal services would be held at Pedan's Pond the following Sunday morning after church.

The day was bitter cold, with a strong north wind sweeping across the prairie. The entire congregation accompanied the candidates for baptism to the pond, where men had already cut a narrow passage through the foot-thick ice from the bank to a spot in the pond deep enough for immersion. While the people stood on the bank, singing hymns, the minister waded out to the baptismal pool and stood in the waist-deep water as the candidates waded out to him, one by one, and were immersed.

All her life Grace had been deathly afraid of water in anything larger than a washtub, and her fear of walking down between the walls of ice into the cold black water was almost overpowering. But as she listened to the old familiar hymn, "If Jesus Goes with Me," her fear melted away. When her turn came, she walked calmly into the icy water.

As the converts came out of the pond, waiting families and friends quickly wrapped them in warm quilts, hustled them into the buggies and up the hill to the Pedan farmhouse where they changed into dry clothes. Neither the minister nor those he baptized that frigid day caught cold or suffered any other ill effects from the experience.

In the spring of Grace's eighteenth year, her father decided to move to the Birdwood, some 65 miles to the northwest. The new home would be in a sparsely populated area, a new open range frontier. The young woman had mixed feelings about the move. She and her older sisters were enjoying their social life in the valley, mostly centered around the Walnut Grove church and the Roten Valley schoolhouse, where they and their friends and beaus attended church services, literaries, box socials and parties. The only advantage to the move was that they would be living on the edge of the big ranch country, cowboy country. There she might, at last, meet a real cowboy.

The move entailed many hardships for the family: another small, crowded house, hard work and loneliness. However, the lovely, sparkling Birdwood Creek that gurgled its winding way past the little house, and the big cottonwood trees beside it were a delightful change from the dry, treeless plains of their first homes. But their pleasure in that first summer on the creek was marred by the near-fatal illness of the husband and father, stricken with appendicitis that July. At that time (1900) the malady was known as "inflammation of the bowels," and there was little that could be done for it.

The nearest doctor daily made the thirty-miles-long round trip to the small house, did what little he could to ease the sick man's frightful pain, shook his head hopelessly and drove away. Eventually the appendix ruptured, and the family watched the suffering man sink lower and lower. One evening, when they did not expect him to live through the night, a cowboy came to the door. Grace answered his knock.

Tall, slim, grey-eyed, he stood hat in hand on the step. He explained that he was summering cattle on Squaw Creek, a few miles to the north, that he had heard that Mr. McCance was sick and he had come to see if there was anything he could do: help with the chores, sit up with her father that night. She thanked him, told him there was nothing anyone could do and that the family would watch by his bedside that night.

Sadly she watched him mount his handsome grey horse and ride away, wondering if she would ever see him again. Then she hurried back to her father's bedside. But Charles McCance survived that awful night, and the hot days and nights that followed, to eventually win his way back to health again.

That frontier, too, was settling fast and by the next year there were neighbors, parties and Sunday-school services in the new schoolhouse. There, under Grace Jeffers (older sister of William Jeffers, later president of the Union Pacific Railroad), a dedicated teacher who, as one of a large and poor family, had struggled to obtain a high-school education and become an educator herself, Grace crammed all the education she had missed during the years she had been her father's boy into that final year at home.

Inspired by Miss Jeffers, Grace was determined to be a teacher herself. Before she could obtain a teaching certificate, she would have to spend eight weeks in school in North Platte, the county seat 30 miles distant. With her father as co-signer of her note, she borrowed $35 from the bank. The sum, Miss Jeffers had told her, would be sufficient for books, tuition and eight weeks' board and room while she completed a concentrated high-school course, the old-time "summer school" for teachers. She finished the course, sat for the county examinations, passed and received her third-grade teacher's certificate.

That winter Grace taught a six-month term of school (two pupils) in an isolated area 60 miles north of the Birdwood. Before leaving home to head out into the unknown as a passenger in a single-seated, two-wheeled mail cart behind two lively mules, she spent a part of the last dollar of her borrowed money for several yards of calico, enough for a quilt top—the first she was to make from whole goods, rather than scraps.

After all the years with her lively brother and sisters, Grace found the quiet loneliness of the ranch-home school almost unbearable and, she said later, if it hadn't been for the pleasure she derived from cutting and piecing her quilt, she would have died of boredom.

Her wages were $15 a month, plus board and room: enough to pay off her note, buy new clothes and go to summer school again. That fall she went back to the bank, borrowed $60, bought a horse and buggy, roomed at home and drove to her new school, five miles away. The Birdwood was so well settled by then that she had sixteen pupils of all sizes and ages. Her salary was double that of the year before, and again she used her first two months' wages to pay off her second loan.

In the meantime she had seen the cowboy two or three more times, always unexpectedly and to her own disadvantage. There was the day she and her sisters rode horseback into the hills on the far side of the creek to pick wild fruit. When she saw that her horse had pulled loose from the bush to which she'd been tied and had crossed the creek and headed toward home, Grace ran after her. Pulling off her shoes and stockings and tucking her long skirts above her knees, she waded the stream and tried to catch the mare. Well knowing who was master of the situation, the pony kept just out of reach as Grace hopped along through the stickery grass. At that moment, the cowboy rode around the nearest hill, almost in front of her.

The embarrassed young lady hurriedly pulled down her skirts as the cowboy caught her horse, led it to her, tipped his hat politely and rode away. The romance later took a turn for the better and the cowboy came riding to her home one day—as if straight out of her dream—for the led horse carried a fine sidesaddle. Grace mounted it gracefully and rode off into the lovely fall-tinted hills with him. That afternoon he proposed to her.

In October 1903, Grace married her cowboy, Bert Snyder, and went to live with him on his Sandhills ranch, 20 miles to the north. The first of her three dreams had come true.

Her marriage coincided with the twilight years of the open range. Within the next few years, settlers flocked in to occupy every previously empty valley, and fences began to stitch the land. The far-flung established ranchers helped their homesteader neighbors "make do" for the five years needed to "prove up," then bought them out and ran cattle again where the little claim soddies and shacks had stood so briefly.

The forty years Grace spent on the ranch were good ones, even though they brought their quota of blizzards, prairie fires and drouths. She was busy raising turkeys of her own, tending big gardens, baking bread, churning butter, canning and curing the vegetables, beef and pork that supplied her table, sewing for herself and her three daughters—and piecing quilts.

She helped out of doors, too, mostly in the hayfield. Putting up the hay for winter feed was the big job every summer. Grace and her husband, with one or two hired men, made up those early hay crews. Her part was always the same: she ran the rake. She could rake straighter, evener windrows than any man he ever had, Bert said, and she loved doing it. With a gentle team to pull the rake, she drove up and down the meadows, spinning the straight, fragrant rows of hay behind her.

The problem of what to do with the children while their mother spent her afternoons in the hayfield was solved by bolting a stout wooden box to the rake frame at her feet. There her first child, a girl, rode contentedly; and when her brother took her place in the box, the little girl played beside the big haystacks where her father on the hay sweep and the hired man on the stack could keep an eye on her. Later the girl and the boy became a part of the crew, driving the stacker team that lifted the big loads of hay to the stacks. Still later, when they were old enough to handle the mowers, their two younger sisters graduated from the box on the rake to driving the stacker team, and then to mowers of their own. But, for more than twenty years, Grace kept her place as top rake-hand on the ranch.

Schools, or the lack of them, have always been a problem in the sparsely settled ranch country. When her two eldest children were ready for school, there was none near enough to send them to. Grace taught them herself. Later they rode horseback to a new district school five miles distant, as did the two younger in their turn. In time telephone lines bridged the distances between the ranches, bringing the neighbors closer. Following the Second World War, power lines stretched across the many miles of hills, making modern conveniences possible for the isolated ranch homes, and good roads and automobiles brought the distant towns within easy reach.

The Snyders bought their first automobile in 1912, quite a few years before there were any roads. A wooden-bodied Ford, precursor of the Model T, it was a marvel—but not exactly practical. Both Grace and Bert drove it—or perhaps "pushed it" is a better description. The crooked, sandy trails that so long served as roads in the Sandhills made driving a car about as easy as wrapping two watermelons together. Progress was slow, considering stallings on uphill grades and in bad spots—and each time the engine died, someone had to get out and crank it to life again.

But the Snyders and their neighbors were persistent. Bert and Grace had their second Ford by 1920, the year the passage of the Nineteenth Amendment gave women the vote. For the first time since she had lived on the ranch, Grace set out with her husband, that bleak November election day, for their polling place: a schoolhouse 15 miles distant.

The roads were dry and sandy, and they had to push the car up so many hills and through so many bad places that they were all day getting there and back—but Grace had cast her first vote, a significant milepost in her life, and a privilege she exercised faithfully from then on.

Over the years, the art of quilt making had never lost its fascination for Grace. She spent all her spare time cutting, piecing or quilting, and especially in the long winters, when they were sometimes snowbound for weeks at a time, did her pastime stand her in good stead.

The bright, pretty quilts she made for everyday use on the family beds were fashioned from sewing scraps, but when she turned to designing her own patterns she began to buy carefully matched colored percales, and to turn out the masterpieces that were to make up her collection of show quilts. After her daughters were married and gone from home, Grace set up her quilting frames in the sunny bedroom that had been theirs. From then on, she always had three quilts under way at a time: one in the frames, one being cut and another being pieced. When the ends of her fingers were sore from quilting, she cut out pieces; when she wore blisters on her hands with the scissors, she sewed pieces together. Lovely quilts seemed fairly to flow from her skilled hands.

During her final years on the ranch, Grace made most of the spreads that were one day to win recognition for her as the maker of some of the most beautiful quilts in the world, "one of the most extraordinary quilt artists America has ever produced," according to one brochure, "Quilt Fair '78," describing her work. These included the large, colorful "Mosaic Hexagon," made of more than 50,000 dime-sized hexagons, and her unbelievably beautiful "Flower Basket Petit Point" of 87,789 tiny squares and triangles—pieces so small that eight of them, sewed together, make a square smaller than a regular-sized postage stamp.

Interestingly enough, parts of her finest quilts were pieced while she sat in her car beside a Sandhill windmill, or a gate or a section of barbed-wire fence. Bert had continued to drive as long as Ford manufactured his planetary-shift models, but when the new gearshifts became the only cars available, he told his wife and daughters they could do the driving. He would go horseback. But going horseback wasn't always practical and it came to pass that he frequently asked Grace to drive him to some distant pasture to check a windmill, or to repair a gate or a stretch of fence. Picking up an ever-ready box of quilt pieces, she took him where he wanted to go and sewed pieces together while she waited for him.

Grace's parents, after all the hard frontier years, finally prospered, then sold their good Nebraska farm and retired to California, where they lived out their lives. Six of the nine brothers and sisters had also moved to the West Coast, and Grace and her remaining Nebraska sister (Florry had died in 1909 at the birth of her only child) visited occasionally. On one such visit, near the end of the Second World War, the two of them went to California by train.

Grace, ready to come home before her sister was, made her third dream come true by exchanging her train ticket for passage on a plane and flying home above the clouds. From then on, she never passed up an opportunity to fly. When she was invited to show some of her quilts at the Womans International Exhibition in New York City, and the Eastern States Exposition in West Springfield, Massachusetts, she flew to both cities. When coming down over New York City at night, with the millions of lights below giving the clouds a pink glow, she said it seemed that she was sinking into an enormous bowl of pink ice cream.

Grace's son had built a new home on the ranch, near his parents' house, and brought his bride there to live. When their first child was ready for school, there was none for him to go to; the little frame schoolhouse where his father had gone had been torn down during the war. As the only child in the big district, some other solution had to be found. His father solved the problem by buying a small plane and flying him down to Tryon, the only town in the big county. The plane could make the 24-mile round trip in a few minutes, whereas it took two to three hours to travel the same distance in a good car.

Naturally, Grace often flew with her son. She loved looking down on the meadows where she had raked so many miles of windrows, or on the roads, where she had so often pushed the old Fords through the sand or snowdrifts. The plane was handy for checking the windmills and fences, or for zipping down to North Platte, 50 miles away, for some shopping, a trip that needed at least six hours by car when the so-called roads were good, an indefinite time when they weren't.

However, Grace was to see the day, some years before she and her cowboy retired to their comfortable home in North Platte, when a paved road reached all the way from the city to the ranch, and beyond. Though a winding road through the limitless grassy hills, she could then drive comfortably, day or night, from the ranch to town in ninety minutes—and not have to push even once.

Though she is too frail to travel anymore, and stays home in North Platte, Grace enjoys reports brought back to her of the fame accorded her and her quilts. In July 1978 her Flower Basket quilt was the star of the big show at the select Congress of Quilts in Arlington, Virginia. The following December, eleven of her quilts were hung in a "one-woman quilt show" at the Great Expectations Quilt Fair in Houston, Texas. In July 1979, they were the "centerpiece" of the huge Quilt Symposium of Palo Alto, California. With an insurance value of nearly $100,000, the quilts are far too valuable to be shipped as baggage on any plane. Yet they are in such demand that the big shows are willing to pay for a seat of their own on the plane, next to Grace's daughter who accompanies them. Featured the past few years in the leading quilt magazines across the nation, the collection is a top drawing card at any show.

Plans are now in the making for a "Grace Snyder Room" in a museum in Lincoln, Nebraska's capital city. Long the acknowledged Quilt Queen of her home state, the title is now being awarded her all across the nation. Now in her ninety-eighth year, Grace looks back on her long life with satisfaction. She has seen all three of her impossible dreams come true in most dramatic fashion.

———————

Nellie Snyder Yost was born in a Nebraska sod house in 1905. She is the author of nine books on the history and biography of the Great Plains from Texas to Montana. The first book published in 1951, all are still in print, some in paperback. She has won W.W.A.'s Golden Spur Award, 1969, the Golden Saddleman, 1975, and the Cowboy Hall of Fame Wrangler, 1978. She has just recently retired as Secretary-Treasurer of Western Writers of America.

BIBLIOGRAPHY

"Three Wishes" is based on the recollections of Grace Snyder, the author's mother.

5

Heroine of Honey Creek

by LYLE BRUERE and RUTH VAN ACKEREN

Kate Shelley, at age fifteen, had one big, exciting adventure that lifted her to national prominence and continued recall and honors almost a century later, as the Heroine of Honey Creek.

N.S.Y.

There had been no twilight in the Iowa farm valley, that rain-lashed evening of July 6, 1881; none of the usual burnished darkening of little hollows and the twitter of small nesting things.

Wind and rain and early darkness had rolled together above the Des Moines River where it crossed farmlands between Boone and Moingona. The storm swept along the Chicago–North Western railroad tracks and over Honey Creek, to beat against the trackside home of Michael Shelley's widow and four children.

When the rising creek threatened to undermine the stable, young Kate Shelley had run down from the house to open the latched door. Their few horses and cows scattered to safety on higher ground as she moved some baby pigs to shelter and beat her way back up the slope through wind and rain. At age fifteen, she was her mother's most dependable helper and guide to the younger children.

In Michael Shelley's thirteen years of section labor, his wife and children had watched him walk the track and cross the railroad bridge at Honey Creek. They knew the signals of numbered engine whistles, and members of the track and train crews.

The July storm swelled into heavier gusts, and the Shelleys watched from the window as lightning flashes lit the wet ground and tossing trees. The old clock ticked away the hours as the younger children—Mayme, John and Margaret—dozed near their mother, but Kate shared her vigil. Flashes showed the creek rising higher on the slope, rolling and frothy between its scattered burdens of boards, leafy tree limbs, and fence posts. Could Honey Creek bridge stand against this strain? Would the even greater force in the Des Moines River wash out its long wooden bridge?

Between fragments of prayer, asking intercession of all the saints, they listened for reassuring sounds from the railroad track, where the Chicago Express passenger train was due from the West about midnight.

Eleven o'clock . . . Then a whistle pierced the drumming of the storm, and a backing engine's headlight wavered through the rainy darkness. It was near the bridge at Honey Creek; the helper engine that was available at Moingona for assistance to trains or short delivery runs or safety checks. How many times Kate's father had gone to that bridge after heavy rains, waiting for the helper engine to be backed across the Des Moines River bridge and the shorter one above Honey Creek. Sometimes he climbed into the engine cab to ride with the engineer and fireman to Boone and back, or stood on the running board behind the tender with Pat Donahue, the section boss, both holding their lanterns before them and watching for damage to the roadbed.

"Run to Boone and return to Moingona regardless of all trains," such orders would read. If there was question of the track's safety, the engine might stop while the two men walked the endangered stretch, their lanterns wheeling the shadows of their legs.

Kate pressed against the window frame as they watched the engine light back slowly onto the creek bridge. Suddenly the light tipped and disappeared. Above the wind and rain, they heard sounds of crashing timbers and squealing brakes, then the engine's shuddering fall. Men shouted in the darkness for a moment. Then everything was still, and Kate's own scream was echoing in her ears as she jerked on her coat and hat and reached for the lantern. The wick had burned down to its last shred, and she hurried to cut a strip from an old felt skirt, coaxing it into the wick slot as she turned aside her mother's anxious protests.

Kate knew the risks out in the storm, but was driven to help if she could. Only two years earlier, Kate's brother James had drowned while swimming in the Des Moines River. Mrs. Shelley's eyes were wise and sad, but she knew the dangers others might be meeting. Every moment might make the difference between rescue and disaster for the helper-engine crew. And someone had to warn the crew of the midnight passenger train, due from the West in less than an hour.

Margaret Shelley pushed the lantern nearer to her daughter's hand. "Go, then, in the name of God, and do what you can," she said gently.

The railroad track near the Shelley house was covered by water, so Kate climbed the bluff behind the house and hurried southwest in a curving detour to a point where the track cut through low hills. She ran along the ties then, hoping the men could see her lantern. When she reached the broken bridge, she swung the lantern and shouted into the darkness.

The answering call came from the bank below and near the bridge, and in the next flashes of lightning Kate could see engineer Ed Wood and his brakeman, Adam Agar, but the wind and rain drowned out their words. They had pulled themselves into trees overhanging the swollen creek, and Kate knew that they couldn't hear what she called about getting help from Moingona. She had to trust that they would be safe in the trees, and hurry west. It was only a mile to Moingona, but to get there she had to cross the Des Moines River, flooded and churning in the storm. The only way across was the long wooden railroad bridge. And on that bridge she might, before long, meet the passenger train that was sweeping that way, somewhere beyond Moingona.

What had happened to fireman Olmstead, she wondered as she ran toward the river bridge. Had Pat Donahue been with the engine crew when they backed onto the creek bridge? Sometimes the gusts of wind turned her half around, and she bent against the drenching rain for an instant, gasping into her cupped hand.

Kate knew that pedestrians were forbidden to cross the narrow railroad bridge, where they might meet a train at any time. Some reckless ones had continued to cross it anyway, and there was talk that the bridge and building gang might have to take up the plank walk that was there for use of the C&NW men.

They had done it, too, she saw when she reached the bridge. On a still day in broad daylight, such a crossing on just the great slabs of ties could stop a heartbeat in fear, but this was wind and blackness that reflected the wet ties and tossing river only in the lightning flashes.

The swollen river was much nearer the ties and rails than Kate had ever seen it before, and as she knelt to crawl the slippery ties, close inside one guiding rail, she listened and looked again toward the far end of the bridge, some four hundred feet ahead. No head-lights of the midnight train—no sound of its whistle—so she crawled across the last tarred timber of the ground track onto the ties and rails beamed between the great wooden pilings.

The next gust of wind blew out Kate's lantern. She had no match, even if there had been a dry spot for striking. The lantern's dim light had been a help and comfort in the blasts of rainy wind; without it, she had to stretch one hand ahead to explore while she clung to the rail with the other. The now-useless lantern hindered her, but she pushed the wire hoop higher on her arm and reached toward another tie. Every child in the Shelley family knew the precious value of their few possessions.

Sometimes her drenched skirt caught on a splintered edge, and her bent knee was jerked down between ties; she clawed in terror until she saw again that no headlight split the rainy darkness.

Tears and rain ran down her face together when a great flash of lightning showed the western bank some two hundred feet ahead. She had come halfway; there was still no sign of the midnight train —and then she saw the great uprooted tree rushing toward her on the rolling water.

In her first terrified reaction, Kate rose to her knees and clasped her hands, but instinct bowed her close against the rail that must be her anchor if the tree lodged against the bridge.

The lightning flash was gone and it was dark again when the bridge creaked mightily and the huge tree slid between two piers. Foam and wet leaves pelted the girl who pressed against the rail. She pushed the lantern higher on her arm again and scrambled on, knowing that every foot she gained toward the bank was bought with time that brought the night train closer. The Chicago Express made no stops at such small towns as Moingona; it would rush on past and toward the broken bridge at Honey Creek unless she got it signaled to a stop.

Kate could run when she reached the western bank, and she left the ties, dangerously uneven in the dark, for the safer gravel on the shoulder. The lantern banged along her thigh as she held her aching side and ran toward the depot, where she fell against the door. Two startled men inside it helped her to a bench. Kate gasped out her warning, and as the men saw her torn and rain-soaked clothes, her cut hands still clutching the unlit lantern, one of them muttered, "She must be crazy."

"That's Kate Shelley!" Agent McIntyre reproved him, and under his hand the telegraph key vibrated in the Morse code's dots and dashes, telling an agent farther west to stop the Chicago Express.

Without a word from the agent, night operator Ike Fansler pulled the lever that set the red reflector in the lighted semaphore. That red light high above the roof level would stop the train if it had already passed the next town west. To a bystander whose look was questioning, Ike said only, "Mike Shelley's kid would know."

A moment later, the yard's second helper engine was sounding the short, sharp whistles that signaled emergency to all railroad employees within hearing distance. Townspeople came running, too, and Kate was helped into the engine cab with the rescue party. There was little talk as they slowly crossed the bridge above the river. Then the broken bridge at Honey Creek was reached, and Kate guided the men to where she had last seen the engineer and brakeman.

Daybreak came early in midsummer, and a rope was cast to engineer Wood. The cast was repeated again and again until he was able to catch it. He made it fast to the tree and came hand-over-hand to the bank, where a dozen hands clutched him and drew him to safety.

A boat was sent to rescue brakeman Agar, and both men were hurried into comfortable quarters after their drenching and exposure of more than five hours.

After that daybreak rescue on Thursday, there was no rest for Kate, or anyone else in the little trackside house. All day long the valley residents came and went. On Friday the reporters came, checking the sites of Honey Creek's broken bridge and Kate's incredible crossing of the Des Moines River. They questioned Kate and neighbors and railroad employees, and some followed the party searching for the two men who had been swept downstream from the helper engine.

Saturday passed, with a weary Kate and engineer Wood being asked again and again if they had seen either fireman Olmstead or foreman Donahue after the creek bridge collapsed. Buzzards were seen on Sunday, circling above a cornfield which was higher than water had ever been known to rise. Donahue's body was found there.

Olmstead's body was never found, and Kate's overwrought nerves gave way before the loss of those longtime family friends. It was not until October days ripened the valley's beauty that she was able to resume her duties of house and farm.

In the three years since her father's death, Kate had planted the crops and harvested them. The July flood had swept away the corn and oats. In the crisp October days, there was fuel to be cut and hauled, with such help as the younger children could give, and Kate's blue eyes were shining as she dug and sorted potatoes to be stored for winter use. Even in her diminished strength, it seemed so good to work and look across the sunny valley. The Shelleys were grateful for the help offered them after the story of Kate's bravery was printed and reprinted in so many publications.

The Chicago *Tribune* had raised a fund which reduced the $500 mortgage against the quarter-section farm, and Kate's small earnings as speaker at various meetings were applied against the balance until it was cleared. Both parts of the C&NW railroad's tribute delighted Kate. On the practical side, she was given $100, a substantial supply of food and coal and a lifetime pass over the system. The handsome gold medal presented her by the company was a source of joy and inspiration to her throughout the years.

Another gold medal, designed by Tiffany of New York, and a check for $200 were presented to Kate by the State of Iowa, and many other honors were paid her by schoolchildren, citizens' groups and various organizations. In time she became a teacher in rural schools and her pupils shared her pleasure when, in 1901, twenty years after she had crawled the long river bridge, a new iron railroad bridge spanned the river and was named for Kate Shelley.

In 1903 Kate became the railroad station agent at Moingona. The railroad world of timetables and tickets, lanterns and keys and train orders had framed her life since her earliest memory, and its wondrous blend of order and variety were hers until her death at the family home near Honey Creek, January 21, 1912.

A bronze plaque, placed at her grave seventy-five years after her heroic act, bears an outline of the lantern she dragged across the rolling Des Moines River, and that lantern has an honored place in Iowa's museum of the State Department of History and Archives. A copy of each published story about Kate makes an impressive display in the Kate Shelley Memorial Park and Railroad Museum at Moingona, and few heroines are subjects of as many ballads as the girl from the trackside homestead.

Perhaps "Kate Shelley's Longest Mile" by Edith Newhouse tells best the story of Kate's bravery, and how it is retold when summer storms roll through that farmland valley. This is the last of the eleven rippling stanzas:

When summer storms lash Honey Creek and skies are dark with
    rain,
  Sometimes a ghostly whistle drifts across the misty plain,
And lightning flares above the treetops tossing in the gales
  To show the phantom figure of Kate Shelley by the rails.

Ruth Van Ackeren's writing on historical subjects includes the book she edited, Sioux County: Memoirs of Its Pioneers, *and scores of story-length biographies appearing in national and regional magazines. She serves on the book-rating panel of Western Writers of America, and she and Nellie Snyder Yost co-edited the book,* Bartlett Richards, Defender of the Grasslands, *now in process of publication by Nebraska State Historical Society.*

Lyle Bruere, daughter of Ruth Van Ackeren, is the author of numerous articles and stories. Mrs. Bruere and her husband live in Cedar Rapids, Iowa. Her current activities include serving on Western Writers of America's book-rating panel and membership in Iowa's Fort Atkinson Foundation.

BIBLIOGRAPHY

BOOKS

Beitz, Ruth. "Kate Shelley—Railroad Heroine," Shenandoah, Iowa: *The Iowan*, September 1, 1967.

Grant, Donald. "Ogden Relives the Story of Heroic Kate Shelley." *Des Moines* (Iowa) *Register,* July 4, 1965.

Henson, Fred C. "Apprentice to Greatness," Cedar Rapids, Iowa: *The Conductor and Brakeman,* November 1955.

Hubbard, Freeman. "The Legend of Kate Shelley," *Railroad Avenue; Great Stories and Legends of American Railroading.* San Marino, California: Golden West Books, 1964.

Hughes, R. O. "Broken Lamp Lights Way to Legend," Cedar Rapids, Iowa: *The Conductor and Brakeman,* June 1956.

Knauth, Otto. "Iowa Fund Drive Begins for Kate Shelley Memorial Park." *Des Moines* (Iowa) *Register,* July 13, 1975.

Lamberto, Nick. "Seek to Save a Landmark Near Boone." *Des Moines* (Iowa) *Register,* June 30, 1968.

Levi, Sister M. Carolissa. "How Kate Shelley Saved Train, Became Iowa Legend." *Des Moines* (Iowa) *Register,* July 4, 1965.

Lewis, J. F. "Heroic Deed of Kate Shelley Recalled." *Des Moines* (Iowa) *Register and Leader,* January 28, 1912.

McElravy, Robert C. "Kate Shelley." *Des Moines* (Iowa) *Register and Leader,* January 24, 1912.

Meek, Loyal. "Mt. Vernon Man Built the Bridge Kate Crawled Across." *Cedar Rapids* (Iowa) *Gazette,* July 10, 1956.

Novotne, Sharon. "Up in Smoke Goes $90,000 Boone Landmark Project." *Des Moines* (Iowa) *Tribune,* November 12, 1970.

Shelley, Jack. "Kate Shelley's Nephew Recalls Her Exploit," *Des Moines* (Iowa) *Register,* October 1, 1967.

Shelley, Kate. Lecture by Kate Shelley, 1888. Photostatic copy of original manuscript in files of Order of Railway Conductors and Brakemen, O.R.C.&B. Building, Cedar Rapids, Iowa.

Swisher, J. A. "Kate Shelley." Iowa City, Iowa: *The Palimpsest,* State Historical Society of Iowa, Vol. 6, No. 2, February 1925.

Zielinski, Mary. "Iowan Still Remembered for Her Act of Heroism." *Cedar Rapids* (Iowa) *Gazette,* May 23, 1976.

Editorial. "A Heroine." *Boone* (Iowa) *News-Republican,* January 27, 1912.

Editorial. "Editorial Comment on the Life and Death of Kate Shelley." *Boone* (Iowa) *News-Republican,* January 27, 1912.

The Roving Reporter. "Kate Shelley." *Clinton* (Iowa) *Herald,* October 6, 1955.

STAFF-WRITTEN ITEMS

"Pride of Iowa Visits." *Dubuque* (Iowa) *Daily Telegraph,* November 20, 1881.

"Kate Shelley Appointed Station Agent, Moingona." *Davenport* (Iowa) *Democrat*, November 17, 1904.

"Miss Kate Shelley Visits the City," *Boone* (Iowa) *News-Republican*, April 27, 1909.

"Miss Kate Shelley, the Famous Heroine, Passes Away Sunday." *Boone* (Iowa) *News-Republican*, January 22, 1912.

"Special Train: Shelley Funeral." *Boone* (Iowa) *News-Republican*, January 22, 1912.

"Governor Gue's Story of Miss Shelley." *Boone* (Iowa) *News-Republican*, January 22, 1912.

"Miss Shelley Was Brave in Death." *Boone* (Iowa) *News-Republican*, January 24, 1912.

"Resolutions for Miss Shelley." *Boone* (Iowa) *News-Republican*, February 10, 1912.

"The Story as Told by Miss Kate Shelley." *Boone* (Iowa) *News-Republican*, June 24, 1912.

"Local Man Saw Shelley Save Train." *The* (Ames, Iowa) *Daily Tribune*, September 16, 1941.

"Kate Shelley Raced Death to Save 200 Aboard Express." Cedar Rapids, Iowa: *The Conductor and Brakeman*, June 1955.

"Archives Swell with Kate Shelley Lore." Cedar Rapids, Iowa: *The Conductor and Brakeman*, December 1955.

"Kate Shelley Plaque Now on Display in State House." *Boone* (Iowa) *News-Republican*, February 9, 1956.

"All Rails Lead to Boone." Cedar Rapids, Iowa: *The Conductor and Brakeman*, May 1956.

"Kate's Own Account." Cedar Rapids, Iowa: *The Conductor and Brakeman*, June 1956.

"Heroine Kate Shelley Is Honored." *Cedar Rapids* (Iowa) *Gazette*, July 8, 1956.

"Kate Shelley Story Consigned to Bronze and Stone." Cedar Rapids, Iowa. *The Conductor and Brakeman*, August 1956.

"Rail Heroine's Depot Endangered." *Cedar Rapids* (Iowa) *Gazette*, May 8, 1964.

"Kate Shelley Saved Train 62 Years Ago Today, Recall," *Boone* (Iowa) *News-Republican*, July 6, 1943.

"Iowa Centennial Recalls Heroic Story of Boone Girl Who Saved Train." *Des Moines* (Iowa) *Tribune*, July 9, 1973.

6

The Lure of Gold

by CAROLYN NIETHAMMER

The lure of gold brought Irish-born Nellie Cashman from the Cassiar Mountains of British Columbia to Tucson, Arizona, and finally to Alaska. She established boardinghouses, restaurants and stores for miners, and raised funds to build a Catholic church in Tombstone. In 1897 she joined the gold stampede for the Yukon, established another restaurant in Dawson, then became a claim owner herself. She was convinced there was a river of gold under the rocks of Nolan Creek, north of the Arctic Circle.

N.S.Y.

It was late fall in 1875, and the harsh cold of winter was already settling into the Cassiar Mountains in the interior of British Columbia. Most of the prospectors searching for gold in the district were digging in to withstand the bitter winter.

Nellie Cashman, the first white woman to penetrate to that remote area, had spent the last year running a miners' boardinghouse and looking for gold in the creeks. But with the onset of winter she decided to spend some time in milder Victoria, stock up on supplies, and return to her business the next spring. She also had $500 to deliver to the Sisters of St. Ann—money she had collected from the miners for the new hospital the sisters hoped to build in Victoria.

Nellie was hardly settled for the winter when she received word that many of the men who stayed behind, some of them her former boarders, were sick from scurvy. Immediately she gave up her idea of escaping the cold in front of a cozy urban hearth. Within a day she had purchased potatoes, lime juice and other supplies and talked six men into accompanying her on the hazardous, icy trek into the Cassiar.

Later Nellie said, "At Wrangel the U.S. Customs officers tried to dissuade me from what they termed my mad trip and in fact, when we had been several days up the river on our journey they sent up a number of men to induce me to turn back." In fact, Captain Campbell at Fort Wrangel had received word from an Indian that a white woman had died up the creek. Knowing that Nellie Cashman was the only white woman for hundreds of miles, he concluded that it must be she. The soldiers he sent in for her body found her sitting in front of a roaring fire near her tent. She warmed them all with a cup of hot tea before they returned to the fort—without her.

The winter was very severe that year. Hauling supplies weighing 1,500 pounds, the little party had to break trail through the snow accumulation on the frozen Stikeen River. Some days they made only five miles. But Nellie did her part, plowing ahead on snowshoes, dragging a heavy sled by means of a harness around her neck.

The journey seemed endless; six, seven, eight weeks. One dark, frigid morning, concerned that the trip was becoming too much for a woman, one of the men decided to pamper Nellie by taking a cup of coffee to her tent. But her tent wasn't where it had been the night before. He called the others and they began a search. A quarter mile down the river, they found her, struggling out of the massive snowdrift that had moved down the hill during the night, carrying Nellie with it.

Seventy-seven days after the rescuers left Victoria—sixty-six nights camping in the snow—they reached their destination. Nellie began distributing the supplies and nursing those men who were desperately ill. She was happy to accept money from those who had it, but those who didn't received the same generous portions of the health-restoring foods. In later years she was fond of recalling that not a single man died after she reached the camp.

Tales of such exploits—and this is only one of many that filled Nellie Cashman's long and fascinating life—suggest a heroine of brawny amazonian proportions with manners as raw as the frontier on which she lived. Quite the contrary is true. Petite Nellie was barely over five feet tall. Despite a life spent in some of the most remote mining districts and the roughest camps, Nellie Cashman always kept her femininity and good looks. She had fine, delicate features, wavy brown hair which she kept tucked into a bun, and clear, smooth skin. At the time of her rescue mission to the Cassiar miners she was in her early twenties and weighed less than 100 pounds.

Several years previous, around 1867, Nellie, her sister Fannie and her widowed mother Frances, had fled their native Ireland, a land overcome with political and economic disaster. They landed in Boston, where Nellie worked as an elevator operator. In 1869, soon after the completion of the transcontinental railroad, the family again moved, this time all the way across the continent to San Francisco. Nellie was now halfway around the globe from Queenstown, Ireland, her city of birth.

Fannie and Thomas Cunningham, another Irish immigrant, married and began to raise a family. But Nellie was anxious for more adventure.

She first went to Virginia City, Nevada, where rich silver finds had turned some Irish immigrants into barons; then it was on to the neighboring town of Pioche, where her short-order cooking made such a reputation for her that the miners called her "Nellie Pioche."

After nearly four years in British Columbia, Nellie passed through these Nevada towns again, looking for a place to settle. But they had seen their heyday and were on the decline. The talk was of the Arizona Territory. The Southern Pacific Railroad would soon push into that undeveloped area, and a boom would surely follow.

The fall of 1878 found Nellie in Tucson, Arizona Territory. Once again she was the first single white businesswoman in the area, and she lost no time in setting up a restaurant. She named it The Delmonico and advertised it in the *Arizona Citizen,* a newspaper run by a young editor named John Clum.

The Delmonico was a success, but Tucson was still a sleepy pueblo, much attached to its Mexican heritage. It didn't take Nellie long to find out that the real action was 140 miles to the southeast, in a new camp where not long before Ed Schieffelin had discovered silver in the rolling brown hills bordering the San Pedro River valley. At that time, the Apaches still considered the area their own, and many white settlers who weren't careful ended up in lonely desert graves. Fort Huachuca had been established to deal with the Indian problem and the soldiers there knew the risks. When they found out where Schieffelin was prospecting they warned him, "That area is barren and dangerous. The only thing you'll find out there is your tombstone."

But Ed Schieffelin managed to keep away from the Apaches and eventually to find silver. In honor of the soldiers' prediction, he named his first claim "The Tombstone." The town was named after the mine.

In the summer of 1879, the first bullion from the Tombstone mines arrived in Tucson for deposit in the bank and eventual shipment to the East. The stage had refused the risk of carrying the shipment, so Ed Schieffelin had driven it in himself in the back of a wagon. All Tucson turned out to look at the dull silver bars worth $18,744.50.

No doubt Nellie Cashman was in the throng crowding around the wagon; by the following spring, she had established two businesses in the growing camp of Tombstone. John Clum had also moved to Tombstone and started a newspaper called the *Epitaph,* in which appeared advertisements for Nellie's Nevada Boot and Shoe Store as well as her Tombstone Cash Store, which sold "groceries and provisions of all kinds."

The businesses thrived, fulfilling one of Nellie's life priorities: to be successful and make lots of money. Now she turned her attention to an even more consuming passion: civilizing the community and raising money for charitable causes.

A devout Catholic, Irish Nellie was concerned that there was no church of her faith in Tombstone. The bishop responsible for the area resided in Tucson, and when Nellie laid her complaint before him he struck a deal with her: if she'd get a church, he'd come up with a priest. Nellie had the more difficult part of the bargain, but she was undaunted and started canvassing the town for contributions. After she raised $700 by personal subscription, she then organized Tombstone's first amateur theatrical production: a musical comedy called *The Irish Diamond* which was followed by a grand ball. All proceeds went to the church fund, and the bishop had to make good on his promise.

Nellie was also instrumental in organizing the Miner's Hospital Association and the Tombstone branch of the Irish National Land League. As treasurer for both groups, she was continually planning benefits to raise funds. It must have taken some pretty fancy talking to inspire enthusiasm in the townspeople who at that time were a generally rough group of cowboys, miners, gamblers and ladies of the night. But never did Nellie lack for supporters. As John Clum wrote fifty years later in a reminiscence of his friendship with Nellie: "If she asked for a contribution—we contributed. If she had tickets to sell—we bought tickets. If she needed actors for a play—we volunteered to act. And although Nellie's pleas were frequent, none ever refused her."

Though Nellie's own reputation was always unimpeachable, she never snubbed those of her sex who had chosen a different path. She recognized that the women of the camp's netherworld were a good source of support in a crisis. Years later a former Tombstonian wrote: "All oldtimers will remember Nellie Cashman always called for help from Black Jack, known as the queen of the red-light district and Nellie said her greatest help came from the back street which had no name on the map."

In spite of this whirl of activity, Nellie apparently began to miss cooking for a crowd. At any rate, it was about this time that she took over the Arcade Restaurant and Chop House.

She was indeed the belle of the town—advertisements for her businesses were found in every issue of every newspaper, and the news columns carried word of her activities. Then, in the late summer of 1881, she received a telegram that brought it all to a halt.

Her sister's husband had died of tuberculosis, leaving Fannie alone with five children, one of them a baby. A typical Irishwoman, Nellie was high on family loyalty. Selling her businesses as quickly as possible, she started for San Francisco. Once she got there, it was apparent that it would be best to move the little family to Tombstone where she could more easily support them.

By autumn Nellie was back in business in Tombstone, this time as a partner with a fellow named Pascholy. Their enterprise was called the Russ House, and it was one of the finer hotels for travelers and boarders. The elegance of their bill of fare helped give Tombstone the reputation for having the best restaurants between St. Louis and San Francisco. Diners who took Sunday dinner at the Russ House on October 30, 1881, could choose from a menu which included brook trout, lamb with caper sauce, chicken fricassee à la crème, beef a l'Espanol, calf head, corned beef, dressed veal, pork with applesauce, lobster salad, beets with horseradish, turnips, mashed potatoes, assorted pies, New York plum pudding, grapes and walnuts.

Although Nellie superintended the restaurant operation and did much of the cooking herself, she did have help. One of her cooks was a Chinese named Sam Lee, and when Sam decided to visit his homeland he asked Nellie for a picture of herself. Several months later he returned with a beautiful oil painting photograph.

During this time, Nellie helped her sister Fannie get set up in a boardinghouse business, and they shared the care of the children. It wasn't easy riding herd on such a brood in a rough town like Tombstone. Legend has it that one of Nellie's nephews, Mike Cunningham, was walking home from school on the afternoon that the Earp brothers and the Clantons and McLowrys decided to have it out in what history now calls the gunfight at the O.K. Corral. When the shooting was over, two McLowrys were dead and young Billy Clanton was mortally wounded. Bystanders carried Clanton into the Crystal Palace Saloon and put him on a table. Little Mike ran to get the nineteen-year-old cowboy a glass of water. When he returned, Billy Clanton was dead.

Mike seems to have been the friskiest of the five youngsters. Another story tells of the day he and a young friend took a couple of burros and headed out of town to play "prospector" during a period when Geronimo and his band were on the rampage, terrorizing ranchers in the area. Tombstonians had been warned to be careful outside the city limits, but with the heedlessness of children, the boys didn't give a thought to any danger—at least, not when they left.

When suppertime came and went and the boys were not yet home, Nellie became concerned and started asking around. An old prospector who had come into town for a good meal volunteered that he had seen the two boys heading for the mountains outside of town. Nellie threw off her apron, hooked up her buckboard and within minutes was driving out to the dark desert. She had an idea where the boys might be. As the horse picked his way over a barely discernible road, Nellie saw Apache signal fires flicker, then die on the mountains surrounding the town.

At last she pulled up to a decrepit abandoned ranch house. Inside she found two frightened children huddled in a corner. She hurried them into the wagon and took off for town. Years later, when Mike Cunningham was a leading Arizona citizen and president of the Bank of Bisbee, he told how scared he and his buddy were when they heard the approach of a horse, and how relieved they were to hear Aunt Nell's voice calling out to them through the darkness.

In spite of Nellie's help with child care, the burden became too much for Fannie and she fell ill. For a while Nellie ran back and forth between Fannie's boardinghouse and her own kitchen until that became too hectic and she sold out her interest in the elegant Russ House. Later, when Fannie rallied, they completely refurbished her boardinghouse, reopening it with great fanfare as the American Hotel.

Less than four weeks later, one of Tombstone's periodic devastating fires swept the town and flames surrounded the beautifully redecorated hotel. Nellie's many friends formed a bucket brigade and kept the structure wet, but three times the building caught on fire, and three times Nellie and Fannie and brave volunteers rushed toward the flames with pails of water. When at last the fire was quenched, the business section of the thriving town lay in charred smoking ruins. The American Hotel still stood, but the entire wardrobe of the family was destroyed in the lower rear rooms and the rooms directly above were useless. Fannie's hair was so badly singed it had to be cut, and Nellie's arm was severely burned. The destruction was estimated at $1,500.

But during Nellie's years on the frontier she had seen fires wipe out entire towns. Her good business sense told her to be prepared. The building was insured for $3,000.

When May arrived in 1883, Nellie had a bad case of spring fever. For almost two years this vigorous adventuress had concentrated mainly on business and raising children. She was aching to get away for a while. Reports were drifting up to Tombstone concerning the rich placer gold finds in the deserts of Baja California. Nellie hired competent help for Fannie, organized a group of twenty-one leading townsmen, and dug out her overalls, flannel shirt and a wide-brimmed hat. The party left town on the Modoc stage headed for Guaymas, Mexico, where they bought burros and chartered a ship to take them across the Gulf of California.

Weeks went by. No word was heard from the prospecting

group. Papers all over the West printed stories of their demise. Then at last, on June 11, the editors of the *Tombstone Evening Republican* received a letter from a member of the Cashman party. It read, in part:

It took four days to cross the gulf on our trip out, the distance being 111 miles to Trinidad Bay. Thence we went to the placers on foot, the distance being 95 miles, through a country devoid of vegetation and over a rough trail, where water was very scarce. Nellie Cashman, with a party of four men started from Trinidad Bay ahead of the rest of the party. Nellie and two of her party came near dying of thirst, but were rescued by the rest of the party overtaking them the second day out. When we arrived at the placers we found what there was of them completely worked out. . . . I saw over 100 batches worked without a color.

The story concluded: "Since the receipt of the above dispatch Miss Nellie Cashman has arrived in town and confirms the above in every particular."

With her hopes for a rich gold strike dashed for the time, Nellie returned to business in Tombstone, once again taking over the Russ House, buying some small mines near town and making a few speculative investments by way of grubstaking prospectors with the understanding that she'd get an interest in whatever they found.

About this time, Fannie's health faltered. It was tuberculosis—the same disease that had taken her husband. There was no doubt that the end was near, and she longed for the comfort of being near her own mother, now an aged woman living in San Francisco. When Nellie put Fannie on the train for California, she knew neither she nor the children would ever see her again.

Even with the responsibility for the support and care of her new brood, Nellie could not resist involvement in community affairs, which included imposing her own brand of Irish Catholic morality on the town.

In the spring of 1884, five men were being held in the Tombstone jail under sentence of death for the cold-blooded murder of four innocent bystanders during the robbery of Goldwater's store in Bisbee. The citizens of the entire county were outraged by the senselessness of the murders and looked forward with great relish to the spectacle of the simultaneous hanging of these five brutal outlaws.

Sheriff J. L. Ward had issued tickets to as many "official witnesses" as the courtyard could accommodate, but that excluded a majority of the would-be observers. An enterprising and mercenary carpenter stepped into the breach and on a nearby vacant lot built a grandstand that overlooked the courtyard. Tickets sold as fast as ice-cold lemonade at a picnic in June. The whole affair was taking on a carnival atmosphere, and everyone was delighted. Everyone except Nellie Cashman.

Two of the condemned prisoners were Catholics, and Nellie had taken it upon herself to assist the priest in ministering to their spiritual needs. The story goes that she was so sincere and earnest in her faith that the other three outlaws also embraced Catholicism before their final hour.

The prisoners could hear the pounding of the hammers building the grandstand and were worried that their deaths be turned into a circus. They appealed to the sheriff, who found himself in a delicate political position because the townspeople were so hungry for spectacle. He told the men he could do nothing for them.

Nellie knew of the prisoners' concerns and agreed that no matter what their crime, they deserved a measure of dignity at their death. But she knew that her usual straightforward tactics would not work this time. Although there were a few people who thought as she did, most of the others were being carried along with the mob spirit.

With cool-headed forethought, she convinced the mayor and sheriff that the streets should be cleared by midnight the day before the hanging for fear a riot might break out due to the intensity of feeling.

On that night, when the streets were quiet and dark, all carousers having been sent home to bed, Nellie Cashman emerged from the back door of the Russ House followed by a small group of miners carrying picks and axes. It was 2:00 A.M. Before daybreak, the grandstand was reduced to splinters and deposited in a nearby arroyo.

The hanging took place as planned, but without the additional onlookers, and the five bodies were buried. But how long the bodies would stay in the ground Nellie wasn't sure. There had been talk that the corpses would be sold to a medical school for dissection. That evening after dark, two prospectors left the Russ House carrying bedrolls and frying pans and headed out of town into the darkness. Throughout the night and for ten succeeding nights they slept next to the fresh graves watching to see that the bodies were not desecrated.

This story, which has no doubt become elaborated through time, joins others which tell of Nellie's helpfulness: her raising of $500 for a miner who fell from a scaffold and broke both legs, her putting up a family of seven until the father, a recent immigrant, could find work, and her courageous rescue of a mine superintendent when her own friends, the miners, planned to lynch him for what they wrongly thought was his part in the reduction of their wages.

The lowering of miners' pay and the subsequent strike and bank failure was the beginning of the end of Tombstone's grand days. The shafts were filling up with water, the price of silver was declining and the mines began to close. By the beginning of 1886, there were so few children in the camp and such a small tax base that the public schools were closed. Nellie sent her nieces and nephews off to Catholic boarding schools and closed the Russ House.

The few old-timers in the town perpetuated Nellie's memory, calling her the "Angel of Tombstone." When they retold tales of Tombstone's heyday and they came to the part about the group that went off to Baja to look for gold, it became Nellie Cashman who had struck out into the desert to bring back water for the rest of the group who were dying of thirst, rather than Nellie herself who had to be rescued.

But Nellie wasn't around to hear their stories or correct them. Although freed of the day-to-day responsibilities of child care, she was still financially responsible for her brood.

The next decade found her traveling through the West's mining frontier, chasing the excitement and the challenge of each new boom town. At one point she lived in Kingston, New Mexico, where she ran The Cashman House and employed as a dishwasher a young man named Ed Doheny, who later was to become an oil multimillionaire. "One of the best pearl divers I ever had," Nellie remembered him.

In 1895, when her work had taken her to the north, probably the Coeur d'Alene district in Idaho, Nellie decided on a whim to take a little vacation in Juneau. There she encountered a group of miners she had known in the Cassiar. Later she remembered:

At the time, I said I believed the northern country would yet prove the richest, but I did not go into the interior because I had too much at stake in several western mining camps. My brief trip to Juneau was vividly impressed on my mind for one reason. You see, many of the boys were just about to go into the interior to prospect, and when I arrived, they seemed glad to see me. They built a huge log fire and made me sit by it and talk of the old Cassiar days. They said it looked natural to see me sitting by a campfire as in days of yore.

So Nellie's old friends went north and she returned to Arizona to open the Buffalo Hotel in Globe and later to set up a camp kitchen in a place west of Phoenix called Harqua Hala.

Meanwhile, far up in the Yukon Territory, a fur trapper named George Carmack and his Indian wife and two brothers-in-law discovered gold in a small stream called Rabbit Creek; a tributary of the Klondike River close to where it joins the mighty Yukon. Those miners already in the area, presumably Nellie's friends among them, converged on the creek, renamed it Bonanza, and began scooping up gold nuggets.

On July 17, 1897, the steamer *Portland* arrived in Seattle and discharged sixty-eight miners from the Yukon, all of whom left the ship staggering under the weight of the gold bags they carried. The newspaper wire services flashed the news around the globe, and within days Nellie read about it in the Phoenix paper.

All around the world, clerks, farmers, merchants and miners dropped whatever they were doing and headed for the Yukon. It was the greatest gold rush in history.

Nellie could not resist. On September 15, 1897, the *Arizona Daily Star* reported that Nellie Cashman had passed through Yuma telling of her plans to head north as soon as possible. She was looking for six good prospectors and an investor with $5,000.

Apparently she found neither, but by mid-February she was in Victoria, British Columbia, outfitting for the trip north and awaiting her oldest nephew Tom Cunningham who was to make the trip with her. Victoria was packed with eager stampeders swarming through the streets, buying provisions and jockeying for berths on the dangerously overcrowded ships headed for Dyea and Skagway, jumping-off points to the Yukon.

Even with all the people in the city, Nellie's presence was noticed, so well-known had she become by that time. A reporter for the *British Daily Colonist* wrote of her: "She is out now for the big strike, nothing more or less than the Mother Lode of the far-famed Klondike region. She says if her experience in quartz mining will stand her in good stead and her proverbial good luck in mining matters stays with her she will have a chance at least to stake out a few claims in the mountain of gold which is thought to enrich all the north."

Nellie and her nephew joined with two men they had known in Tombstone to make the trek over the treacherous and nearly perpendicular Chilkoot Pass which stood between Skagway and Dyea on the coast and the Yukon River, which the stampeders used as a watery highway by which to reach the goldfields. More than half of the nearly 100,000 stampeders who set out on the Trail of '98 turned back when they faced the incredibly steep barrier of rock, ice and snow. But Nellie Cashman, in her late forties by now, struggled over, making many trips to carry the 900 pounds of supplies that the Mounties were requiring each person to provide. Once over the pass, the party built a boat and followed the Yukon River to Dawson City.

On their arrival, Nellie and her friends found that every inch of ground on the rich creeks had been staked. Undaunted, Nellie opened a café instead, calling it the Cassiar Restaurant. Later, when some other entrepreneurs "got cold feet both literally and figuratively," she bought out their grocery store located in the basement of the Donovan Hotel. Nellie was dismayed to learn that many of the prospectors spent their evenings in the bars and gambling halls simply because they could not endure the loneliness of their tiny dank cabins, especially during the winters when the sun sometimes didn't rise above the horizon. She scrounged some furniture and filled up an extra room in the grocery store, called it "The Prospectors Haven of Retreat," and passed out free cigars and coffee to those who dropped by.

About this time, Nellie herself became ill with an infected intestine. She was taken to the hospital run by the beloved Father Judge. While there, she learned how badly the overworked priest needed help and funds, and she began soliciting for the hospital all up and down the creeks. When the Sisters of St. Ann arrived from Victoria to help Father Judge, Nellie was there to meet them at the dock. She continued to lend them her support and friendship as they struggled to deal with the diseases and injuries that plagued the residents of this remote corner of the world.

By the turn of the century, Dawson City began to empty out. Gold had been discovered in Nome, and many miners went there; others had had enough of life in the frozen north and returned to their farms and stores. Nellie had staked claims on several moderately paying creeks, but by 1901 she and five partners were able to buy 19 Below Discovery on Bonanza Creek. When after the first year her partners had as much money as they wanted from the claim, Nellie bought them all out and held onto it for another year. One of her friends remembered that she had made $100,000 in Dawson City, but had sunk every penny of it back into the ground, looking for more.

By 1904 even Nellie had to concede that Dawson City's days were over. She moved to the new town of Fairbanks, where she ran a grocery store. But city life could not compare with the thrill of mining and prospecting, and by the summer of 1905 Nellie had installed herself in the wildest, most remote area in all of the Alaska Territory: the Upper Middle Koyukuk River. Her first base for exploration was Coldfoot, 60 miles north of the Arctic Circle. Then she moved even farther north to a cabin near her claims on Nolan Creek; so isolated that it was 40 miles from even the nearest mail service.

Nellie was the only woman for many miles, but that did not bother her in the least: "I have mushed with men, slept out in the open, siwashed with them and been with them constantly, and I have never been offered an insult. . . . A woman is as safe among the miners as at her own fireside. If a woman complains of her treatment from any of the boys, she has only herself to blame. . . . I can truthfully say that there was never a bigger-hearted class of men than the genuine sourdoughs of Alaska."

Nellie was getting older, and she was determined that she was going to find her life's big payoff in the Koyukuk. There was a river of gold somewhere under the rocks of Nolan Creek, and she was going to find it. But moving all that earth required expensive machinery and capital to buy it. She formed the Midnight Sun Mining Company, had stock certificates printed up and made several trips "outside" to raise money by selling shares in her enterprise.

Getting in and out of the Koyukuk area was always difficult. In 1924, when she was nearly seventy-five years old, Nellie earned the title of champion woman musher of all Alaska when she covered 750 miles in seventeen days, running through snow and driving a team of dogs.

On that trip she headed for New York City to speak to a potential investor, to Washington, D.C., to confer with President Coolidge concerning the problems facing Alaska, and to Bisbee, Arizona, to visit her favorite nephew, Mike.

Mike tried to persuade her not to return to Alaska—he saw no need for a woman her age to be struggling with life in the frozen northland. "I've got plenty of money to take care of all of us," he told her. But Nellie would have none of it. Her "boys" were waiting for her on Nolan Creek—she was needed.

"It'll be a long time before I reach the cushioned-rocker stage," she told him.

On the way back to Alaska in the spring of 1924, Nellie caught cold, but she kept pushing on, figuring she'd rest up in her cozy cabin on Nolan Creek. By the last week in May, she had gotten as far as Koyukuk River and was heading north on the first mailboat of the season when she became too ill to continue. She was taken back to the hospital in Fairbanks, where doctors gave a diagnosis of double pneumonia and marveled that she had been able to withstand the vigorous river trip.

But Nellie hadn't planned on spending the precious warm months in the hospital; she was determined to get back to her mines. Later in the summer she started out again. This time got to within 80 miles of her camp before she became so weak that her friends became alarmed.

As she had helped others all her years, without regard for their creed, now she was so aided. Helping hands dressed her in her fur coat and hat and settled her into a boat guided by an Episcopal deacon and an Indian. They rowed down the Koyukuk until they met a steamer owned by Sam Dubin, a Jewish trader. Sam immediately turned his boat around and took Nellie to the Sisters of St. Ann who had a mission at Nulato, where the Koyukuk meets the Yukon.

After she had spent another month in the Fairbanks Hospital,

Nellie realized that it was September and another rough icy winter would soon be on the land. She decided to head south, where she might use the time to round up some more investors.

But Nellie made it only as far as Seattle. There she asked to be taken to St. Joseph's Hospital in Victoria, where she would be near the Sisters of St. Ann, many of whom had been her close friends for many years.

She refused to be taken to her room in a wheelchair, but once settled, she told a sister, "I have come home to die."

The end came nine weeks later, on January 4, 1925. Nellie Cashman was buried next to the sisters' plot at Ross Bay Cemetery in Victoria, high on a bluff overlooking the ocean.

Newspapers throughout the West, in big cities and tiny hamlets, carried her obituary, often adding information about the time she had spent in their city or state.

One anonymous editor said it as well as anyone when he wrote: "There haven't been many like her nor will there be again. She had beauty without ostentation, wisdom without education, and a flaming unquenchable spirit that was nonetheless familiar with the paths of true humility."

Carolyn Niethammer has written for national and southwestern magazines and has published two books: American Indian Food and Lore, *a cookbook of Indian plant foods; and* Daughters of the Earth: The Lives and Legends of Indian Women. *She is presently at work on a novel based on the life of Nellie Cashman.*

BIBLIOGRAPHY

BOOKS

Adney, Tappan. *The Klondike Stampede of 1897–1898.* Fairfield, Washington: Ye Galleon Press, 1968.

Faulk, Odie. *Tombstone: Myth and Reality.* New York: Oxford University Press, 1972.

Myers, John Myers. *The Last Chance: Tombstone's Early Years.* New York: E. P. Dutton, 1950.

ARTICLES

Brophy, Frank Cullin. "God and Nellie." *Alive,* October 1973, pp. 2–3, 28.

Clum, John P. "Nellie Cashman." *Arizona Historical Review* 3 (1931): 9–34.

Lake, Ivan Clyde, "Irish Nellie: Angel of the Cassiar." *Alaska Sportsman,* October 1963, pp. 19, 42–45.

NEWSPAPERS

Alaska Weekly (Seattle, Washington), February 13, 1925

Arizona Daily Citizen (Tucson), September 15, 1897

Arizona Daily Star (Tucson), January 7, 1925, January 12, 1925

Arizona Sentinel (Yuma), April 16, 1898

Arizona Silverbelt (Globe), February 1, 1896

Arizona Weekly Star (Tucson), October 10, 1897

Bisbee (Arizona) *Daily Review,* July 15, 1934

British Daily Colonist (Victoria), February 5, 1875, February 15, 1898

Cariboo Sentinel (B.C.), July 17, 1875

Cordova Alaska Times, May 19, 1924

Fairbanks Daily News (Alaska), July 23, 1908

Fairbanks Daily Times (Alaska), July 22, 1908

Klondike Nugget (Dawson City, Yukon Territory), October 28, 1899

Phoenix Weekly Herald (Arizona), May 24, 1883, May 27, 1897

San Francisco Chronicle, June 12, 1883

Seattle Post-Intelligencer, July 17, 1897

Tombstone (Arizona) *Epitaph,* May 1, 1880, June 26, 1880, October 6, 1880, November 1, 1881, November 8, 1881, January 3, 1882, May 1, 1882, May 27, 1882, February 10, 1884, April 2, 1886

Tombstone Nugget, October 19, 1880, June 8, 1881, October 30, 1881, November 4, 1881, December 30, 1881, January 21, 1882, April 8, 1882, April 30, 1882

Tucson Daily Citizen, April 5, 1965, April 19, 1971

Victoria (B.C.) *Daily Times,* January 10, 1925

MANUSCRIPTS

Bisbee, Arizona. Cochise County Recorder's Office. Mining Claim Records.

Fairbanks, Alaska. Recorder's Office. Mining Claim Records.

Seattle, Washington. University of Washington Library. W. C. Fonda, Scrapbook No. 1.

Seattle, Washington. University of Washington Library. Photo Archives.

Tucson, Arizona. Arizona Historical Society. Brophy Collection.

Tucson, Arizona. Arizona Historical Society. Cashman Collection.

Tucson, Arizona. Arizona Historical Society. Cunningham scrapbooks, manuscript of speech.

Tucson, Arizona. Arizona Historical Society. J. P. Gray boxed material.

Tucson, Arizona. Arizona Historical Society. Anton Mazzonovich memoirs.

Tucson, Arizona. Arizona Historical Society. Ed Schieffelin. Schieffelin Small Collection.

Whitehorse, Yukon Territory. Yukon Territorial Archives. Mining Claim Records.

OTHER

Boutin, Sister H. Thelma, personal communication, September 1978.

Cashman, Nellie to Cunningham, Mike. January 31, 1920. Personal collection of Natalie Denney, Phoenix, Arizona.

Cashman, Nellie to Cunningham, Mike. April 15, 1923. Personal collection of Natalie Denney, Phoenix, Arizona.

Denney, Natalie. Phoenix, Arizona. Interview, May 1978.

Loyola, Sister Mary to Devere, Evelyn. n.d. Collection at Rosetree Inn, Tombstone, Arizona.

San Francisco Census, 1880.

7

A Good Old Gal

by MARY'N ROSSON

Sarah Jane Creech Orchard, a many-faceted woman of early New Mexico, made her own excitement if none was available. Her career extended from London's Limehouse district to a stagecoach route in the Southwest in pioneer times. A hardhearted businesswoman, she raised flowers on her windowsills to decorate graves that otherwise would have had none, and saved sufficient funds from her brothels and hotels to build a church.

N.S.Y.

The tiny woman, trim in dark tailored skirt and white cambric shirtwaist, grabbed the proffered hand of a bearded miner and with a provocative glimpse of a lace-frothed petticoat and slim ankle, scrambled up to the driver's seat of the big red and yellow stagecoach. With a wiggle, she settled herself comfortably on the leather seat, tightened the chin strap of her black hat and laced the reins to the four restless horses expertly through gloved fingers. She flung a wicked wink at the man who gave her a hand up, kicked the foot brake off with a bang, yelled a few unladylike oaths at the horses and was off down the road in a swirl of dust. The diminutive driver was Sarah Jane Creech Orchard, making the regular run of the Mountain Pride Stagecoach Line from Kingston, New Mexico, through Hillsboro and Lake Valley and on to the Santa Fe railroad terminus at Nutt in 1886.

Towering, rugged cliffs hovered over the Kingston-Hillsboro route. For most of the seven miles, the stage shivered and shook its way through the rocky bed of the Percha River, whose spring floods made the road extremely hazardous. The trip southward to Lake Valley and Nutt, over sharply rolling hills, was mainly uneventful.

Sadie, as she was usually called, later told an interviewer:

The roughness and isolation of the Kingston-Hillsboro route was surely trying and a real test of my courage. I stayed alert, held tight to the reins and rested my boot heel on the brake, ready to stop if the need arose. My old shotgun, nestled at my side, gave me an added feel of safety. I always thought the drive through the beautifully wild Black Range Country exciting and challenging. I never felt terribly in danger although sometimes I could sense there were Indians and bandits lurking around.

Often, as the stage rumbled along its route, Sadie's thoughts turned back to the circumstances that brought her to New Mexico. As Sadie Creech she landed in New York City from England around 1885. She felt lost in the big city and decided that her future lay in a smaller town. One day, while out strolling, her attention was caught by a handbill in a store window. Its praise of a territory called New Mexico aroused her curiosity. The handbill read:

> Ho! For the gold and silver of New Mexico
>   Fortune hunters, capitalists and poor men,
> Sickly folks, all whose hearts are bowed down;
>   And ye who would live long and be healthy,
> And happy; come to our sunny clime and
>   See for yourselves!

Visions of gold dust danced in Sadie's head, and in a short while she left New York City for the unknown regions of New Mexico. Sadie first stopped in Georgetown, near Silver City, which was enjoying a brief moment of the glory of gold. The moment was over quickly, however, and the miners began moving to the Black Range. Sadie, relentlessly on the trail of easy money, followed.

The Black Range is a series of densely wooded mountains so savagely rugged the natives called them Sierras Diablo, or Devil

Mountains. The range, when viewed from a distance, appears to be wrapped in ebony velvet; hence the Black Range name. On the slopes, within a 40-mile radius, Kingston lay to the west; Hillsboro was in the center; Lake Valley and Nutt were to the south. The first three communities were in the midst of tremendously rich ore discoveries.

Sadie Creech came first to Kingston, which was then dubbed "Gem of the Black Range" for its fabulous strikes. Unskilled and low on funds, Sadie determined to survive, even if it meant going into the "oldest profession." She found a small house on Virtue Lane, employed several pretty Cyprian Sisters (as the girls were then called) and opened a bordello, which proved to be very prosperous.

At this time Sadie was thirty-five years old and a five-foot, 100-pound whirlwind of energy. She emphasized her petite high-bosomed figure by showing off her womanly curves in fashionable dresses. She wore her glossy dark hair piled high with soft ringlets framing her delicately chiseled features. Sadie was especially proud of her shapely white hands and small, dainty feet and wore only the grandest of imported butter-soft leather gloves and shoes. Her aristocratic appearance turned the hearts and heads of the woman-hungry men in Kingston. They were more intrigued, however, with Sadie's coarse Cockney accent, oath-filled vocabulary and ribald good humor. Sadie's business flourished.

Kingston got its name from the first strike, the Iron King Mine. The many mines that opened made the little settlement a beehive of activity. Thirty thousand feet of lumber was freighted from Lake Valley in a single day to build homes and businesses. A brick hotel was built and named Victorio, in open defiance of the Apache chief who raided the ranchers and miners. Another building housed the Percha Bank, whose huge vault was usually crammed with gold and silver. The town sported twenty-two saloons and no church. Life was cheap in Kingston. A young miner named Pete Lewis lies in an isolated grave by Mineral Creek. He was slain in a quarrel over a fifty-cent piece.

This rowdy mining camp saw the beginning of the legend of Sarah Jane Creech Orchard. She counted among her many good friends Ed Doheny, who later struck it rich in oil, and his mining partner, Albert Bacon Fall, the future Secretary of the Interior, later to be imprisoned for his part in the Teapot Dome scandal.

Sadie brought Lillian Russell, the queen of the stage, to perform at the Kingston theater. The two women had been actresses together during their leaner years in London and had remained good friends. These people were only a few of the more prominent people who showed real affection for the frank and rough-speaking madame known as Sadie.

Two incidents, partially substantiated, reveal Sadie's ambivalent personality. As with many women of her profession, she yearned for respectability. On learning that Kingston had many saloons and no church she swung into action. Rounding up her idle girls, she sent them out to pass the hat in the saloons and stores. Sadie went after her own customers and bade them contribute generously or face her wrath. She set an example by placing her favorite diamond lavalier in the hat.

Gamblers donated ruby stickpins and snake-eye rings. Miners tossed in small bags of gold dust. The Cyprian Sisters, swept along by Sadie's urging, dropped in earrings and brooches. The grand total was $1,500—enough to build a small stone church.

Sadie was proud of her efforts in getting the church built. However, her rewards were few. One Sunday she dressed in her best, gathered several of her girls together and attended services. She was stunned by the cold shoulder she received from the ladies in the congregation and embarrassed by the sly smiles of the men. Humiliated, Sadie and her brood swept from the church with heads held high, vowing never to return.

The bold, bad side of Sadie emerged in the second incident, that nearly proved fatal for an innocent victim. One of her friends, tiring of her husband, asked Sadie's help in getting rid of the "old bore." Sadie agreed to aid her friend, and the two women plotted for days before coming up with what they considered a surefire, if cold-blooded, scheme.

On the appointed evening, the wife invited Sadie to partake of a lavish dinner that had been prepared especially to please the husband. The unsuspecting man enjoyed the delicious meal and the tender, loving care bestowed on him by the two females. Later the victim, stupefied by the heavy meal and good liquor, fell asleep in his chair. The two plotters moved quickly. They tied several sticks of dynamite together, slipped them under the snoring man's chair, lit the fuses, then ran like wild things into the street. The dynamite blew with a deafening roar, sending the screaming man sailing through the roof. He lay unconscious for days before recovering. Records fail to reveal whether the two culprits paid for their unholy deed, but Sadie's friend was never again bothered by her husband.

By 1886 Kingston was no longer the "Gem of the Black Range." Lack of ore closed the mines and forced the miners to leave. Sadie's business also fell off. She cast her greedy eyes toward Hillsboro and Lake Valley, both of which were still prosperous. Lake Valley was famous for its bountiful Bridal Chamber Mine, a natural vault crammed with black-horn silver, so pure it was shipped directly to the mint. But Lake Valley was isolated, easy prey to Indians and outlaw gangs.

Hillsboro appealed more to Sadie. There Dave Sitzel and Dan Dugan had found a float which assayed $160 in gold value per ton. They staked out the sites as the Opportunity and Ready Pay mines. There were other rich ore-producing mines too. In one winter's spree, prospector George Wells enriched Hillsboro's shops and saloons with $90,000 in gold dust taken from Wick's Gulch.

This report of easy money sent Sadie's adrenaline flowing. She moved to Hillsboro and settled in a thick-walled white adobe house built around a patio lush with green grass, shade trees and brilliant-hued flowers. Her thoughts eventually turned to marriage, which she believed was the true road to respectability. During one social evening, she was introduced to James W. Orchard, owner of the Mountain Pride Stagecoach Line. Orchard was also the duly elected River Commissioner and the boss of the Kingston-Hillsboro toll road, which charged $.10 a horse and $.25 a wagon. Orchard was shy and weak, a perfect target for a woman of Sadie's domineering character. He was intrigued by her sweetness and beauty. After a whirlwind courtship, the strangely matched pair were united in marriage in Sadie's flower-bedecked parlor.

No children were born to this union. A small boy had accompanied Sadie to Hillsboro, and he became a part of the Orchard family. An aura of mystery surrounded the child. To any questions about his parentage, Sadie answered with a brusque "None of your business!"

The boy was frail, completely blind and mentally retarded. He was an object of pity to the townspeople, but not to the devoted Sadie. At a time when handicapped children were kept hidden and seldom mentioned, Sadie proudly and openly took the boy shopping and visiting with her. The lad was in no manner neglected and always appeared neatly dressed and well fed. He died young and was buried in Hillsboro's windswept hillside cemetery. The mystery of his birth was never solved, and today no one remembers his name. Sadie lavished all the maternal love she possessed on this small, sightless child.

The Orchards' first years of marriage found them doing fairly well. Sadie was in full command. Orchard and Bill Holt, one of the stage drivers, operated the line from Silver City to Mogollon. This route was a difficult 100 miles of an up-and-down road that was hardly more than a trail. It was mountainous and periodically alive with marauding Apaches and robbers. It was miraculous that during his ownership of the line neither Orchard nor his drivers ever had a holdup, fought with Indians or crashed a stage over a cliff.

Hardships of the route and the difficulty of finding courageous drivers prompted Orchard to sell the line. He started the Kingston-to-Nutt route which was rough but not quite as dangerous. This line had three relay stations along the way, complete with cedar-post corrals.

Later Sadie spoke proudly of the Mountain Pride Line:

We had sixty-five handpicked horses, also an express wagon and two yellow and red Concord stages. The Concords were built by the Abbott-Downing Company in Concord, New Hampshire. Each weighed twenty-five hundred pounds and was sturdily built. Nine passengers rode inside on padded leather seats and six others could perch on top with the luggage. There was also a leather boot [storage box] on the back of the stage. The coaches cost $1,250 and were the finest money could buy. They surely played a vital part in settling the West.

Our time schedule called for the stage to leave Kingston at six o'clock. I drove often. I could handle the four horse team and the heavy stage from the high driver's seat on top of the front of the stage and I could kick the foot brake with the very best of them! I recall one time renegade Indians, decked out in their favorite white beaver plug hats—or castors, the miners called them—appeared suddenly in the road right in front of the stage. I kicked the foot brake on quickly and pulled hard on the reins to stop the horses.

It made me so mad! I knew they wanted to steal my horses. I didn't stop to think, I just lit into them with all my might, flaying about with my bullwhip and screaming at the top of my voice. The Indians were probably shocked or amused that a small woman could make so much noise and do all that damage. Believe me, they really scattered.

She finished that speech with lip-smacking satisfaction.

Sadie had another story to tell:

Bill Holt and I schemed to foil the holdup of the stage when it was carrying a large sum of money. The line was consigned to take almost $100,000 in cash to the newly built railroad spur at Lake Valley. It was one of the largest shipments of money ever made and the responsibility was great.

Several days before the transfer, friends warned Bill and me that a band of white road agents might be planning to hold up the stage before it reached Lake Valley. Well, we couldn't allow that. Bill and I put our heads together and worked out a plan.

Came the big day. The passengers were loaded on the stage and Bill put the money chest on top of the stage, waved good-bye and drove away. The passengers, unaware of the valuable cargo, were somewhat apprehensive when, as instructed, Bill stopped the coach in a secluded grove just beyond Hillsboro. He made sure the spot was safe from prying eyes before removing the thick, heavily padded collars from the horses' necks. Holt opened the lacings on the undersides of the collars and pulled out the straw stuffing. He repacked the collars with the money, threw the empty chest and stuffing in the brush, replaced the collars on the horses and continued on his journey. A few miles further on, masked men blocked the road with their horses.

"Throw down the money chest!" shouted the leader. "Throw it down and be damned quick about it!"

"Sorry, boys," grinned Bill. "Madame Orchard took the money down yesterday."

Unbelieving, the bandits searched the stage but found no money. They reluctantly began to depart. One of the band, hating to give up the loot, shouted in defiance, "I've a good mind to shoot your horses and make you walk home!"

The defiant one, however, holstered his gun in disgust and the stage went safely on its way. If the horses staggered from their golden burden, no one seemed to notice.

We really outsmarted them robbers. We were so clever in those days.

Sadie spurned the brothel business during her marriage to Orchard. He deeded her a lot for a dollar on which she promptly built a first-class restaurant and hotel called the Ocean Grove Hotel. She later added the Orchard Hotel next door.

The Ocean Grove was neat, comfortably furnished and reasonable. The liquor was top quality, and the restaurant became noted throughout the territory for its superior meals, prepared by the Chinese cook, Tom Ying.

On one occasion, the food at the Ocean Grove did not please a customer, a visiting lawyer. He went to Sadie's for breakfast and ordered two eggs, bacon, toast and coffee. After a long wait, he was served a few slices of underdone sowbelly, two sad-eyed eggs, a slice of stale bread and a mug of lukewarm Arbuckle coffee. He was regarding the unappetizing food with curled lip when a shadow fell across his plate.

"What's the matter with them eggs?" a deep voice asked. "Do you want them doner?" The startled man looked up to see Sadie, wearing her most ferocious don't-you-dare-complain expression.

"Oh no, ma'am," the customer stammered. "Everything's just fine."

With an unbelieving snort, Sadie turned away. After she left the man hustled the eggs and sowbelly into his red bandana and stuffed the package into his shirtfront. He drank the coffee, paid the bill and sidled out the door, successfully dodging Sadie. Later he learned that Tom Ying, the cook, was ill; and one of Sadie's girls had done the cooking.

Hillsboro's prosperity began to falter as the big mines started to play out. The Mountain Pride also suffered, and Orchard was unable to pay the mortgage. Sadie refused to help her husband, and he was forced to sell the line to Fred Wister. Soon afterwards, Orchard disappeared. A story made the rounds although his wife refused to discuss the situation.

James Orchard relished "forty-rod" whiskey, a very strong liquor. Sadie, who liked a nip now and then, thought Orchard over-

did his drinking and told him so—often and loudly. Sadie gave her
husband little money; she forced him to peddle bootleg whiskey to
keep his own supply going. He hid extra bottles around the house
—so successfully that Sadie could not find them.

Sadie owned a beautiful old grandfather clock which stood in
the hallway of her home. Since it was wound weekly, the space beneath the dangling works made it a safe place for Orchard to hide
his whiskey.

One afternoon while Orchard was away, Sadie noticed the clock
had stopped. On investigating she found her husband's cache of
"forty rod." The bottles had fallen against the pendulum, stopping
the works. By the time Orchard arrived home, Sadie was livid with
fury.

"James!" she yelled. "You son of a bitch! Did you think you
could fool me forever? Get your things and get out! This instant!"

Her husband begged and pleaded, but his wife gave him just
time enough to collect his belongings and hitch up the buggy. He
climbed aboard, then turned to give Sadie a last, pitiful look. She
remained unmoved and shouted, "Now git and don't come back!"

When the buggy was about 100 feet away, Sadie hefted her
shotgun and fired at her husband's back. Then without a backward
glance she stomped into the house, still cursing. People who saw
Orchard later said he was not seriously hurt—only that his protruding ears resembled small colanders. Sadie never saw Orchard
again.

As the county seat of Sierra County, Hillsboro retained some
prosperity from the many trials held in the courthouse. Sadie also
prospered as the judges, lawmen and witnesses for the trials pa-
tronized the Ocean Grove. Other visitors stopping at the hotel included rich miners, renegade young sons and the territory's most
powerful politicians. Sadie, who had little use for phonies or hypo-
crites, was the pet of the visitors. Outspoken and completely devoid of tact, Sadie's feisty personality only deepened the men's
affection for her.

Sadie was also very shrewd. She kept a daily journal of the important men, recording the pet names she gave them, their com-
ings and goings, the plottings and sordid affairs. Should one of her
customers balk at committing himself to one of Sadie's pet projects, a casual reference to the diary usually brought him into line.

This small form of blackmail meant success for a number of Sadie's plans which often benefited the community.

Sadie's head was not always filled with business. As a child in England, she dreamed of riding to the hounds, sitting gracefully atop a prancing steed, dressed in an elegant equestrian costume and trailed by admiring men and jealous women. Growing up did not dim the dream, it grew only more possessive.

One sunny day Hillsboro was startled to see Sadie riding side-saddle on a black horse down Main Street. She was gowned as if for a queenly ride to the hounds. She wore a long grey velvet skirt with grey silk ascot tucked neatly into the neck of a white shirtwaist. Well-fitting boots enhanced her small feet, and three-quarter length gloves protected her hands. A tall silk hat sat jauntily atop carefully arranged curls. A lustrous mother-of-pearl-handled riding crop completed her ensemble. A small black boy named Boots, who looked after the black horse, was her only retinue.

Hillsboro reacted to Sadie's strange appearance with hoots and jeers, but the ridicule failed to deter her. At least once a week, for many years, she made her stately ride down Hillsboro's Main Street.

Sadie's days in running the hotel were often routine. Then one Saturday morning some Indians appeared again to ruffle her composure. The ladies of Hillsboro, as well as the hotel, baked bread every Saturday morning. The Indians, lured by the delicious aroma of baking bread, came down from the mountain to beg for a loaf. Tom Ying, at a knock on the door one Saturday, was startled to see several Indians with hands outstretched. They refused to leave, and Ying grabbed his meat cleaver and chased them out of the yard. Next morning the corral gate was found open; the horse Sadie rode wearing her "hunt" outfit was gone. He was found later, with his beautiful mane and tail covered with burrs.

The following Saturday, Sadie greeted the redskins armed with her shotgun. The men again left with no bread. That evening Sadie found her clothesline, hung with her satin bloomers, lace camisole and silk stockings, lying in the mud. She decided then it was better not to fight over a loaf of bread. In the future the Indians got their bread and Sadie suffered no more pranks.

In 1896 the mysterious disappearance of Judge Albert J. Fountain and his nine-year-old son Henry stunned the Southwest.

Fountain had been asked to investigate a widespread cattle rustling gang. His evidence gathered, the judge prepared to leave his home in Las Cruces, New Mexico and drive the long distance to the winter court sitting in Lincoln. He had received death threats, and his anxious family begged him to delay the trip. Fountain refused, but agreed to taking his young son with him, reasoning that no one would harm a small boy.

Fountain presented his evidence to the court and was granted cattle-rustling indictments against wealthy rancher Oliver Lee and his two cowhands. Court over, the judge and Henry started home.

On the trail, Fountain was told by Mescalero Indians and a mail carrier that three men were trailing him. The Indians and the carrier were the last people to see Fountain and his son alive.

Posses were sent to search for the judge after his failure to return home. They found the deserted buggy. Henry's hat and Fountain's cartridge belt, with twelve bullets missing, lay on the buggy floor. The posse followed the trail of three men almost to Oliver Lee's ranch. The sign was lost by cattle being driven across the tracks.

The two bodies were never found. Two years later, Lee and his men, fearing for their lives, surrendered. Feeling was running so high in Las Cruces that Judge Frank Parker, in a change of venue, moved the trial to Hillsboro.

The trial spurred Hillsboro into new life. Lawmen, witnesses and the curious poured into town. Lee's followers camped at one end of town. Fountain's took over the other end.

Sadie's hotel was crammed with important personages. She was right in the middle of all discussions. Lee was her friend, and she voiced a strident opinion to any who would listen. Had it been the year of picket lines and placard bearing, Sadie would have headed the march toting the biggest "Free Lee" sign and making the most noise. She was in her glory.

Sadie's Tom Ying prepared hearty meals for the prisoners. The first day of the trial, the men stuffed themselves on pork chops, collard greens, sweet potatoes, hot biscuits and apple pie. Every day bountiful meals were delivered and served by Sadie to the men on trial.

The trial lasted fifteen days. Albert Bacon Fall headed the defense while Thomas Benton Catron led the prosecution. From the first day, the proceedings took on the trappings of a circus. Fall's thundering histrionics were no more theatrical than the sight of Sadie and her girls trooping in every day to place fresh flowers on the defendants' table.

Fall argued that since no bodies had been found, no murders had been committed. This convinced the jury, which returned a fast verdict of not guilty. The freeing of Lee set off a celebration Hillsboro long remembered. Guns boomed, firecrackers popped and liquor flowed freely. Sadie led the dancing in the streets.

The remains of Fountain and his son were never found. Their disappearance is one of the great mysteries of the Southwest and is still widely discussed today.

In the early 1900s Sadie felt she needed more money. She returned to her onetime profession and opened two brothels: one at each end of Hillsboro. She hired young, pretty Mexican girls who taught Sadie the art of swearing in Spanish. The girls were clean, well dressed and personable. Sadie found a fat cook named Charlie who provided both houses with wholesome meals.

After the day's work at the Ocean Grove was done, Sadie dressed in her finest and played hostess at the bordellos. She wore stylish silk gowns with a marabou feather boa slung around her shoulders. Snowy egret plumes graced her elaborate coiffure. A common touch was a showy necklace of five-dollar gold pieces worn around her neck. Sadie was a standout in any crowd, and the men agreed she was all woman.

The year 1914 saw the beginning of tragedy for Hillsboro. Spring rains filled the Percha River and sent a wall of muddy water through the town. Mrs. Hattie Givens described her feelings as the water rose almost to the second floor of her home: "Then a terrible crash of falling timber and glass told us the front of the drugstore had fallen out; another crash and the back of the store gave way; further down the street we could hear crash after crash as the terrible waves demolished building after building. It was the most fearful disaster we had ever experienced."

There was one death from the flood. Tom Murphy's body was found in the brush some fifty feet above the normal waterline of the creek. Sadie's only loss was several cases of beer that washed downstream.

Hillsboro was slowly recovering from the flood when influenza struck almost every family. Panic gripped the town as deaths rose daily. The acrid scent of burning bedlinen and clothing belonging to the victims filled the air.

This terrible tragedy brought Sadie's basic goodness to the surface. She closed the hotel, shut the closet door on her silken gowns hanging on their scented coathangers, donned a starched calico dress and set out to help the stricken people. Many weary and heartbreaking days and nights followed for Sadie. She was physician, nurse, friend, minister, undertaker and provider for those who needed help. She tended the sick, cooked and cleaned house for the ill families. She found homes for the orphans and laid out their parents. She shopped for "them chippies on the hill" and took over the support of a family whose father was in jail for stealing.

Sadie was affected most by the pitiful plight of the children; perhaps their suffering reminded her of the small child she had loved so devotedly. The barren pine coffins upset her, so she cut up her silken gowns and lined the tiny caskets with the material. Ofttimes Sadie would hitch up her buggy and bear the small remains to the cemetery herself. Her final gift of love to the little ones was a bouquet of red geraniums from the pots growing in her living-room window. If live flowers were unavailable, she plucked artificial blooms from her hats and made nosegays for the graves.

Eventually the influenza epidemic ran its course, but fate was not finished with Hillsboro. A great drouth was followed by a merciless depression. The most devastating blow came in 1938, when Hot Springs (now Truth or Consequences) wrested the county seat from Hillsboro. The town fought bitterly against losing the county seat, but the voters of Sierra County supported the change.

Only the old folks without a future and a few stubborn ranchers stayed with Hillsboro. The entire countryside lay in a deathly stillness, almost as if in a hypnotic trance. The soft wind moaned through the bare branches of the once lovely cottonwoods. To all appearances, Hillsboro had become a ghost town.

Sadie Orchard, like Hillsboro, had reached the end of the glory trail. The passage of time, the relentless struggle to survive, had taken its toll. There was no business. The girls had left long ago. Sadie's failing health finally forced her to sell the Ocean Grove restaurant to Tom Ying. He chose to call it The Chinaman's Place.

Sadie spent most of her time rocking in the sunlit patio of her home. She relived the days when she was young and beautiful and daring enough to drive a stagecoach, when she wore diamonds in her hair and was on a first-name basis with the most important men in the territory.

Sarah Jane Creech Orchard was nearing ninety, penniless and alone, when she passed away. Foreclosures on her property had been filed. Gone was the treasured equestrian outfit, the feather boa, the necklace of five-dollar gold pieces. She had outlived most of her friends. Even as the once-spunky little woman lay dying, scavengers picked through her poor belongings looking for something of value. There were few to weep or bring flowers when Sadie Orchard was consigned to a pauper's grave in the hillside cemetery.

Today the Black Range District is more ghostly than robust. Lake Valley is a true ghost town, with only caretakers to guard the shuttered mines. Kingston has become an art colony; its Percha Bank serves as home for the Black Range Artists' Gallery. Hillsboro has several hundred residents and bubbles with enthusiasm during its October apple festivals.

Sadie Orchard's Ocean Grove Hotel is now the Black Range Museum. The kitchen of Tom Ying, who lived to the venerable age of one hundred and four, is just as he left it. There is wood in the big black stove, ashes in the bucket and Tom's black skullcap lying on the table. All seem to be waiting for their master to return.

In death as in life, Sadie's personality dominates the museum. Her photographs dot the walls; a bright red felt runner that topped her piano is prominently displayed. Sadie's black silk stockings, a few pieces of tarnished jewelry and her cherished riding crop are mute reminders of this common yet uncommon woman who clawed her way to survival by matching the toughness of the world around her.

What kind of woman was Sadie Orchard? Women who knew her stated emphatically that she was hard as cold steel and capable of doing almost anything. The men, who were perhaps better acquainted with Sadie, admitted she was a rough fighter, yet insisted, "Sadie was a good old gal."

Distasteful as her profession was to some people, even the most rigid moralist could agree that, in spite of her calling, Sadie was, in her own way, a Lady.

———————

A native of Cleburne, Texas, Mary'n Rosson has lived in El Paso since the early days of World War II. Finding herself fascinated with the color and vitality of life as it existed in the old West, in 1970 Mrs. Rosson began writing articles based on the history of that era.

Her work has now appeared in all leading Western publications.

BIBLIOGRAPHY

BOOKS

American Guide Series. *New Mexico.* New York: Hastings House, 1940.

Fergusson, Erna. *New Mexico.* New York: Alfred A. Knopf, 1955.

Gibson, A. M. *The Life and Death of Colonel Albert Jennings Fountain.* Norman, Oklahoma: University of Oklahoma Press, 1965.

Keleher, William A. *Fabulous Frontier.* Santa Fe, New Mexico: Rydal Press, 1942.

McKenna, James A. *Black Range Tales.* Glorieta, New Mexico: Rio Grande Press, 1969.

Metz, Leon. *Pat Garrett.* Norman, Oklahoma: University of Oklahoma Press, 1974.

NEWSPAPERS

El Paso Herald Post, November 7, 1936, May 5, 1943

El Paso Journal, July 7, 1936

El Paso Times, June 10, 1899, March 10, 1963, October 13, 1935, April 1, 1965, November 6, 1938

MAGAZINES

Black Range Museum Pamphlet, no date

Findlay, J. "Sadie Was a Character." *Password*, Vol. XVI, No. 1
    Spring 1971.
Florin, Lambert. *New Mexico Ghost Towns,* 1971.
Robbins, Louis. "Sadie." *Real West,* 1970.
Simmons, E. E. "Sadie Was a Lady." *Southwesterner,* January 1962.

MANUSCRIPT

No byline, no title, unpublished, in possession of Mary'n Rosson.

INTERVIEW

Key, Lydia. Curator of Black Range Museum, Hillsboro, New
    Mexico.

8

Polly Pry

by MARY LOU PENCE

In the days when it was decidedly unladylike for a woman to have anything to do with newspaper work, Leonel Ross O'Bryan rose to fame under the pseudonym of "Polly Pry" as the Denver Post's front-page girl and often scooped her sneering male contemporaries.

N.S.Y.

Denver in the 1890s was the largest city in the Rockies. It was the center of a new empire, and it was not unusual to find women as proprietors of eating houses, running laundries, owning millinery shops, teaching school or testing their talents on the boards of the frontier theaters. But the female journalist was yet to make her appearance.

On an autumn day in the nineties a couple of men bought up the old *Evening Post* and changed its name. They changed its location, too, and they had their executive quarters painted flame color. It was called the "Red Room." They changed the all-male equanimity of the newsroom by hiring a female front-page reporter who could write with gusto. She was known as "Polly Pry," and for three decades she was to be one of America's most courageous and colorful journalists.

Soon after Polly invaded the *Denver Post*'s inner sanctum of masculinity, the partners' Red Room was to be renamed more aptly "The Bucket of Blood." For it was here an episode of horror was enacted, and Polly Pry, with unequaled courage and daring, saved her publishers, Fred Bonfils and Harry Tammen, from a crazed man's bullets. She was to earn her spurs from her male colleagues for this heroic feat.

But in the beginning, when the new owners of the *Post* chose the banner slogan "So the People Will Know," and assigned their front-page girl to crusade "for things as well as against them," the men then working in the newsroom heatedly resented this blond beauty with her flouncing skirts and big-brimmed hats invading their city room. "Good Gawd," they'd groan, "do we have to put up with the likes of those Eastern sob-sisters—Nellie Bly, Jenny Lind, Annie Laurie, Penelope Penfeathers?" The paper boys, too, snickered behind her back as she made her way towards the Red Room.

Polly went to work and got in the thick of the newsmaking; she viewed a fire and counted the dead; visited mine cave-ins and consoled the bereaved; rushed into the violence of a labor strike and got her stories. One by one the men grudgingly admitted that "for a woman, Polly Pry was pretty damned good!"

Polly Pry was born Leonel Ross Campbell, daughter of Mary Elizabeth McKinney and James Nelson Campbell on November 11, 1857 in antebellum Kentucky. The Civil War brought her father's lush plantation to economic chaos, and the good days of the Old South were over for the Campbell family. It was then that Nell, as she was known, was selected to benefit by the generosity of a rich relative and was enrolled in a girl's school in St. Louis.

Here she met George Anthony, a member of an illustrious and wealthy Kansas railroad construction family. She was but fifteen and he was many years her senior, but the lonely, homesick Nell was fed up with the world of giggling and tittering schoolgirls. She became enamored of the attentive and romantic George.

One dark night, attired in her most stylish grown-up gown of black velvet, she slipped out of her dormitory window, ran across the grassy campus and hopped over the fence into the ready arms of her lover. Their elopement, in the luxury of the Anthony private railroad car, took them south of the border, where George had accepted a commission from a Boston banking firm to build the Mexican Central Railroad, a concession granted by Mexico's President Porfirio Díaz.

A new, wide wonderful world now opened to Leonel, and her inquisitive mind began absorbing the language of the people, their customs and something of the economic status of the country. As the wife of an important man, she found herself in the role of gracious hostess entertaining influential personages—both her husband's business associates and high Mexican diplomats. In return, the Anthonys were frequent guests in the glittering palace of Mexican President Porfirio Díaz. Here the dazzling American señora was a delight. She was rapidly becoming fluent in the language of her hosts. Her blond beauty was accentuated by the latest Worth gowns imported from Paris and the exquisite and expensive jewels with which George adorned her. At afternoon functions, her plumed chapeaux brought admiring exclamations from the native señoras.

But the soirées of society were too restricting for Leonel's unfettered adventurous spirit. After five years, chafing at the shackles imposed by society and the bonds of matrimony, she walked out of her husband's deluxe traveling palace. Her marriage on wheels went on the rocks as she headed for New York and the golden dome of the Big Town's *World* Building.

Not one to start at the bottom, she went to the top, to publisher John Cockerill who was also her father's friend, and told him she wanted a job. Cockerill protested that she was too young and pretty to be put through the hoops of big-time journalism: "I ought to spank you and send you back to your husband."

But there was no brushing aside this persistent young woman; he hired her at $6.00 a week. Because this was the era when it was considered unladylike to use real names, Leonel chose the pen name "Polly Pry." She was assigned immediately to the tune of screeching fire sirens to cover a tenement district holocaust. She wrote a sizzling account, beat the deadline and impressed the city editor.

It was the beginning of her adrenaline-paced career which would take her quick-tripping feet many times to the scenes of violence and horror. She was given a raise and a foreign assignment: to South America where she poked into secret diplomatic business for her paper.

When she returned to New York, she had garnered a vast amount of experience and background material. With an itch to write fiction, she quit the *World* and under her assumed by-line began concocting romances for Street & Smith magazines at the rate of one love affair per week. She was now earning her own way, with enough left over to help her financially distressed parents.

Her concern over her father's accumulating debts and her brother's failing health took her out of New York and linked her destiny with the West. While enroute to visit her family who had moved to Denver because of her brother, Nell met dynamic newspaper personality, Frederic Bonfils. Seated across the table in the dining car she was attracted to Bonfils' attire: brown check, braid-edged suit. Then she took a second look and saw he was reading a paper with gaudy red headlines.

"How awful!" Leonel blurted out. And immediately was embarrassed when he proudly told her it was his paper, the Denver Post. Before the meal was finished, some of his enthusiasm had rubbed off on Leonel; before the evening was over, she had accepted a job writing for his "awful" newspaper. She became the first woman reporter in the history of the old he-man Denver Post.

In her spare time, Polly continued to concoct love stories. Her home on West Colfax Avenue became a beehive of activity. Here she was equally adept at entertaining Sarah Bernhardt at tea, interviewing political candidates and consoling that strange Colorado man-eater, Alfred (also spelled Alferd) Packer. It was this cannibal that brought her worldwide acclaim, and because of him, she became the heroine in the drama of near-tragic proportions in the Red Room the day she saved the lives of her bosses, Bonfils and Tammen.

When Polly had come into the newsroom in 1898, her publishers were instigating a reform crusade and assigned Polly to get the lowdown on Colorado's institutions. "Our insane treatment of the insane," was her first exposé. At the penitentiary in Canon City, she came upon a gaunt black-haired man who refused to talk to anyone.

"Who is he?" she asked the guide. She was told she was in the company of a man-eater, doomed to forty years for killing and devouring his companions during a blizzard in 1873 in the San Juan Mountains.

The morose-eyed man piqued Polly's curiosity. After several visits, she gained his confidence. And his story. "You understand that was a long time ago," Packer told her. "My liberty was taken away from me. . . . I am innocent of the hideous crime with which I am charged."

Packer's act of cannibalism had occurred in 1873. He was arrested in 1874, but escaped from the adobe jail and was not apprehended until nine years later, when he was brought back for trial at Lake City. Some of the *Post*'s reporters reminded Polly of the story (though of doubtful validity, it had found its way into Colorado folklore) of how when the jury rendered the guilty verdict, an illiterate bartender attending the trial circulated the supposed outbursts of Judge Melville Gerry when he sentenced Packer: "There was sivin Dimmicrats in Hinsdale County, but ya et five of thim, ya voracious man-eatin' so-and-so!"

Polly thought the saloonkeeper's account disgusting. She had read stories of the unwritten law of the high seas—cannibalism was permissible—and she believed it could also be applied to blizzard conditions. Besides, Polly was convinced of Packer's innocence and her heart ached to help him. She pleaded his case to her employers and they gave her the go-ahead. Next, she went to Governor Charles Spalding Thomas about Packer. His abrupt dismissal of the subject infuriated Polly, so she poked into the governor's parole board files and came up with some fifty-seven names Governor Thomas had granted clemency to in the year 1899. She reminded her readers of the fact that of this "whole troop of ravishers to whom the Tender-Hearted Thomas" had given freedom, there were "eight with criminal histories of such blushing acts as rape and murder, yet His Honor refuses Packer, and he is a sick old man."

Despite her insistence via the Denver *Post*, Governor Thomas told her, "Under no circumstances will there be executive clemency for Packer." But he did not reckon with this indomitable and determined female reporter.

"Heaven surely forgives when one of his sons is no longer able to distinguish right and wrong and a man in the last throes of starvation cannot surely be considered responsible," her stories emoted. She also confided to her public that Packer was now a diabetic and was in desperate need of good, clean mountain air. Free air!

She had Bonfils and Tammen sold on her crusade of amnesty for the aged Packer. They hired lawyer W. W. Anderson, better known as "Plug Hat," to handle the legal end.

During the years that Packer had been confined to prison, he had busied himself with handiwork—making hair ropes, bridles and other knickknacks which he sold to cowboys. He had saved well over $1,000. When Plug Hat entered the scene, he found the old man not penniless, as he had supposed, so he pocketed the prisoner's hard-earned funds. "For my services," he told Packer.

When Polly found out about it, she headed directly for her publishers' office. They were furious at Plug Hat. Bonfils began cursing "the damned double-crosser," and Tammen suggested, "Let's sic Packer on him!"

They resolved to terminate Plug Hat's services and sent Polly across Curtis Street to tell him so, and that furthermore he'd not receive the fee they'd promised him.

The attorney was feeling pretty smug with Packer's money safely tucked in his pockets when Polly burst into his office. She informed him he was fired. Plug Hat reached for his short topcoat and told her that he was a gentleman from Missouri and he'd show those two scoundrels over at the *Post!*

Gathering up her gored alpaca skirts, Polly rushed out ahead of him. Back in the Red Room, she breathlessly warned her bosses. She had barely finished when Plug Hat appeared, his hand thrust deep in his coat pocket. The men began hurling harsh language back and forth. "You're a damned robber!" Tammen shouted. The lawyer's face went white.

Then Polly saw him reach into his pocket. "He's got a gun," she screamed.

Bonfils rushed at Anderson. With a well-planted uppercut, he had his assailant sprawling on the floor, and he was on top battering him with his fists. Blood was spouting from a gash in Anderson's cheek when Polly stopped Bonfils. "The scandal will be all over town, and it's not worth it," she reasoned.

Bonfils let Plug Hat up from the floor. "Now get out, you thieving skunk!" Bonfils ordered.

As Anderson made his way toward the door, the partners continued snarling accusations and contemptuous epithets at him. But not for long. Almost at once the door swung open again, and Plug Hat, revolver now cocked to a vantage point, fired first at one and then the other of his enemies. Polly saw Bonfils go down, a bullet clipping his shoulder and another thudding into his chest. Now the trigger-crazed Anderson moved upon Tammen, one bullet grazing the publisher's wrist and a second bouncing into his shoulder.

Polly rushed to Tammen's aid, her full skirts shielding him from the mad man and blotting him out as a target. Then she grabbed the gun just as Anderson aimed again. In the scuffle, he hissed at her, "You'll get it next!"

She faced him squarely, still struggling for the revolver. "Go ahead. And you'll hang for it!"

Plug Hat was looking into the blazing eyes of the tall Polly. He recognized his match in this lady wildcat and backed out of the room.

All this time, Polly was protecting Tammen with her skirts. She could see Bonfils unconscious on the floor, his breathing harsh and heavy. Two men arrived from the street below to see what the commotion was about.

But Anderson was gone. He'd calmly walked out of the *Post* building and into police headquarters, where he gave himself up. He thought he'd killed "those two skunks" and in so doing, he figured he'd done Denver a good turn and was willing to hang for it.

He was mistaken. The partners recovered and brought their would-be murderer to trial. Appearing as one of the witnesses in the case was Alfred Packer. He was an object of curiosity in the courtroom.

Polly Pry was also summoned to testify. But the trial resulted in a hung jury, and Plug Hat went free. Anderson later reported that while he was in jail, he received an anonymous note and a bouquet of roses. He insisted it could have come from none other than ex-Governor Thomas. It referred to Polly's bosses: "I congratulate you upon your intention, but must condemn your aim."

Meanwhile Packer, having tasted the perfume of freedom, renewed his pleas for liberation. Polly again took up his cause, and her columns waxed emotionally in sympathy for the pathetic old man whom many had observed those days in court when Plug Hat was being tried.

Polly circulated a petition signed by more than a hundred Denver citizens, including the mayor, the city attorney, the police chief, a district judge, a bank president, and T. M. Patterson, owner and editor of the competitive *Rocky Mountain News*. She also directed an attack against Agent Mears of the Ute Indian

Reservation, whom she suspected of conniving with and influencing the Colorado governor.

It was a great day for her and her cannibal when Governor Thomas announced on January 7, 1901: "Alfred Packer, Number 1389, heretofore made application and the parole denied has since been renewed. Without changing my opinion concerning the offense I am constrained to grant application. The prisoner to be confined to the State of Colorado. Signed Charles S. Thomas, Governor."

On the same day that the Governor made this announcement, he resigned his office. He later wrote that "regarding Packer himself the *Post* bedeviled the life out of me, during my whole term as Governor, to pardon him . . ."

On January 10, 1901, the freed Packer left the prison. Polly advised her readers: "Let Packer forget the unholy events of the past . . . refrain from epithets as 'man-eater, human hyena and ghoul!' "

Her pleas were answered, for on the first days of liberation, her benefactor was issued tickets to boxing events, and he was also presented complimentary invitations—even one to an opera performance. But in the days to come, Packer was to prove somewhat of a pest to Polly, for he continued to hang around her desk, leaning over her and her typewriter.

Hardly had she got Packer out of prison when her bosses sent for her. "Get us a front-page story concerning those murder mysteries in the Western Federation mines."

The explosiveness of the mining situation in Colorado at this time was an aftermath of the depression of the 1890s. Many unskilled laborers and immigrants were available for the smelting works and mine fields. The struggle resulted in the union leaders bringing in agitators to intimidate or forcibly drive off the non-union laborers. It was the plight of the working man being victimized by these drastic methods that was turning the public to revulsion, and the exposure of the agitators and their leaders was a challenge to Polly.

Equipped with notepad and pencil, she set out for the mine pits. When told by labor leaders Big Bill Haywood, Charles Moyer and Vincent St. John that women weren't allowed underground, she disguised herself in masculine work clothes and, with pick and lantern, accompanied the miners down the shafts. Her printer's ink caused these leaders many sleepless nights as she assailed and hurled charges against them. "Why not work the wage scale out with the mine owners? Why kill or maim the workers?" she asked.

In 1902 Polly was sent to Telluride's Smuggler Mine, where a worker named Arthur J. Collins had been murdered. She visited the mine, talked to the mine owners and the men. She interviewed Vincent St. John, president of the Labor Federation. In a piece for her paper she quoted St. John in his callous defense of murder. Mr. St. John repudiated the story, and his unions boycotted the *Post*. Suddenly Bonfils cooled off on Polly's pursuits and only halfheartedly supported her crusades. Next he began picking quarrels with her and even went so far as to intimate that Polly might not be telling the truth concerning her interview with labor's boss.

This slap in the face was simply too much for Polly. After all, when a lady is brave enough to risk her life wrestling to save her bosses from a smoking pistol, she is not apt to take an insult.

When Bonfils would not back her campaigns, there was nothing Polly could do but quit! As she handed him her resignation, she militantly accused the publisher of being cowardly in his bowing to St. John, and of not standing on his own feet for the sake of the victimized working people.

To prove she had no fear of St. John, Polly single-handedly launched her own news magazine, a weekly, *Polly Pry*. It took some doing getting it rolling, but she owned her home on West Colfax Avenue, and it now became her place of business. She bought a secondhand press and hired two printers. She sold subscriptions at $4.00 per year and engaged a hawker at the downtown newsstand. In her second issue, she announced, "Sorry you couldn't get *Polly Pry* last week, but we were completely sold out."

In every issue she continued her spirited campaign against the vicious tactics of the labor agitators. Concerning the mining war in Las Animas County, she wrote: "I was there last week and not one day passed without its murders, killings and assaults." Her presses rolled red-hot from her Colfax home.

Polly Pry was an oddity in which she not only beat the drums for her pet project and causes, but also included choice bits of town gossip: "Denver," she announced in her first edition, "was just big enough and just lively enough and just naughty enough to need a weekly paper . . . as desperately as a lively boy needs his Saturday-night tubbing."

In another issue, she played up the big social event—the 1903 automobile show—calling it the Go-Devils Parade. She took the society gals to task for not being up on the latest motoring attire of dust jackets, chauffeur capes and goggles. "They might as well wear a muslin gown on a cross-country hunt or go burro riding in a ball dress as to wear fluffs and filldals in an auto!"

She poked fun of the local women's bridge games: "The grocer waits while the buxom matron snitches a few dollars off the bill here and there trying to catch up with her bridge debts."

She related gleefully "tales of the *nouveau riche* and socially prominent." She printed a story, "The Expectorates," which was told to her by the former Leadville Cinderella, Mrs. Margaret (Molly) Tobin Brown. While flitting around the world, Molly Brown had rented her mansion to a former Colorado governor. On her return, she called his wife's attention to the condition of her walls and rugs. "But," reminded Governor X's spouse, "you didn't furnish cuspidors."

Then on January 16, 1904, the issue told of an attempt to assassinate her: "For the past several weeks I have been receiving anonymous letters warning me . . . that I would be killed and my office blown to atoms."

On a dark night, her doorbell had rung. When she answered it she had a quick glance at a strange figure. "Some instinct or apprehension warned me, and I stepped behind the door. A bad light, a black dress and a poor marksman saved my life." She described her assailant as "a tall man in dark clothes and a derby, with a dark mustache and a scarred face."

The police found the traces of two bullets: one in her desk and the other which had bounced off the wall. The police chief stationed guards around her home, and Governor Peabody offered the aid of the militia. A corps of newsboys from the city's big dailies arranged around-the-clock security and kept an eye open for suspicious loiterers.

Polly refused to quit. "I am going to keep right on running my magazine and writing what I think proper," she announced. For two more years her presses rolled, although she changed the name of the paper to the *Saturday Sun* and gave it a more metropolitan

treatment. When she was offered the important position of Colorado Commissioner for the World's Fair, she sold her weekly.

The next few years found her on special assignments covering
Wild West rodeos, mining booms and other riotous happenings in
the Rockies.

Her second marriage in 1910, to handsome Denver attorney
Harry O'Bryan, did not slow up her fast-paced career. For a time,
she presided as hostess at their Gaylord Avenue home, but the
printer's ink would never drain from her veins, and she was soon
back on the front page with the fires, the murders, the unfortunate
juveniles. She was now front-page girl for John Shaffer's Denver
Times. Although she tried to cover up with the crispness of her
style and the sharpness of her tongue and typewriter, her stories
spread sympathy like jam on toast for the plight of the frustrated
and downfallen. And her paychecks continued to be divided
among her own impoverished relatives.

Now, in 1914, a break threatened relations between the United
States and Mexico. With an itch to be in the thick of things, she
jumped at the chance to be johnny-on-the-spot when Shaffer of
the *Times* proposed to send a correspondent into revolutionary
Mexico.

Equipped with rare courage and shrewdness, together with her
years' experience of life in Mexico, a knowledge of the language
and a notebook and camera, as well as a piece of lucky jade, a
rabbit's foot, and an accident policy, Nell left Denver on March
15, 1914. An arrangement had been made by the American government for her to cross into Juarez by way of El Paso. It was
while she was thus enroute that she received word of the death of
her husband in Oregon. She could not turn back now.

"I have had some rough trips in my days—stagecoached over
the Andes to Peru, and the Sierras in Mexico, pack-trained
through the tropical forests of Ecuador and have been on a storm-
wrecked steamer between Guayaquil and Santiago. I have waited
in the vilest of holes, dipped into the slums of New York, but nowhere have dreamed of anything like the car into which my handful of luggage was thrown as I scrambled aboard the train under
way at Juarez," Polly later wrote.

She was now back in the land where she and George Anthony
had spent those early years. But everything was changed—changed

by one of the most daring, but romantic rascals in history—
Francisco "Pancho" Villa.

She remembered how in those other days the vast haciendas had
reared their cream-colored walls and flowers had filled the patios.
She recalled how she had watched the droves of horses and burros
disputing the wild pastures with the ever-increasing herds of cattle.
She found now that blood-stained horrors had replaced the
blooming desert of northern Mexico, and as she made her way
along the war-torn villages, she had to step over dead bodies piled
high. Where she had so often banqueted in the governor's palace,
there was now rioting for corn. The cracked bell of the centuries-
old chapel which had called the faithful to worship was stilled,
and the gentle padre's voice went unheeded.

Polly Pry rode the railroad car at her own risk. She moved between armed guards with a military pass in her hand. She was bent
on interviewing the brown rogue of the big hat and three-inch
rowel spurs who had brought about this state of affairs. She was
headed for the palace where Pancho Villa was headquartered.

There was a wait in his parlor for the rebel chieftain was a busy
man. Polly observed the roses, bougainvillea and trailing vines
adorning the table. As she stepped back to view the effect of the
floral decor, she heard a high-pitched voice: *"Bien, señorita. Está
muy bonita."* And Pancho Villa in his olive-drab uniform was
leaning against the door jamb.

"You Americans are crazy to meddle in affairs which do not
concern you," he told her fiercely, his beady eyes cruel and cold.
Then, as a cool statement of fact, he added, "The day may come
when I shall have to fight all foreigners and Colorados, too!"

"But not an American woman," Polly smiled. "Not a woman
who has come all this way to see you."

"Never!" he shouted with swift transition, and then laughed
with good humor.

Then Señora Villa appeared and Polly, speaking in Spanish,
knew she had an ally in this woman. "I find," the presswoman
wrote to her paper, "that love questions bind this soldier the same
as they did Napoleon, whom he is trying to imitate. I find Señora
Villa with him at the front."

Not only did Polly get her interview with Pancho, but she went
where American men dared not go, and saw what they dared not
see. She saw Torreón fall—the burning, flogging, maiming. She

watched the flies buzzing over the dead bodies. She witnessed the half-breathing humans shoved into trenches and covered with earth. She viewed the enormous funeral pyres as they illumined the city in every direction.

"I went about unarmed and alone at times among that hostile and war-infested country, among a primitive and semi-civilized people more than two-thirds of whom were Indians. . . . But I was accepted and the rebel officers invited me to make myself at home. I was given the freedom of the camps."

Then she went into the Federals' headquarters. At Mazatlan the blue-uniformed Francisco Valenzuela was amazed. "A correspondent? It is incredible what the American ladies can do!"

Once amid this poverty and destitution, she tried to snap a picture of the hungry people in line at the Prefectura, but a policeman stopped her. "Just then a shell screamed over our heads and there was a terrible explosion. In the ensuing panic a soft-voiced old peon pushed me through a door and into an empty office from which another door led outward, and I rushed for the carriage and the hotel." Thus she just missed the Plaza Republic explosion, which wounded dozens and killed many.

In July this undaunted reporter, to get her story for the Denver *Times,* went through the hot and menacing lines from the Federalists to the Constitutionalists. The hostilities of both armies of Mazatlan ceased while Polly crossed to the side of the besiegers. It was almost noon and the two officers invited her to lunch with them and their staff—*frijoles* and fresh tortillas in a boxcar dining room. From where Polly sat, partaking of their hospitality, she could see the wide spreading arms of an ebony tree "from which hung limp and grotesque forms, heads resting on shoulders, bare feet reaching for the soft earth."

For six hours the flag of truce waved and then Polly, with the nauseating memory of hanging men twitching at her elbow, or "mayhap it was the breeze stirring them," was escorted through the lines of battle-hardened soldiers to her waiting party. She was only too glad to be off by train for Modesta. Yet not once did she "show the pale feather of fear," the rebels reported, as she moved onward in this land of bandit warfare.

She was the guest of a rebel paymaster on a wild bullet-dodging ride with two months' stipends which had to get through to eight thousand fighting men. The car lit out, with Polly propped against the strongbox, through the rough passes, between the foreboding hills and into a dry arroyo of Tepic country. There she was met by General Obregon.

Polly Pry returned to Denver and reported her exciting adventures—describing how the copper-colored followers of Villa were routing the Federalists out of Mexico. Then, with a trace of nostalgia, she spoke to friends about those other days she had known when there was abundant romance for her in the land south of the border.

But Polly Pry was not one to dwell on the past. Although hostilities between divided Mexico had now ceased, there were other stories breaking. A world war—the first—was commencing; although Polly was now in her sixties, she volunteered for foreign duty with the Red Cross. Despite the threats of enemy submarines, she set sail. She served in Albania and Greece, and her accounts of the torn and ravaged countries were syndicated.

She had proposals to remain abroad as a foreign correspondent, and in New York the big Eastern dailies tried to entice her with lucrative offers. But Polly was homesick for the Rockies, so back to Denver she went. She organized the Rocky Mountain region's first "Poppy Day" to benefit the French orphans. She was named by *Redbook* magazine as one of the five most interesting women in America.

By the late twenties, Polly Pry had retired from active reporting. She began writing her autobiography, *My Life as a Reporter*. Sitting like a queen on her high-backed gold chair, she had an audience, too, during winter evenings, when college girls—would-be journalists—visited her.

With misted eyes, she recalled for them those early days when she was the only woman on the old *Post;* how those magnetic bosses "kept the whole staff hopping like Mexican jumping beans"; and how she had stepped right into that Bucket of Blood. "You can get what you want out of life if you make up your mind what it is, and at the same time are willing to hustle for it!" she counseled the students.

But Polly Pry's autobiography was never completed. She was eighty-one when she was taken to St. Joseph's Hospital with a heart attack. Her faithful colleague, Pinky Wayne, wrote an obituary for their old paper:

July 16, 1938: After three decades of brilliant reporting Mrs. Leonel Ross O'Bryan passed away. . . . Just before she had raised herself on an elbow and said to an attending nurse, "I must be up . . ." Yes, she was conscious that there were still stories to be scooped and even in death she ached to be the first on the scene.

Polly Pry was interred in Fairmont Cemetery surrounded by her beloved Colorado hills.

It has been written that her old bosses, Bonfils and Tammen, never quite forgave her the stigma of which they were so self-conscious: that they owed their lives to a woman's skirts. Still, there are those who are in the know that will tell you Harry Tammen and Fred Bonfils never quit a friend in need. During the last years of Polly's life, she was in financial straits. Some of the final words of Harry Tammen to his wife had been about caring for "the fellows and the girls down at the office." Mrs. Tammen remained faithful to her husband's wishes, and the end of Polly Pry's life was brightened by Agnes Tammen's generosity.

In summing up the achievements of this remarkable newspaper woman, topflight journalists of today agree that few reporters have been able to compete successfully with her record. "Polly Pry— beautiful, wild, fearless." Yes, she was almost a legend.

———————

Mary Lou Pence, a third-generation Montanan, is a charter member of Wyoming Presswomen and a longtime member of Western Writers of America. Her publications include The Ghost Towns of Wyoming, *which won the American Association for State and Local History Award of Merit;* Petticoat Rustler, *a Western Writers of America anthology chapter in* Tales and Legends of the Old West, *1962, which won the National Federation of Presswomen's top citation for feature writing;* The Laramie Story, *official publication commemorating the town's centennial, 1968;* Boswell—The Story of a Frontier Lawman, *1978. She has also written for the Denver* Post, Time-Life, Empire, *the Portland* Oregonian, *and a number of historical journals.*

BIBLIOGRAPHY

BOOKS

Fowler, Gene. *Timberline*. Garden City, N.Y.: Garden City Publishing Co., 1933, Chapter 13.

Ishbel, Ross. *Ladies of the Press*. New York: Harper & Brothers, 1936.

Ubbelohde, Carl, Benson, Maxine, and Smith, Duane A., *A Colorado History*. Boulder, Colorado: Pruett Publishing Co., 1972.

NEWSPAPERS AND PERIODICALS

The Denver *Post,* January 14, 1900; January 8, 1901; January 10, 1901; January 16, 1938.

The Denver *Times,* April 18, 1914; April 21, 1914; April 30, 1914.

Polly Pry, weekly, Denver, Colorado, vol. 1–4, September 1903–August 1905.

Saturday Sun, September 1905–06.

MAGAZINES

Contemporary, Denver Post, "The Adventures of Polly Pry", Eva Hodges, February 18, 1968.

Empire Denver Post, The spelling of Packer's first name (Alfred or Alferd) explained; Zeke Sher, November 21, 1976.

INTERVIEWS BY AUTHOR

The late Joseph Emerson Smith, Denver and Georgetown, Colorado, who knew Polly Pry all of her Denver lifetime.

The late Al Birch, Denver *Post* staffer who worked with Polly Pry on the old Denver *Post*.

BIRTH AND BURIAL RECORDS

Fairmont Cemetery Association, Denver, Colorado. O'Bryan-Campbell plot, May 13, 1958.

9

Mother Joseph

by LUCILE McDONALD

Quebec-born Esther Pariseau came West to serve mankind in the name of God. As Sister Joseph, she built her own quarters with hammer and saw in 1856 and set about putting up the first Catholic school, mission and orphanage in Vancouver, Washington. She then designed and helped build the four-story brick building that followed it. As Mother Joseph, she spread her work throughout the Pacific Northwest and is today considered the region's first architect.

N.S.Y.

The group of five women seemed dowdy and ill at ease. Persons around the hotel who regarded them curiously must have thought they were certainly unaccustomed to travel. After all, New York, even in 1856, was the metropolis of the nation, and these were obviously ladies from a sheltered background—Quaker spinsters perhaps. But why had their families permitted them to set forth unaccompanied on what was evidently the beginning of a long journey? It was whispered that they had engaged passage to Panama.

The mysterious quintet had arrived from Montreal, Canada and spoke French. They appeared extremely timid about going on the street. Just how their identity was discovered by the hotel management is not known, but suddenly the erect, strong, grey-eyed woman who seemed to be the leader was asked, "Sister, why are you afraid to wear your habits? No one will harm you if you do. In this country you do not need to go in disguise."

"We were warned to do so because of danger to us," Esther Pariseau replied. "If you say it is safe, gladly will we put on our robes. We are more comfortable in our customary garments."

Looking much relieved, the five Sisters of Providence donned their wimples and black attire and trooped off to board the ship that was to carry them on the first leg of the journey to the new world they had set out to conquer. While they were babes in the wood when it came to foreign travel, they were unafraid to face the problems that lay ahead on the opposite side of the North American continent.

In the five weeks that followed, while the contingent journeyed 6,000 miles—first to the Isthmus of Panama, across it by narrow-gauge railroad, and north once more in a ship to the Columbia River—Esther Pariseau had much time in which to meditate upon the events which had carried her so far out into the raw world from her Canadian home. Born April 16, 1823 in Saint Elzear Parish, Quebec, she had grown up in the stone farmhouse of Joseph and Françoise Pariseau. Since earliest childhood, she had watched her father at work in his carriage shop. When she was old enough, he taught her to handle tools and understand the qualities of wood. Before she was ten, she could recognize various kinds of timber, how they had to be seasoned and which were most durable. In another two years, she was using hammer, chisel, drawing knife and saw. One winter she fashioned a sewing box as a gift for her mother.

Carpentry was not the only skill she acquired; she learned to sew and to cultivate the garden. She proved extremely capable at whatever she tried, and her mother had to teach her not to be overbearing and imperious in her relations to her sisters and others.

When Esther was sixteen, her mother became ill as the result of the birth of her tenth child; the two oldest daughters had to take over much of the work of household and farm. They received only such education as their mother could give them in reading and writing until a boarding school opened in a nearby community in the fall of 1840. As the carriage shop and the farm were prospering, Esther was given an opportunity to attend, for Mme. Pariseau perceived in the girl a disposition to exercise her talents beyond the bounds of her family.

Esther proved an amazing pupil, and there was almost nothing in the way of practical arts that she did not try. She was adept at spinning, weaving, needlework, baking and cooking. She could garden, create small household articles in the carriage shop and was good at penmanship. She had acted as nurse for both her ailing mother and the young children. She sang well and had a genius for organization. After two years in the school, her ambitions had been directed toward emulating heroines of earlier times—especially nuns who had accomplished good works. From childhood she had felt at home in the church, and the idea of undertaking a novitiate was agreeable to her family. She was considering what order to enter when she was told of the formation of the Sisters of Providence and that they were seeking funds for a new asylum for the care of aged and infirm women. This appealed to Esther, but on account of her mother's health, she delayed taking action until the day after Christmas, 1843, when her father accompanied her to Montreal. He introduced his daughter to Sister Gamelin, the Mother Superior, explaining that she was now twenty years of age. "She is healthy and strong and eager to serve God," he added. After telling of her many talents, he predicted, "She will someday make a very good Superior."

Esther was the thirteenth woman to take vows of the new order. Years of scarcity and frugality followed, for the order was short of funds. The young postulant learned to deal with the economy of privation and became wise in the use of substitution and alteration, how to make the best of what was in her care. She completed her novitiate on July 21, 1845 and became Sister Joseph, taking the name of her father because she thought it would make him happy.

Canada had been interested in the Oregon country because of the fur-trade companies which had penetrated the Far West. The Hudson's Bay Company established Fort Vancouver on the Columbia River in 1825, and Abbé Francis Norbert Blanchet had gone out from Montreal to become a missionary to the Indians. After spending six years working in the new territory with Abbé Modeste Demers, Blanchet returned east and was appointed bishop of Oregon. Sister Joseph helped sew his vestments and linens.

By the end of 1848, Sister Joseph's duties had increased: she was infirmarian, pharmacist, community seamstress and general bursar at the convent. The House of Providence took on the duties of aiding the city of Montreal through epidemics of typhus and cholera.

In 1852 Bishop Blanchet was again back in Eastern Canada, asking this time for sisters to volunteer to go to Oregon. Five were accepted, but not Sister Joseph, who also applied. She was considered too important in the mother house in her role as bursar. When the group of volunteer nuns reached their destination, the bishop was absent in Mexico and they had no instructions as to where to go. After waiting for him in Oregon City, they left for California and eventually went to Chile, causing great regret that the expedition had been so badly bungled.

Three years went by, and Bishop Blanchet was once more back in Eastern Canada, asking for sisters to go to Vancouver. This time he would personally conduct them the entire distance (although as it turned out, in New York they were not under his supervision). Sister Joseph insisted that she wanted to go, so she was named superior of the new foundation. She was now known as Sister Joseph of the Sacred Heart. Because of a misapprehension about the dangers of travel, her group departed in secular garb, but when they stepped ashore on the bank of the Columbia River they were easily recognizable as a new breed: "women blackrobes."

Vancouver was larger than they had expected; the Hudson's Bay fort had been replaced with an American military post manned by two companies of soldiers. A church had already been established; also a small residence for the bishop. No arrangements had been made to house the sisters, partly because the vicar general, who had been in charge during the bishop's absence, did not concur in the plan to settle the nuns at Vancouver. He thought they should be in Olympia, the capital of recently organized Washington Territory.

The only place for lodging the contingent was a shed, open to the weather, but the bishop could not see the nuns going there; instead he offered them the unfinished attic of his home. Their first task was to clear it of rubbish and clean it before they could attempt to bed down. This was extremely rough accommodation for five women, but when a small house was finally ready for them, it had to be used as a chapel while the regular church was being repaired. The sisters made the best of the situation and moved into the housekeeper's room off the kitchen. It measured 10 by 16 feet, but Mother Joseph at once went to work to make it habitable. She applied her knowledge of carpentry and hammered together five bunks while another sister fashioned ticks stuffed with clean straw. Sister Joseph went on with her construction and produced a rough table hinged to the wall. Boxes served as chairs, and other boxes were nailed to the wall to hold dishes and tableware.

A few months later, a new convent was ready: a small wooden building 16 by 24 feet, with four windows. A stairway led to the attic dormitory. A small room was walled off and fitted as a chapel; Sister Joseph constructed the altar and its furnishings. The nuns proceeded to open a school; their first pupil was a three-year-old girl abandoned by her mother. Seven more children were admitted in April 1857. They now were caring for a second orphan, a boy scarcely more than an infant. The improvised convent had already become a house of refuge. Its next inhabitant was a penniless man of eighty-five, whom they permitted to sleep in the kitchen.

Thus the nuns' work began in the little community in the great Oregon country, where Indians still outnumbered whites. Of the sisters, only two were capable of teaching in English; the other three spoke the French of Eastern Canada, including the mother superior, who felt greatly frustrated in her work. The sisters had arrived during the Yakima Indian war, east of the mountains. Though Vancouver was some distance from the conflict, it was stirring with martial activity. In the resulting disorder, some Indian and half-white children were orphaned. They were left to stay with the sisters; some for a few months, others for years.

From the first, the sisters had made it their duty to visit the sick. They needed a hospital, and the vicar general stirred up interest in forming a nondenominational committee to discuss how it could be organized. Limited funding directed attention to Sister Joseph's construction skills. She had just completed quarters for a laundry and bakery and, since the partitions were not yet in, she was willing to offer this modest edifice for a hospital. It measured 16 by 20 feet and was 8 feet high. Walls and ceiling were covered with muslin fabric and wallpaper. The committee provided four beds and four small tables and chairs. Thus St. Joseph's Hospital came into being. Before it was finished in June 1858, there were applicants for admittance and it was filled to capacity. Additional space had to be found for convalescents.

The five sisters were overworked; they had to do all the house-keeping that went with their two enterprises. Late in 1858 three more nuns were sent out from Montreal to join them: one in the hospital, another to preside over the classroom and pharmacy and the third to help wherever needed. That year a bill was passed in the territorial legislature to allow the Sisters of Charity of Providence to incorporate, with Sister Joseph as their head. This allowed them to acquire income property and "to engage in the care of orphans, invalids, sick and poor and in the education of youth."

Sister Joseph's next effort was directed toward building a home for orphan boys. Colonel George Wright, commander of Fort Vancouver, permitted her and her workmen to take lumber for additions and repairs from the abandoned premises of the Hudson's Bay Company, the last of whose officials departed for Victoria in the summer of 1860. Fortunately, much useful material had been left behind, and the sister superior hastened to take advantage of the colonel's offer. She personally selected timber and fittings and remained supervising the project until the annex was completed. Then she summoned a couple of the sisters to do the painting. The bishop had kept his promise to pay for the workmen on the job if the sisters would furnish the construction materials. While she was building the annex, Sister Joseph accomplished something for herself: she acquired an office of her own for the first time.

Three local postulants increased the number of her staff when they turned to their next enterprise in behalf of neglected persons. In 1861 they undertook the care of mental patients, and within five years had twenty-five insane housed. They were first placed in the small buildings on the mission grounds, then later moved to another structure built west of the military reservation. Sister Joseph obtained from the territory a contract to pay $8.00 a week for each patient's lodging, board, washing and medical attention. Unfortunately, this remuneration was not received in coin, and a paper dollar was worth $.60. When Sister Joseph protested against this discriminatory practice, the contract was not renewed; her dream of founding a much larger asylum for mental patients went flitting. She converted the asylum building into a new St. Joseph's Hospital.

By 1864 Sister Joseph had 100 children, half a dozen old people, 40 hospital patients and the sisters to feed and shelter. Among the crises she already had coped with was the disastrous loss of the potato and grain crops when the Columbia River flooded in 1861, leaving her to find a means of provisioning her community that winter. Money was badly needed. She set out to raise it herself, going on begging tours east of the mountains, traveling by boat and horseback to mining towns and scattered communities in Idaho and Montana. A tale is told of one stop she and her sister companion made at a log-cabin restaurant when two swarthy men sat down at the table opposite them. The strangers were intent on listening to the nuns' conversation and this alerted Sister Joseph as to their probable intentions. The men continued to watch and follow them. One afternoon they accosted the sisters in the road. Eyeing the bag which hung from Sister Joseph's arm, one asked, "Ain't you 'fraid to travel this way?"

She answered shrewdly, "Surely you don't think we keep with us the money we are collecting. What are express offices for?"

This turned the men off for the time being. A few days later both were in jail, charged with murdering a miner for his nuggets. Meanwhile Sister Joseph followed her own suggestion and deposited $2,600 at the first express office she found.

Another time masked men held up a coach in which the nuns were riding on a rough mountain road. An account published in "The Bell and the River" (written by Sister Mary of the Blessed Sacrament McCrosson) gives this version of what happened next. The baggage was collected in one pile after the passengers were routed from the coach. They were then told to get back in, but Mother Joseph lagged behind and addressed one of the bandits: "My boy, that black bag. Please give me that black bag."

"Which one?" he asked.

"That one, to your right."

While the other passengers watched breathlessly, she pointed to an ample carpetbag. "Yes, yes, my boy, that's it. Give it to me."

Astounded by the courage of the nun, the robber picked up the desired piece of luggage and dropped it at her feet.

"Thank you. God bless you, my boy," she responded.

The men looted the other bags and rode off, leaving it to the passengers to gather what remained of their possessions. The account concludes: "Mother Joseph winked at Sister Mary Augustine, whose gasping was still audible, and confidently patted the bag. Two hundred dollars were still safe among her clothing."

The years were passing, and Mother Joseph was getting no younger. As she had acquired additional property for the House of Providence, she was imbued with a great desire to build while she was still around to accomplish her purpose. A change in her fortunes came in 1866, when it was announced that she was no longer head of the Vancouver mission, but was to become bursar for all the western missions. Then the sisters were ordered to vacate their original mission claim to permit expansion of the military reservation. At that time, the nuns had 200 homeless persons on their hands, housed in seven little buildings, and Sister Joseph visualized her fourteen years of planning and labor wiped out.

Fortunately, citizens of the town protested, and the order was suspended until Sister Joseph could prepare a program to meet the contingency. She had already formulated plans for a new House of Providence on property owned by the order, but more money was needed to finance it. In 1873 a visit from the superior general turned the trick. Inspection showed the inadequacy of the seven small buildings on disputed land, and consent was given to proceed with the project. At the end of the following year, the new building designed by the architect-sister was ready for occupancy although it was encumbered with debts. Again the nuns canvassed the miners, on one trip going clear to Colorado. As soon as one financial crisis was passed, another seemed to arise, but Sister Joseph surmounted all of them.

Her new House of Providence in Vancouver was reputed to be the largest building north of San Francisco. The imposing structure was in the form of a cross, three stories high, of brick on a stone foundation. It covered about two acres. One wing was devoted to day scholars and boarders, another to orphan girls, the central portion was occupied by the sisters and the boys' orphanage was in the rear. As funds became available, improvements were made, but it was not until 1888 that the hardwood flooring was laid, and it was 1892 before the building was pronounced complete. Mother Joseph put considerable of her own handicraft into the design of the chapel; it was considered her finest work. She made and clothed all of the wax statues, carved benches and made molds for the scrolls at the pillar tops and also carved the five altars.

Having been the architect of this imposing structure, Mother Joseph went on and planned many others for her order, among them St. Mary's Hospital at New Westminster, British Columbia, St. Joseph Academy in Sprague, Washington, a school and a hospital in Olympia, St. John's Hospital in Port Townsend, St. Eugene Indian School in Kootenay, British Columbia, St. Elizabeth Hospital in Yakima, Washington, St. Ignatius Hospital in Colfax, Washington, and Sacred Heart Hospital in Spokane. Her last planned structure was an orphanage in New Westminster, British Columbia. Although then in her seventies, Mother Joseph stayed right on the job with her building program, climbing ladders to test beams and inspect the work.

She died of a brain tumor on January 19, 1902 at the age of seventy-nine. In 1953 the American Institute of Architects acclaimed her the Pacific Northwest's first architect. The West Coast Lumbermen's Association also recognized her as "the first white artisan to work with wood in the Pacific Northwest." One editorial writer said of her: "She was adept in nearly all the arts and trades. She was skilled in wax works, the most delicate embroidery, but her genius found its strongest expression in architecture."

She is credited with having led the foundation of eleven hospitals, seven academies, five Indian schools and two orphanages. She had a long wait to reach the national Hall of Fame, but seventy-six years after her death, she was chosen to represent Washington State there: the first woman from the Northwest, and the first Catholic sister.

———————

Lucile McDonald has been a writer all her life. She spent thirty-six years in the newspaper business and though now presumably retired, she contributes a weekly column to the daily Journal-American *in Bellevue, Washington, where she lives. Widely traveled, she was twice a foreign correspondent. She is author or co-author of twenty-six books, juveniles and adult nonfiction.*

Mrs. McDonald, a descendant of Pacific Northwest pioneers, was born in Portland, Oregon and knows the region well. She is the recipient of numerous awards for her writings on historical subjects.

BIBLIOGRAPHY

BOOKS

"The Bell and the River," by Sister Mary of the Blessed Sacrament McCrosson, Palo Alto: Pacific Books, 1957.

"The Legacy of Mother Joseph," in the Sisters of Providence periodical vol. 4 number 2, Seattle.

"Mother Joseph of the Sacred Heart; Her Contribution to the Growth of the West," by Dolores Schafer, S.P. 1971, a manuscript in the Washington State Library.

Two articles by Lucile McDonald based on interviews and published in the July 10, 1966 and August 17, 1968 issues of the *Seattle Times* Sunday Magazine.

10

Pioneer Doctor

by JUDY ALTER

Women who pioneered in the medical field found it rough going; men had long considered medicine their exclusive province. Dr. Georgia Arbuckle Fix was a homesteader as well, and was said to have been the first physician to successfully use a silver plate in brain surgery.

N.S.Y.

It was the kind of accident that happened too often on pioneer homesteads in western Nebraska. Eli Beebe had been helping his father-in-law dig a new well on the Eikenberry family homestead. They used a windlass and bucket to hoist the dirt out as they dug, and Beebe slowly cranked another bucket to the top. Then, his hand slipped from the handle of the windlass, the heavy load of dirt crashed to the bottom of the well, and the whirling windlass struck him full force in the head, fracturing his skull.

Word was sent for Dr. Georgia Arbuckle, but her soddie cabin was a long, hard ride from the homestead in the upper Mitchell Valley. As soon as she heard she was needed, Dr. Arbuckle threw on her well-known cowhide coat, grabbed her medical kit and started across country with the buggy and team that had carried her on many similar journeys.

The ride across the prairie was long and lonely, with only an occasional sod house rising from the landscape. There were no roads, and landmarks to guide her were few, but Georgia Ar-

Ma'am Jones. *Courtesy Opal Clarke.*

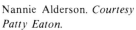

Nannie Alderson. *Courtesy Patty Eaton.*

Martha James Bull Waln, age 75. *Courtesy Paul Frison.*

Grace and Bert Snyder, wedding photograph. *Courtesy Nellie Snyder Yost.*

Nellie Cashman. *Courtesy Arizona Historical Society.*

Teenager Kate Shelley. *Courtesy Iowa State Historical Department, Division of Historical Museum and Archives.*

Dr. Ellis Reynolds Shipp. *Courtesy Utah State Historical Society.*

Allen Street, Tombstone, early 1880's. *Courtesy Arizona Historical Society.*

Sadie Orchard (right) and friend. *Courtesy Black Range Museum.*

A cartoon from Polly Pry's own newspaper, satirizing her competitors. *Denver Post Photo.*

Polly Pry. *Denver Post Photo.*

Mother Joseph. *Courtesy Sisters of Providence.*

Providence Academy, Vancouver, Washington. *Courtesy Sisters of Providence.*

Dr. Georgia Arbuckle Fix.
Courtesy Esper Clary.

The Great Western in Monterrey, from Samuel Chamberlain's diary of the Mexican War, *My Confession, Written and Illustrated. Courtesy Harper & Row.*

Esther Hobart Morris. *Courtesy Wyoming State Museum.*

Statue of Esther Hobart Morris in front of the State Capitol, Cheyenne, Wyoming. *Courtesy Wyoming Travel Commission.*

May Arkwright Hutton. *A Bernard-Stockbridge photo, courtesy Eastern Washington State Historical Society.*

buckle had the uncanny sense of direction which blessed many pioneer women. She could set out across a rise in the prairie and go straight as an arrow to her destination.

Eli Beebe was still alive, though in critical condition, when she arrived at the homestead. With great care, Dr. Arbuckle cleaned the wound, gently pulling away fragments of skin, pieces of bone and clotted blood. The skull directly beneath the wound was shattered, and she knew she had to have some way to cover the fragile brain that had been exposed.

Casting about in her mind for some readily available material, she took a silver dollar from her bag and asked for a hammer. Carefully, she pounded the silver dollar into a thin plate of the needed diameter. This plate was then sewn into Beebe's skull in an operation that would be rare enough in those days in a fully equipped hospital, let alone in a primitive homestead soddie. It was probably her most unusual case, but Georgia Arbuckle did not think of its medical rarity. She had simply done what needed to be done.

The lone woman graduate in the nine-member class of 1883 at the State University of Omaha's College of Medicine, Georgia Arbuckle had worked hard to become a doctor. Born in Princeton, Missouri, to an unwed mother, she grew up in straitened circumstances. There are some hints—unproven—that she and Calamity Jane were childhood rivals in Princeton where Calamity, then known as Mary Jane Canary, led a pampered life that contrasted severely with the meager existence of the Arbuckle family.

When Georgia was about nine years old, her mother married Tom Reeves, a contractor, and a few years later the family moved West in a futile search for health for Georgia's mother, who had developed consumption. Georgia stayed behind in Princeton, befriended by a Dr. Dinsmore and his family.

By the time she was sixteen, Georgia Arbuckle was teaching in a log schoolhouse just east of Princeton. At the encouragement of Dr. Dinsmore, she began to study homeopathy, the theory of medicine proposed by a German doctor named Hahnemann who recommended minute doses of medicine for the cure of various diseases. The influence of her study of homeopathy stayed with Georgia Arbuckle, and in her later practice she was noted for diluting medicines with large quantities of water. At that time, people tended to have more faith in strong, bitter medicine, and patients joked about her "river-water cures."

In the early 1880s, the Dinsmores moved to Omaha. Georgia followed them and enrolled in the newly organized college of medicine there. She worked her way through school doing practical nursing, cleaning, whatever was necessary. Fortunately, the three-year program was shortened to two for her because of her study with Dr. Dinsmore.

The new Dr. Arbuckle practiced briefly in Omaha and even served as an officer in the Douglas County Medical Society; an unusual honor for a woman physician in that day. But the open land to the west attracted her. When her stepfather and half-brother decided to homestead in the western part of the state, she went with them. They arrived at Fort Sidney in May 1886.

Georgia Arbuckle chose a homestead site on the north bank of the North Platte at a spot near what is now Minatare, Nebraska. Her claim was marked by three small willow trees—the only trees along the river for miles—that had long been guideposts for men fording the river. She chose the site because its trees reminded her of Missouri. There were no frame houses in the whole valley, but the one-room soddie soon erected on her claim was considered one of the nicest because of things she had brought from Omaha.

She became a familiar figure riding out on calls. Cowboys were always breaking a leg or an arm or collarbone while branding cattle or breaking horses. Georgia Arbuckle set their bones, depending on fellow cowboys to hold them and on the patient to bear the pain stoically.

Georgia Arbuckle was a tall, strongly built young woman. Though no beauty, she had a strong face with square chin and cheekbones high enough to leave a suspicion of Indian blood. Some have tried to attribute her talent for mixing healing potions to a heritage from some Indian ancestor. She wore dark clothes, often a shirtwaist and skirt, and in the winter always wore the long cowhide coat that became almost symbolic to her patients and neighbors.

It was not unusual to see her tall, determined figure setting out across the prairie in the dead of winter. Sometimes her brother Billy or another willing volunteer would drive for her. Other times she drove herself. In the first days of her practice, Dr. Arbuckle drove a nondescript buggy. Later, after she moved to the town of

Gering, the stables there equipped a special buggy for her. It had side springs, and the top of the buggy was strapped to the axle so that the doctor wouldn't be bounced off the seat going over a deep rut. For bad weather, there were side curtains and a storm shield which hooked over the dashboard and buckled to the front of the buggy top. The storm shield had an isinglass window for the driver to peer through and a little square hole through which the lines were pulled. In really bad weather, when snow made passage impossible, the doctor simply unhitched one of the horses, mounted it and rode to her destination. The physician who had preceded her in the valley, a Dr. Birney, once refused to go out on a call because it was too stormy. He lost face and left the area soon afterward. Georgia Arbuckle never let the weather stop her.

Nor did long hours of solitary travel bother her if no driver was available. She followed the "roads" of the day: either cattle trails or simply the easiest way to get through. Often she had to ford the wide North Platte by going from island to island. With or without a driver, the doctor caught what rest she could on her far-flung house calls.

One farmer told the story of waking one morning to see a team and buggy stopped between his house and barn. When he went to investigate, he found Dr. Arbuckle and a driver, both sound asleep. The driver said the last he remembered was traveling down the road. The team must have turned through the farmer's gate because they had made stops there before.

Another time, the doctor drove over 30 miles to see a sick baby. A woman who was staying with the baby's family said, years later, "I can see her yet, raising up and groping back to consciousness when the team stopped. Her hair was long and black and straight. During the drive it had fallen down. She sat up and mechanically began pinning it back into place in a coil on top of her head. Then she descended from the buggy, brushed her clothes and was ready for work."

Few of her cases required such innovative treatment as Eli Beebe's skull fracture, but many were critical. There was Mr. Pickering, who cut a deep gash in his foot while cutting timber for a new fence. As his son told the story, Pickering doctored the foot the best he could and thought no more of it until it began to cause him severe pain days later. By the time Dr. Arbuckle was called, blood poisoning had set in. The doctor was concerned about whether the foot could be saved. She used quantities of hot water to draw the poison out and saved the foot, although it was some time before her patient was able to walk again.

Another patient who owed the use of his limbs to Georgia Arbuckle was Dan Davis, who lived on a homestead some distance away. Davis chose a still day—or so he thought—to grease his windmill; but while he was at work, an air current caught the fan and turned it violently. His left hand was crushed. A neighbor went for the doctor immediately but Davis had to wait several pain-filled hours for her arrival. She cauterized the wound, then made a rough splint from a shingle. After setting the broken bones, she taped the hand to the shingle. It healed in several weeks, and Davis had full use of it.

She was never hesitant to admit when she was puzzled by a case or even when she had made a wrong diagnosis. One such case involved Frances, a girl in her teens, who told Dr. Arbuckle she was not feeling well enough to go to school. There had been a typhoid scare in the area, and scores of patients had imagined themselves into symptoms. When Frances appeared, the doctor thought she, too, might be malingering and dosed her with one of the river-water cures. The girl failed to improve; after a few days, it became evident that she did indeed have a bad case of typhoid. No one was more concerned or upset than the doctor who had missed the symptoms. Frances developed a high fever which did not immediately respond to the treatment with which her doctor had so much success. Customarily, Dr. Arbuckle gave her patients a specially brewed mixture of sage picked from the neighboring hills and wrapped patients in damp sheets, often wrung out in milk. In this case, she made eighteen trips to the girl's bedside, including several in the dead of night, before Frances passed the crisis.

There were no dentists and few preachers in the territory. Georgia Arbuckle filled both roles when necessary. One cowboy found his toothache unbearable one night and took a friend with him for comfort when he went to waken the doctor. When she was dressed and ready for business, Georgia Arbuckle told her patient to sit in a chair and grab both arms tightly while his friend held his head. The patient sat with his feet straight out in front of him, but when the doctor began to pull the tooth, he slowly drew his feet up. Heavy spurs rolled across the floor and raked the doctor's foot.

She let go the tooth and shouted, "Careful! I'm no bronc!" Eventually the tooth came out.

Another dental patient recalled that when Dr. Arbuckle practiced in Gering, a dentist came to town every Tuesday. This man had a tooth that always ached from Wednesday until Monday. Finally, it became so painful he could no longer stand it nor wait for Tuesday, so he asked the doctor to pull it. A woman who lived with the doctor held the patient's head this time, but the tooth proved reluctant. By the time it finally came out, the patient was almost on the floor, bleeding profusely, and both women were, in his words, "nearly hysterical from their exertion." The patient worsened things by laughing at the ludicrous situation, leading the women to fear that he was either hysterical or demented. It was the only time he had seen the fearless Dr. Arbuckle ghost-white with worry.

It was a much more serious matter when the doctor had to take the preacher's place. Early in her practice, she was called on to bury a young man who died of smallpox. She and a driver had attended him through the illness, but were unable to save him. There being no one else, the driver made a coffin and dug a grave, and the doctor said a last prayer.

Another time she was called to a family who lived in an area where there was no cemetery. They lost a child to typhoid, and the neighbors made a coffin while Dr. Arbuckle prepared the child for burial. Then a spot was selected near a road, and neighbors and friends gathered to hear the doctor conduct a graveside service. Unfortunately, such incidents were not rare in her practice.

The lady doctor could be gentle when the occasion demanded, but she was never one to mince words or action when she felt a principle was involved. Once she asked a friend to accompany her on an "errand of mercy" to a home where a new baby was expected soon. The women swept and scrubbed the house, made the mother comfortable and tidied the children. During their cleaning, they came across twelve bottles of liquor hidden on a shelf. Dr. Arbuckle, always a crusader against liquor, was angry at the idea of the father of a new baby being drunk, so she personally destroyed every bottle. Word had it there was a spot on that farm where grass would not grow for a long time.

In 1888 Georgia Arbuckle was called to testify at a murder trial. In July of that year, a frantic rider came after her, calling that she was needed at the Burton place. Burton had been shot. She arrived to find there was nothing she could do for the man who lay dead where he had been shot by a hired hand in a dispute over pay. The murderer escaped, but was later arrested and brought to trial in December of that year.

Along with several neighbors, Dr. Arbuckle was called to Old Fort Sidney to testify at the trial. She and young Gwynn Fix made the trip a wedding journey and were married December 9. Gwynn Fix, a handsome man somewhat younger than his bride, was from a well-to-do family and was noted for driving a fast team with a good buggy and a fine lap robe. He was not noted for the strong ambition that characterized his wife, and many of her friends wondered at her choice. Georgia Arbuckle met Gwynn Fix during the first year of her practice in the area, when he became seriously ill with typhoid. Her care of him through a long illness led to a romance; though some suggested that he appealed to her maternal instinct and her need, left over from a lonely childhood, to have someone of her own to love.

It was not a happy marriage. Gwynn Fix resented his wife's medical practice and constantly urged her to devote more of her time to housewifely duties. Dr. Arbuckle Fix, as she was now called, was torn, but could not abandon her patients. After two years, she moved from her original homestead to a claim further east, at her husband's insistence. But she was often called to treat patients in the west end of the valley, a long, hard ride for her. In 1892 she moved her practice and office to the town of Gering, feeling that she could better treat her patients from a central location.

Gwynn Fix came to Gering for short periods and drove the doctor on her house calls when he was there, but he kept his cattle interests near their homestead and was gone much of the time. There is a story that Dr. Fix once caught her husband kissing another woman, but their most serious disagreement was over finances, rather than infidelity.

Doctors in those days had no set fees. A ledger of Dr. Fix's shows figures varying from $.50 to $4.00 for either medicine or treatment. Like other doctors of her era, she probably charged only what she thought the patient could pay. Often, doctors were paid in kind. Eggs, chickens, butter, fresh-picked wild fruit—all were brought in payment of services. Cattle were cheap in those

days, and it was not too unusual for payment to be a yearling calf
if the case had been especially difficult or the patient was unu-
sually grateful. Over the years, Dr. Fix built up a small herd that
ran with her husband's cattle. But, without consulting her, Gwynn
Fix sold both herds for less money than they were worth and
pocketed the money for his own use.

The marriage lasted unevenly until 1909, when Dr. Fix finally
filed for divorce. In later years in Gering, she was the subject of
some gossip and criticism, in spite of her loyal friends. She realized that as a divorced woman and one who disregarded the feminine conventions of the day, she was inevitably the target of such
whisperings; but the fact that they stung nevertheless is marked by
a terse comment in her notebook: "You cannot sew buttons on
your neighbor's mouth."

At the time Dr. Fix moved to Gering, the town was only five
years old; but it had grown from a cluster of log shanties and soddies to a busy village with stores, a hotel, a stable and the first
newspaper in that part of the territory. She set up practice in a
brick building that had briefly been used as a schoolhouse but,
finding that she needed larger quarters where patients could stay,
she bought property and had two houses moved across the frozen
river in the winter. The two were put together and remodeled into
a two-story house that became known as "The Sanitarium." It was
a landmark in Gering for many years.

The sanitarium, surrounded by trees which the doctor had ordered from Denver at the high cost of $40, became a community
center for the town and a haven for all. The women's exchange,
started to raise funds for village improvements, began there, as did
the women's missionary society and the women's library club.

Not only the sick but also the discouraged found comfort at the
sanitarium. Dr. Fix was ever ready to talk, listen or read the Bible.
Schoolgirls in need of help and encouragement found a friend in
the doctor, who remembered all that the Dinsmores had done for
her. Several of the girls and some of their teachers boarded at the
sanitarium from time to time, and the doctor was always pleased
when her home was chosen as the place for a wedding.

The story is told of one young couple who wished to be married
there but would invite only the minister, two friends and the doctor. Other young people living at the doctor's house hinted
broadly for an invitation, but none was forthcoming. At the very

moment of the wedding, by coincidence, one of the young men who was not invited was carried in by a group of friends. He had broken his leg. The patient was placed on a couch where he watched the wedding, in great pain, with his friends ringed around him. After the ceremony, the patient made a remarkable and speedy recovery.

The sanitarium, filled with dogs and birds, was a special place to the children of Gering. Dr. Fix had three dogs who were her constant companions: a brown and white mongrel named Jack, a small black one called Jimmy, and Shoddy, a black setter. One whole room, with a large cedar tree set in the middle, was devoted to birds because Dr. Fix felt that cages were too confining for her pets. At one time, there were thirty-three canaries, a poll parrot, and an owl that had been given to the doctor. She gave birds freely to people who would show her they had a spacious cage, but her own bird population was always large. With birds, dogs, visiting children and boarding young people, the sanitarium was bustling with confusion. Patients recalled that it was not a place of peace and quiet.

Dr. Arbuckle Fix actively practiced medicine in Gering until about 1916 when her health, taxed by long hours and hard trips on house calls, began to fail. With a companion, she traveled to California several times and finally established a winter home there. In 1918, when spring came, the doctor did not feel strong enough to return to Gering. She died in July at the age of sixty-six. Georgia Arbuckle Fix had practiced medicine in Nebraska for nearly thirty-five years.

Her story has been told in fact and fiction but is probably well known only to residents of the North Platte valley. Estelle Laughlin's recounting of the doctor's life was published in the *Gering Courier* and in a regional history of Nebraska which had limited publication. But the story of Georgia Arbuckle Fix reached a wider audience in its fictionalized form, a novel titled *Miss Morissa,* written by the late Mari Sandoz. Morissa, the doctor-heroine of the story, is a composite of three early women physicians, and even the casual reader will recognize strong elements of Georgia Arbuckle Fix's life in the book. It is a compelling story.

Judy Alter is a past board member of Western Writers of America, Inc. and has written columns of publishing news and book reviews for that organization's magazine, The Roundup, *for six years. She is the author of* After Pa Was Shot, *a juvenile novel, and the co-author of* The Quack Doctor, *a Texas memoir. Other books include a study of Stewart Edward White for the Boise State University Western Pamphlet Series and* Single Again, *a guide for divorced men. She has also published numerous articles, both Western and health-related, and is a member of Women in Communications, Inc. Her career has also included public relations and editorial work at several osteopathic colleges.*

She holds a Ph.D. in English from Texas Christian University, an M.Ed. from Northeast Missouri State University and a B.A. from the University of Chicago.

BIBLIOGRAPHY

This chapter is respectfully dedicated to the late Estelle Laughlin whose original research on the life of Georgia Arbuckle Fix provides the single most complete source of information on this early pioneer doctor.

BOOKS

Dunlop, Richard. *Doctors of the American Frontier.* New York: Doubleday, 1965.

Sandoz, Mari. *Miss Morissa.* New York: McGraw-Hill, 1975.

Tyler, A. F. and Auerbach, E. F. *History of Medicine in Nebraska.* Omaha: Magic City Printing Company, 1928.

Woods, A. B. *Pioneer Tales of the Nebraska Panhandle.* Gering, Nebraska: Published on his own newspaper press, 1938.

MAGAZINE ARTICLES

Skold, D. Parker. "Nebraska's Mrs. Sawbones." *True West,* June 1975.

NEWSPAPERS

The *Gering Courier*—January 3, 15, 22, 29 and February 5, 1937.

UNPUBLISHED MATERIAL

Private papers of the late Estelle Laughlin, on loan from Mrs. Esper Clary of Scottsbluff, Nebraska.

11

Dame Shirley

by REBA CUNNINGHAM and JEANNE WILLIAMS

Louise Amelia Clappe was a doctor by proxy, the wife of a pioneer physician who practiced his profession in the California gold camp of Rich Bar during 1851–52. Louise assisted him, and wrote of her experiences to her sister back East. These priceless letters, published under the pen name of "Dame Shirley," left us a splendid picture of life in the gold camps of that time.

N.S.Y.

When Louise Amelia Clappe saw her husband's new office in the gold camp of Rich Bar, she sat down on an empty whiskey keg and laughed until she cried. The crude cabin, 10 feet long and 6 feet wide, had a dirt floor. Fayette Clappe's medical library of six volumes served as a table. Medicines were ranged on pine boards nailed to the wall. A cloth-covered window boasted the proud words: *Dr. Clappe's Office.*

When Louise could control her laughter, she knew by her husband's manner that she'd hurt him. He'd spent hours cutting pictures from medical journals to put on the walls for a more professional effect. She only hoped he wouldn't be sorry he'd decided to set up practice here rather than in San Francisco.

Arriving in the boisterous city from their home in the East that year of 1851, Louise had enjoyed walking the muddy streets in the summer rain and breathing in the fog, but the doctor found the climate oppressive and wanted to move south.

Rich Bar lay that direction; a camp that sprang up after two miners found a bonanza. Washing a panful of dirt, they saw the precious gleam—$250 worth of it. In three days, they mined over $6,000 in gold.

Word got out. Within days, five hundred miners swarmed to the camp. They came in herds, like cows to a salt lick. It was life in these diggings that Louise would describe during the next two years in twenty-three letters written to her sister Mollie in New Jersey. The Dame Shirley Letters, so called because of the pen name Louise chose, were used as a basis for stories by Bret Harte and other well-known writers.

Dr. Clappe had gone to investigate Rich Bar. As soon as he had an office, he sent for Louise. Two frisky mules pulled the spring wagon, but as they reached the high mountain passes, the creatures had to dig their hooves sharply into the narrow road to keep the wagon from being dashed to bits in the gorges below.

Somehow Louise smothered her screams and was proud, later, when the bewhiskered driver grinned and said, "Ma'am, yo're the first female I ever drove who didn't yell her damned fool head off."

Even this horrible road ended. When it did, her husband was waiting with a pair of mules and camping supplies. Down the mountain trail they rode, into the crimson waves of the foothills.

There was little sleep the first night. Fleas were everywhere, thick in the air, and Louise was so exhausted from fighting them off that next day she had little appreciation for the scenery, magnificent though it was. The doctor wanted to reach the Berry ranch where they could rest and get provisions, but it wasn't where he'd hoped to find it.

When they made camp that night, Louise was frightened and felt sick. Lying on a mule blanket that did little to cushion the rocky ground, she stared up at the brilliant stars and wished her husband had never dreamed of locating in this God-forsaken country.

Next morning they met a traveler who told them they'd missed the Berry ranch by 20 miles. Louise, ill and disheartened, wanted to rest, but the doctor insisted they keep going.

At the Berry ranch, they had supper and a real bed. Louise simply felt that she wanted to stay right there for the rest of her life, especially when she learned that a couple who had taken the same route they had had been surprised by Indians the day before. The husband had been killed, the wife taken captive.

Despite this, they left early next morning for Rich Bar. A group of Indians did surround them, but they were friendly. Babies stared with large dark eyes; the women pressed close to examine Louise's hat, whip and boots.

One especially beautiful young woman smiled shyly at Louise and touched her things almost reverently. She was dressed only in a dirty strip of blanket. Wanting to give her something, Louise rummaged a package of pins from her pack and put them in the girl's hand. Louise was instantly besieged by the rest of the women and the men, too, all wanting a gift.

That night, camped by a stream, they were kept awake by the uneasy growling of disturbed grizzlies. Only the campfire kept the huge beasts away. Louise found the morning light beautiful indeed.

Weary as she was, she drank in the clean scent of the pines and smiled to see butterflies flit among equally brilliant wildflowers. Deer sometimes were so thick they had to be pushed out of the way, and quail poked their heads out of fallen trees.

It was three in the afternoon when they rode into camp. Rich Bar had one hotel—The Empire—built of planks and canvas. Its barroom was decorated with red calico; a mirror above the bar reflected the array of brandy and whiskey bottles. At the back of the hotel, a small store stocked a confusion of hams, bacon, beans and other eatables.

The Empire had four rooms for guests, a dining area and kitchen. Favored patrons could use a parlor which had a straw carpet and a sofa covered with the same red calico that enlivened the bar.

All the materials for the hotel, built by a gambler, had to be brought in by mule train from the nearest town of Marysville at $.40 a pound. The Clappes' bedroom was furnished with a huge log bed, installed so solidly that only a giant could have moved it.

Louise spent the hazy autumn days trying to make a home of the tent Dr. Clappe had at last been able to rent. He was busy sewing up stab wounds and digging bullets out of the more unfortunate of the camp's thousand men.

There were only three women, and Louise was often lonely. There were no churches, no shops, no parties. There *were* two

newspapers a month at $1.50 each; the letters that took much of
Louise's time cost $2.50 to send.

What would Christmas be like in this place? Louise hoped it
would bring out some softer feelings in these gold-mad miners and
was delighted when the doctor told her plans were being made for
a celebration.

Just before the passes snowed up, a long mule train made its
way in with casks of whiskey, brandy and canned goods. The
morning of December 24 dawned sunny and crisp, and soon The
Empire buzzed as the carpet was scrubbed with yellow soapsuds,
sooty lamp chimneys were cleaned and the bar was trimmed with
new red calico. Boughs of pungent evergreen were at the entrance,
and the gambling room, for the occasion, was rid of its dirty spit-
toons.

Festivities began that evening with an oyster supper, followed
by songs, toasts and speeches. Everyone was toasting everyone
else and animosities were, for the time, forgotten. Louise, golden-
haired, "no bigger'n a bar of soap," smiled at admirers, and
though she thought of her family gathered by the lighted tree in
New Jersey and missed them and the church services, she was enjoying Rich Bar's yuletide.

Then the dancing started. Miners danced with miners. The one
representing a lady wore a piece of red calico on his arm. Drink
flowed and the Clappes soon escaped from the rowdiness, but the
revel continued for three days.

By the fourth day, miners lay in heaps on the barroom and parlor floors. One might raise himself up and bark like a dog, be answered by the call of a bull moose, and both be drowned out by
the hissing of geese—but most of the men were too drunk to do
anything.

That was just as well. Miners who could stagger about tried
boating on the icy waters of Feather River every day. Of those
who fell overboard, several drowned.

After the holidays, winter descended. Five feet of snow covered
the gorge in one day. Trails were impassable. Louise and the doctor had to leave their tent and stay at The Empire.

Since pack trains could no longer reach camp, food dwindled.
Many lived on nothing but barley for days. In desperation, a few
hardy men made it on foot to Marysville and packed the 40 miles
back with all the flour, bacon and beans they could carry. One

hungry miner stumbled through 14 miles of snow to a Spanish ranch. In less than an hour, he consumed twenty-seven biscuits, ham and other fixings, all washed down with plenty of whiskey.

The Clappes had enough to eat, but it was a joy, late that spring, to see pack trains come in with fresh supplies. Salt mackerel, dark hams and canned oysters had become as monotonous as the snowbound days.

Spring also meant more accidents for the doctor to tend. One young man had found good diggings, and, with $4,000 saved, planned to go back home in the East. On his last day in the mines, a stone rolled from the hillside and crushed his leg.

It became a mass of swollen dead flesh. Dr. Clappe had to amputate. After surgery, the miner got typhoid fever. There was no hope for him.

Louise sat by his bed, sponging him with cold cloths, feeding him teaspoons of hot soup. Her heart ached for him and for the mother so far away who would never see her son again.

One evening, he sat up, opened his eyes and whispered, "Do you hear the funeral procession returning?"

Louise soothed him, but in a few days a dozen miners carried his rough wooden coffin up the hill to the burial ground.

Shortly after, the doctor was called to a miner's wife who was dying of blood poisoning after the death of a baby boy. Louise hurried over to help, but the frail little woman was already dead.

The funeral was held in the cabin next morning. The place had only the door for light, but looked as if it had been recently scrubbed. Covered by a sheet, the dead woman lay on a pine slab supported by two butter tubs.

Her husband held the week-old baby while a small girl, her blond hair tangled, ran about the cabin, almost tripping over her long calico dress. Her eyes were feverish with excitement. Sometimes she ran over to the corpse, lifted the sheet before she could be stopped, and called, "Mama, mama!" as if playing a game.

Twenty miners and the three women in camp were at the service. A prayer was offered, one of the women sang a hymn, and the body was covered with dark calico and placed in the pine coffin.

"Magnificent woman, that," said one of the miners to Louise as they walked home. "She earned her old man $900 in nine weeks jus' a washin'. Wimmen ain't common in these parts. Now, if I could find me one, I'd put her to work."

Louise felt uncomfortable. She toiled not, neither did she wash. She felt even more guilty remembering the $4.00 a week she'd paid the little seventy-pound woman for doing the Clappe laundry. And the miners' heavy clothing would have been even harder to scrub on the washboard, rinse, wring, and hang to dry on the limbs of pine trees. Louise was relieved to hear that a grandmother was coming to look after the two children.

Such sad deaths depressed Louise. She was also upset by the fighting, drinking and profanity and longed for her own home, away from the uproar at The Empire. The doctor had promised her a log house after the spring thaws and told her to look for a site.

At the edge of Rich Bar, Louise found a spot with a rainbow of flowers, birds everywhere, and a stream cascading over moss-grown rocks. As soon as the one-room cabin was roofed with crude shingles, she set about making it comfortable.

She covered the mantel above the large fireplace with strips of tin she'd saved from canned goods. Her trunk, draped with red calico, made a toilet table. Ornamented with her silver brush and comb, she thought it looked quite elegant.

A table and four chairs were made by two grateful miners from whom the doctor had removed bullets. Calico curtains brightened the two windows, and a log bed completed the furnishings.

Louise would do most of her cooking at the fireplace, so her utensils were primitive: a huge iron kettle, two copper bowls and a shovel that served as a frying pan. She had three teaspoons, knives and forks. This was much more than any other woman in camp possessed.

Ned, the cook at The Empire, had become friendly with the Clappes and insisted they must have a "coronation" for their new home. One afternoon, he started carrying pots and pans to the cabin. Freshly shaved, he was dressed in a new red flannel shirt and black pants, and refused all offers of help.

"If I live to be a hundred," Louise wrote to her sister, "I'll never forget that meal."

Where Ned managed to get all the delicacies, she would never know. He served the meal with pomp and flourishes, beaming at their astonishment. Roast beef as tender as a woman's heart, ham fragrant with spice and brown sugar, creamed onions, fluffily mashed potatoes. Dessert was mince pie and a pudding made with real eggs and milk followed by nuts, raisins, wine and coffee.

After he had cleared away the dishes, Ned brought out his fiddle. For a long time, he serenaded them with happy tunes. Just before he left, he handed Louise something wrapped in one of the precious newspapers.

It was a gaudy vase with a fake opulence completely out of place in the cabin. Fayette Clappe took one look and told Ned it was much too beautiful for them to accept. At his hurt look, Louise told him it was lovely, thanked him and gave it pride of place on the mantel.

"Miners jus' don't appreciate a purty vase like this here one, anymore than they do good cookin'," Ned said, confirming Louise's suspicion that he'd sneaked it out of a saloon. After he left, she hid it behind the trunk, but she kept it always as a remembrance of the "coronation."

An old half-breed was their closest neighbor. Some warm summer evenings he'd come to sit cross-legged on their doorstep and tell them bloodcurdling tales of massacres in which he'd taken part. These made Louise remember how fearful some of the miners were that the Indians living a few miles south might get too much firewater and attack the camp.

Louise talked to the doctor, and they both talked to their neighbor, who agreed to serve as an emissary. He returned to report that the chief had no wish for war and knew well that his people would be destroyed if they molested Rich Bar: "The Americans are like the grass growing in the valleys, and the Indians are fewer than the flowers on the high Sierra Nevada."

Even with the Indians peaceful, there was constant violence in camp. A young miner known as Little John was given forty-nine lashes with a bullwhip for stealing $400 from a gambling-house proprietor. For allegedly stealing gold dust, another miner was sentenced to be hanged by a self-appointed jury.

Dr. Clappe tried to intervene, but he couldn't stop the mob; nor could he keep Louise from learning that the man did not die quickly, but was hauled up and down over the rocks by the rope until he finally died.

It was from this sort of senseless brutality that Louise found relief in wandering the foothills and mountains, gathering flowers and resting on pine boughs swayed by the wind. She was also cheered by thoughtfulness from the men her husband labored to keep alive and healthy.

One day a young miner brought her a tiny fish he'd found in a mountain stream. It was two inches long, speckled with green, gold and ruby red which emphasized its snow-white belly. "I thought, ma'am, this little feller would keep you company way up here alone so much," he said. He blushed mightily when Louise shook his hand and thanked him.

East of Rich Bar was another Indian band, said to be friendly. One Sunday morning, the Clappes rode over on their mules. The men of the tribe came to meet them, giving the peace sign.

They wore leather leggings and headdresses of leather strips or eagle feathers. Shy, keeping in the background, the women had nothing but bunch grass wrapped around them—some of it green and beginning to sprout. They were filthy and smelled.

This tribe lived in lodges made of tree bark plastered with mud. A hole in the top let smoke escape from the fire below. The only furniture was a firebox and a large stone in the center for grinding nuts and acorns. A large handwoven basket was the only cooking utensil.

Water, nuts and dried grasshoppers were mixed in this to make a kind of hasty pudding which was eaten with the fingers. Louise and the doctor were offered this food, but they signed that they had eaten already and their bellies were full, though they thanked their hosts warmly.

There weren't many women, and all the drudgery fell on them. Several months before, a hostile tribe had invaded the camp and stolen all the children and young women.

Before the Clappes left, the Indians gave them a gift of fresh fish for their supper. They were caught by throwing rocks in the river to frighten the fish to the bottom. Then the Indians dived in and came up with fish in their mouths. The Indians killed them by biting off their heads.

As June ended, the women of the diggings, determined not to be discouraged by the Christmas orgy, but to hold a celebration for the Fourth of July. Mountain flowers and grapevines decorated The Empire. Louise made a flag of red and white calico and placed in the center a blue star to represent the State of California. Along with the feast of fresh trout came toasts and oratory and plenty of whiskey. In the evening, the miners had a torchlight parade and sang zestfully:

> Ye are welcome, merry miners, in yore blue and red shirts,
> Ye are welcome, mid the golden hills of this Fourth of July,
> Tho you've not shaved yore shaggy lips nor cut yore
> shaggy hair,
> Ye are welcome, merry miners, with yore beards and as
> ye are.

The festivities ended with only fifteen fights, which Louise took as a good omen. In the last twenty-four days, there had been only four murders, thirty accidents, two deaths and one hanging!

But the rule of the vigilantes was starting. The Sunday after the Fourth, word came to Rich Bar that a Spanish rancher north of camp had been killed for his cache of gold dust. His black servant was the likeliest suspect. Louise was sorry about that because the man had sometimes cooked for the Clappes and seemed a kind, gentle person.

The vigilance committee tracked him to a cave and smoked him out. The gold bags he had seemed to confirm his guilt. Without letting him explain that the rancher had paid him off so he could visit his mother in San Francisco, the vigilantes hanged him from the nearest tree.

The vigilantes took over Rich Bar, parading through the streets, shouting and swearing. They broke into cabins and tents on the flimsiest excuse. Louise told her sister to give up any thought of visiting the camp, but ended the despondent letter with a touch of humor:

One of my neighbors asked to borrow a teaspoon. As I have three I wanted to loan her my three. But she refused, saying, "This would be too fancy. The folks would think I was 'uppity.' They can just pass the spoon from 'tother to 'tother."

Fayette Clappe knew his wife's nerves were at breaking point. He suggested a vacation before snow closed the passes. Louise was delighted to get out of Rich Bar. They rode their mules across the mountain and into the warm, beautiful American valley.

The Feather River, here undisturbed by flumes and dams, wound its way through the valley which was seven miles long and four miles wide. Turnips grew as large as Louise's waist, and stringbeans could be a foot long.

Many immigrants were putting down roots in this fertile region. A young widow of twenty, whose husband had recently died of cholera, was being courted by all the young men; she was more fortunate than "the long woman," six feet tall, whose husband had died on the journey west. With her nine children, she lived in a covered wagon, worked in the fields and did washing.

The Clappes returned from their month's vacation to find the diggings exhausted. Gambling houses and saloons were closed, The Empire had boarded up its doors, and the flumes that had moaned night and day, like a woman in labor, were silent. The miners were gone.

Louise packed her few valuables in a small bag. On November 5, 1852, she left Rich Bar the way she had come, on the back of a mule.

Glimpsing her last of the cabin in the pines and the gaping diggings, Louise remembered what seemed a lifetime spent in less than two years. She'd seen lives spared and lives taken, raw cruelty and warm kindness. She'd slept on pine boughs, oxhides and stones, lived for days on barley and salt mackerel. Now she was leaving.

She never went back.

Today a few broken tombstones among fallen pines are all that mark a camp where a thousand miners hoped to make their fortunes. The Empire has crumbled, as has Louise's cabin. But the Dame Shirley Letters exist as a priceless memoir of the early days of the gold rush.

Back in San Francisco, Louise began a career in teaching. The Clappes were divorced in 1857. In 1878 Louise returned to the East, where, while living in New York, she gave frequent lectures to women's clubs and other groups.

The Dame Shirley Letters were first published in the *Marysville Herald* in 1851 and 1852. Later, they were serialized in *The Pioneer Magazine* of San Francisco. In 1933 the Grabbon Press published them in two beautiful volumes of a limited edition.

Louise Amelia Smith Clappe died in a nursing home in New Jersey in 1906. She was eighty-seven years old. With her was buried the packet of letters she had written in Rich Bar so many years before.

Born in Iowa, Reba Pierce Cunningham has spent most of her life in Wyoming on ranches and in the lap of the Beartooth Mountains in Montana. She knew many of the old cowboys, roundup cooks, stage drivers and other old-timers. From them came many of the 150 stories and articles she has sold to leading newspapers. She is a member of Nebraska Writer's Guild, National League of American Penwomen and Western Writers of America.

Jeanne Williams published her first short story in 1953, and has since sold over seventy short pieces and forty books, including young adult, gothic, romance and historical titles. Among these are Lady Bought with Rifles, Bride of Thunder, Woman Clothed in Sun, Daughter of the Sword, *and a forthcoming two-volume Arizona saga. A past president of the Western Writers of America, her writing awards include Spurs for the best Western juvenile in 1962 and 1973 for* The Horsetalker *and* Freedom Trail *respectively, and the Levi Strauss Golden Saddleman for* The Horsetalker.

BIBLIOGRAPHY

BOOKS

Clappe, Louise. *Shirley Letters*. New York: Alfred Knopf, 1961.
Edward, James T. *Notable American Women Vol. 1*. Cambridge, Mass.: Belknap, 1971.

MAGAZINE ARTICLE

Rodman, Paul Wilson. "In Search of Dame Shirley." Pacific Review Magazine, 1964.
Also used in the preparation of this chapter were 158 manuscript letters from the California State Library, Sacramento, California, and an assortment of manuscripts from the Morristown Public Library, Morristown, New Jersey.

12

Beloved Healer

by JUDY SKALLA

Brought to Salt Lake in a covered wagon at the age of five, Ellis Reynolds Shipp greatly admired her grandfather, Brother Hawley, for his skill in setting bones. At the behest of Brigham Young, after she was a wife and mother of four, Ellis attended the Woman's Medical College of Pennsylvania and graduated in 1878. She inspired her husband Milford and her sister Maggie to also become doctors, established her own School of Obstetrics and Nursing in Salt Lake City and, still fiery at ninety-two, chided young Utah women: "In a land renowned for its equal opportunities for women, it's amazing so few follow a profession so befitting them."

N.S.Y.

When the Mormons were settling the Valley of the Great Salt Lake, among them was a tiny girl named Ellis Reynolds. She had come West in a covered wagon with her parents and grandparents. The year was 1852, and Ellis was five years old.

Her best friend and hero was her grandfather Hawley. He could set bones! Sickness, pain and death were an accepted part of pioneer life, for on the frontier in those days physicians were as rare as any other luxury. But William Hawley, as a young man back in Iowa, had gone to medical school for a few months. Whenever an emergency involving broken bones arose it was always "Brother Hawley" who was summoned. Ellis was fascinated by his skill.

Years later, as Ellis Reynolds Shipp, M.D., she also gained a reputation as an expert setter of bones. She cheerfully admitted, however, "I learned more from Grandfather about setting bones than I did in college."

If it had not been for the influence of Brigham Young, Ellis could never have become a doctor. She grew from a pensive and introspective child to a poetic and sensitive young woman. Her mother died when Ellis was fourteen, and her father remarried. Ellis felt uncomfortable with the situation and went to live part of the time with her grandfather in the tiny settlement of Battle Creek, south of Salt Lake. Because of this, her education was sporadic.

Then, at seventeen, she received an unexpected opportunity. Brigham Young himself, the revered prophet and president of the Mormon Church, came to preside over a church conference in their community. Ellis had a chance to shake hands and talk with the aging bearded leader. Her lively intelligence interested him. Ellis was invited to come to Salt Lake City, to live at the Beehive House with the Young family, and to go to school there.

Honored and awed, she had gone. Ellis became part of the family in every way. Sister Lucy, one of Brigham's wives, was her special guardian. She studied right along with the Young children under the private tutelage of Karl G. Maeser. She knelt in family prayer with the Youngs and sat in the president's box at the Salt Lake Theatre.

Brigham even expressed fatherly disapproval of Milford Bard Shipp, a young man Ellis was seeing. He was handsome and educated, a just-returned missionary who had come home from England looking for a wife. But he was eleven years her senior and twice divorced. The Prophet did not approve, though Ellis scarcely noticed.

She wrote of Milford Shipp in her diary: "He was to me all the enlivened fancy of girlhood or the matured judgement of woman could picture. . . . So kind and affectionate, so faithful to the cause of Mormonism. . . . He was ambitious, ardent and energetic in all that was noble and laudable. In truth, I never saw a person who could so enchant and fascinate by the power of language."

Ellis and Milford were married on May 5, 1866, when she was nineteen. The newly married Shipps went off to Fillmore in central

Utah to open a store for Milford's father. In ten months they had a son, Milford Bard Shipp II. The Fillmore year was a lonely one for this idealistic and intelligent young woman, used to the lessons and parties at Beehive House in Salt Lake. "It was then I began to realize most fully the blessings of work and mental activity more than I ever had before," Ellis wrote later.

When the business proved unsuccessful, Ellis and Milford returned to Salt Lake City, where Milford soon took another wife: Margaret (Maggie) Curtis. Ellis loved both her husband and her church with such passion that she refused to be embittered by having to accept a sister-wife into the family circle.

Ellis' second son, Willie, was born that year and died a few months later; but a third son, Richard, was born the following spring. Within another few years, two more wives, Elizabeth Hilstead and Mary Smith, joined the mushrooming Shipp family. In a house meant for a single family, all four women and their children made a home, and their charming and well-intentioned husband supported them as best he could. Ellis milked her cow, helped with the household chores and had more children. "And thus began my creed," she wrote in her diary, "the pattern of a weak and unsophisticated life as yet to meet the crucial tests whereby we gain and thus, alas, may lose."

The crucial tests did come, however, and Ellis met them vigorously. Brigham Young made many speeches encouraging the women of the church to join together and learn to improve themselves with the resources available in their mountain refuge. Encouraged by the accomplishments of women around her, Ellis changed her attitude from resigned self-sacrifice to one of dedication and self-improvement. She began by mapping out a pre-dawn reading regimen which she carried out from 4:00 to 7:00 A.M. each day.

As her self-confidence grew, however, the family's economic situation deteriorated. Ellis began teaching at the ward school so "that we might comfortably provide for ourselves without the need of charity."

A problem more crushing than poverty was the ever-present threat of sickness and death. Every woman dealt in her own way with the typically high infant mortality and the frequent illnesses of the remote pioneer communities. The Shipp wives were no exception. They nursed each other and their thirteen children through a diphtheria epidemic with herbs and poultices and loving care. When the birth of a baby was imminent, one of the self-taught midwives in the area was called upon.

In 1873 Ellis' fourth child and only daughter, Anna, became seriously ill. Home remedies failed to save her, even as did a blessing by the priesthood which, since the days of Joseph Smith back in Nauvoo, Illinois, had been the most trusted form of treatment for the sick. Anna died, and the loss of this beloved little daughter ripped at Ellis' already battered soul.

In spite of the difficulties—or perhaps because of them—the four Shipp wives grew close to one another, becoming sisters in the best sense of the word. Ellis and Maggie especially were kindred spirits since they shared a common desire to better their lives and an active interest in learning whatever they could to help the sick and to prevent illness. They were encouraged in this by President Young's recent statements that better medical care was needed for the Saints.

One night as they walked home together from a nursing class, Maggie confessed to Ellis that she wanted desperately to go further than nursing.

"I know I could become a full-fledged doctor," Maggie said.

"How would you do it?" Ellis asked anxiously. She had been harboring a similar dream.

"I'd go to Philadelphia—to the Woman's Medical College there," a pregnant Maggie said with bravado.

The pair walked on in silence, acutely aware of the chances against their ever becoming doctors.

In a few weeks, all of that changed. Brigham Young made the pronouncement in a sermon in October 1873 that "the time has come for women to come forth as doctors in these valleys of the mountains." This extraordinary declaration came soon after Ellis' little Anna had died, and the very thought that there might be some way for Ellis to help alleviate such tragedies in the future must have set her heart to beating in timorous anticipation.

Women doctors among the Saints! The Prophet had reacted favorably to the suggestion of Eliza R. Snow, one of the leading women of the church, that a sure way to stop the unseemly practice of male doctors taking over in difficult obstetrical cases was to train women to be doctors themselves.

The first to go was Romania B. Pratt, who left her five sons in the care of her mother and went East in the winter of 1874. By the following autumn, Maggie Shipp had weaned her baby and had followed Romania. She had been in Philadelphia only one month, however, when the pangs of homesickness forced her back to Salt Lake City. But the tuition had been paid, and someone must fill the vacant spot.

"What a strange fatality!" Ellis wrote in her diary. "This morning I start for Philadelphia to attend the Medical College."

Leaving small children behind while a mother went off to pursue other interests was no great problem in a polygamous household. Many an ambitious wife in those days went out of her home to develop a career both because of the greater financial needs of a polygamous family and because she had no worries that her children would not be well cared for in her absence.

"Go, Ellis," Milford had encouraged when she wavered. Brigham Young also gave her his blessing. They both knew Ellis had the capacity to succeed in her studies.

So Ellis, age twenty-nine, left her three sons in the care of her sister-wife Mary, who had no children of her own, and boarded the train for Philadelphia, traveling with a group of Mormon missionaries going East. Her pent up emotions spilled out in the form of a poem called "Dream of Home," that she wrote while she traveled. Her heart ached as she penned the lines: ". . . fair faces gathered there, Their wistful looks, my empty chair . . ."

At 3:00 A.M. on a cold November morning in 1875, Ellis Shipp arrived in Philadelphia and spent the remainder of the night sleeping on a bench in the railroad station.

Students came to the highly respected Woman's Medical College of Pennsylvania from many parts of the world; that first year Ellis was housed with a black woman and a Japanese. "But," she wrote, "I had no horns, the Negress offered no magic, and the Japanese, though she wore her native costume, became one of us. We all found our places."

Since she had entered late in the term, Ellis had to work desperately hard to catch up. She survived emotionally on prayers and letters from home, though she was still plagued by doubts.

In January Ellis received a letter from Maggie:

You know too well what our home is; noble hearts inhabit the rooms but our circumstances are so unfavorable. Are you not anxious to better your situation, think of your boys, what poor advantages they have, what could you do for them if you were here. You have tried for eight long years. Think of how your heart ached, ached, ached, day after day, and I tell you, . . . it would be no better if you were here again. No, we must get out of this, our children must have a beautiful home, splendid advantages, or they will be as they have been.

Ellis knew that Maggie was right, and she worked harder than ever. She successfully passed her examinations in the spring, but she was exhausted. Yielding to the wishes of her husband, Ellis returned home instead of doing the summer clinic work she had intended. But she would be back.

"Ellis! How can you even think of returning?" Milford and her sister-wives asked in September. The family was in dire financial straits. Her oldest son was ill. And Ellis was pregnant.

Despite their objections, Ellis went. Classmates found her brooding one day and pried from her the news that she was expecting a child in the spring. "We could help you," they intimated. "You don't need to go through with this."

"I came here to learn to save life, not to destroy it," Ellis stormed. Years later, she told her daughter how she had spent all that night on her knees, praying for the strength to go on. At daybreak she felt the sense of peace that an answered prayer brings, and she went to her classes. She did not miss a single session during the school year.

Little money was coming from home now—just the few dollars that a sister-wife sent occasionally in a money order. Ellis took up dressmaking to earn enough food to see her through the winter. For a time she also guarded the hall of cadavers at night, sleeping on a cot in the anteroom.

As the birth of her baby approached, Ellis decided she would go to the charity ward of a nearby hospital. However, when the head of the medical college, the brilliant, white-haired and motherly Rachel Bodley, learned of this, she would have none of it. Dean Bodley arranged for a private room for Ellis and for the best of medical care. On May 25, 1877, Ellis gave birth to a daughter, Olea.

The thick summer heat bore down on Philadelphia while Ellis undertook her required clinical work at the hospital. Olea was left in the care of a landlady, and Ellis rushed home to be with the infant whenever she could. This young Mormon woman medical student far from home felt less alone now with a tiny daughter to love.

"It is to me the crowning joy of a woman's life to be a mother," she wrote in her journal.

The torrid summer in the city had drained her strength, so in late August Ellis boarded a train for the New Jersey countryside. With her baby in one arm and her dressmaking models in the other, she walked from one farmhouse to another until she found a family who would take her in in exchange for expert dressmaking instruction. When the term began for her final year of medical school, Ellis was ready for it.

Pressures mounted from home. The children were ill again and money was scarce. Letters from Milford depressed her. Ellis worked harder than ever in her studies; she knew she could help her family most by becoming a doctor with healing skills and an income.

The simple entry in her diary dated March 14, 1878, reads: "Graduated from Woman's Medical College of Pennsylvania." She neglected to mention that she had graduated with high honors.

Home at last. Ellis let her boys, now ages eleven, nine and four, show her how much they had grown, introduced them to their new sister, and obtained a separate house for her brood so she could open an office there. Her sign outside read: "Dr. E. R. Shipp." She advertised in the local papers as a "Physician and Surgeon; Special attention given to Obstetrics, diseases of women and minor surgery."

Brigham Young, who had recognized her abilities years before, had died while Ellis was away; she could not thank him for his encouragement of her. Mary, Maggie and Lizzie and her still-much-loved husband Milford had anxiously awaited her return, however, and in every way that she could, Ellis repaid them for providing a way for her to become a doctor. The endless questions she answered in the family circle must have lighted an interest in medicine for Milford and rekindled Maggie's ambitions; both of them entered medical schools in the East within a few years, and both graduated in 1883. Later the three Drs. Shipp edited a medical magazine for a time, and Ellis and Milford launched a series of medical lectures "for the ladies."

Nearly a dozen women practiced medicine in pioneer Utah during the last quarter of the nineteenth century—a seeming handful, perhaps, but remarkable in those days. There were very probably more women doctors per capita in Utah at that time than anywhere in the world. But Dr. Shipp was not content to simply be a doctor; she knew she could never do enough alone.

Within months after her return from medical school, Ellis announced the opening of her School of Obstetrics and Nursing in Salt Lake City. Her students came not only from the Salt Lake area, but from Mormon settlements the length and breadth of the West. The only requirement for admission was a sincere desire to help the sick and alleviate needless suffering.

The course took six months to complete, with two classes graduating each year. The students were of all ages and educational backgrounds. This necessitated Dr. Shipp's phrasing her lectures in homespun words and spelling whenever necessary. It was not unusual for the teacher to be holding a student's baby in her arms as she lectured so that its mother could take notes. Neither was it unusual for the doctor to be pregnant herself. Ellis bore four more children after her return from medical school: two boys who did not survive infancy, and two more daughters—Ellis and Nellie.

One of the points Ellis always emphasized in her classes was to "pray in your soul as you hasten to your duty," a practice she followed faithfully throughout her career.

As a doctor, Ellis was on call day or night. Three days before the birth of her tenth child, Nellie, she was asked to attend a difficult obstetrical case. She saved both the mother and child.

Dr. Shipp's fee for prenatal care and delivery was "$25 when it is convenient." Often she was paid with eggs, butter and chickens. Her services also included ten visits to the home afterwards, when she would check on her patients' progress and do anything she could to see to their comfort—including changing the bed and cooking a meal.

Once a young man whose hand had been terribly mutilated in an explosion was brought to her. Dr. Shipp cleansed and bandaged the hand and soothed her frightened patient. Then she worked long hours into the night, gently removing the burned powder from his face. When his wounds had healed, the young man came to show her that he could use the remaining fingers on his hand and that his face carried no scars. Ellis Shipp simply smiled with satisfaction and went on to attend to other patients.

Some ten years after her graduation from college, Dr. Shipp returned to the East for a time to study the latest findings on the new discovery that bacteria causes disease. A few years after that, in 1893, she spent a year in postgraduate study at the University of Michigan Medical School. As one of the best-educated physicians in Utah, male colleagues often consulted her.

Ellis preferred, however, to direct her practice toward obstetrics, gynecology and childhood diseases. "Let men care for their own sex and do the major operations," she wrote. "I never had an ambition to take such responsibilities, for even men [doctors] have fatal cases and, if a woman should have them, [she] would always be condemned because she was a woman!"

Ellis' desire to provide medical care for mothers and children grew also out of her own tragic experiences. Her mother had died young, and five of the ten children she bore did not survive childhood. Many children, she knew, would continue to be brought into the world as an expression of the Latter-day Saint faith. Ellis believed in this tenet with all her heart, but she thought it absurd that so many should die when, with proper medical care, they could live.

For these reasons, Ellis did not feel it sufficient to conduct her classes on nursing and obstetrics only from her office-home in Salt Lake City. Many times throughout the years she would travel to a distant outpost of Mormonism, where she knew that little or no professional medical care existed. It might be Calgary in Canada, the Mormon colonies in Mexico, an isolated community in Idaho, or the desert settlements of Arizona. Ellis would take her three little girls with her and stay for three months to teach a comprehensive course in midwifery and the fundamentals of health.

Naturally she always brought her medical bag on these trips; she expected to render medical services whenever and wherever needed. The day she was summoned from her home in Juarez, Mexico, to travel up the treacherous mountain passes to Colonia Garcia, she gathered her supplies and was ready to proceed immediately. A woman had been in hard labor twenty-four hours, and the baby could not come. Ellis went to her aid as fast as two relays of fresh horses could take her. When she arrived, the unborn child had died, but Ellis was able to save the mother.

At the end of her more than fifty-year medical career, it was estimated that Dr. Shipp had attended some 5,000 births. Those babies delivered by the several hundred midwives she trained added thousands more whose lives were directly affected by her.

A bonus of Ellis' courses was the inroads they made into women's distrust and superstition of men doctors. She invited male doctors to lecture at her school and convinced her students that when their health was at stake, modesty only got in the way.

Ellis was still teaching her classes when she was past eighty years old and was considered the "Grand Old Lady" of Utah. By that time, however, in the 1930s, her emphasis had turned from midwifery to such nursing as was needed by the strengthening medical profession of the West.

Always Ellis deftly combined medicine with motherhood. Her office was inevitably in her home, for the enforced separation from her babes during her medical school years left her determined to keep them near her afterwards. Ellis' love of learning and dedication to her profession inspired her two living sons, Milford II and Richard, to careers in medicine and law.

The boys were grown by the time Dr. Shipp began her sojourns to the remote Mormon communities all over the West. However, Olea, the daughter born in Philadelphia while Ellis was at medical college, and her two younger sisters, Ellis and Nellie, always accompanied their mother on these trips. The daughters, like the sons, were inspired by their mother and went on to higher education. One studied music at the University of Michigan, another received a master's degree from Columbia University, and the third graduated from the University of Utah. The daughter Ellis, named for her mother, eventually compiled and edited *The Early Autobiography and Diary of Ellis Reynolds Shipp*.

Whenever a member of the large Shipp family needed her, Ellis came, though her own muscles ached with exhaustion. She personally attended the births of some of her grandchildren.

Far into the night one Christmas, she twined an ivy wreath for her children that served as their Christmas tree. The poem she wrote to accompany it explains her devotion:

> I twined a wreath while others slept,
> An ivy wreath. I worked and wept,
> It was not for the bonny bride,
> This verdant wreath at Christmas tide.

> It was not for the sombre bier,
> This ivy wreath and briny tear,
> It was for love, devotion true,
> Beloved ones, I twined for you.

Her devotion to the man she had married against Brigham Young's wishes when she was a girl of nineteen lasted throughout her life. Milford Bard Shipp died in 1918.

Somehow Ellis found the time to serve on the staff of the Deseret Hospital in Salt Lake City, serve on the general board of the Relief Society, hold office in several cultural groups and even write a book of poetry, *Life Lines*. Ellis worked on behalf of women's suffrage and was a delegate to the National Council of Women, where she became friends with Clara Barton, Susan B. Anthony and Elizabeth Stanton.

Looking back at the end of her long career, Dr. Shipp, frail and philosophical, wondered "that had I fully realized the magnitude of the undertaking, I would have shrunk from it."

Still fiery at ninety-two, however, she chided young Utah women for not showing an interest in becoming physicians. "In a land renowned for its equal opportunities for women, it's simply amazing such few follow a profession so befitting them." She insisted that the many comforts of life by then available to women had distracted them from challenging callings.

Ellis Reynolds Shipp accomplished fully what she had set out to do that November of 1875 when she left Utah to enroll in the Woman's Medical College of Pennsylvania. She alleviated needless suffering and death for thousands of people throughout the West; her influence reached still further through the practices of her students. And, just as important, she was able to provide for her family in a way that would not have otherwise been possible.

Had all the heartaches and hardships been worth it? Ellis hoped so. "Great minds are they who suffered not in vain," she wrote. "I do not feel my spirit Great. But oh, I have suffered—and pray it has never been in vain."

Like Dr. Shipp, Judy Skalla is a Mormon. Both have known the challenge of raising a large family while pursuing personal and professional interests and actively living their beliefs in The Church of Jesus Christ of Latter-day Saints.

A native of Colorado, Mrs. Skalla spent her early adult years in Wyoming and now lives in Omaha, Nebraska. She has a B.A. in journalism from Colorado State University and has done much free-lance writing. Mrs. Skalla is currently serving as a Relief Society president in Omaha. Relief Society is the Mormon women's organization which focuses on personal development and compassionate service.

BIBLIOGRAPHY
•

Arrington, Chris Rigby. "Pioneer Midwives," Bushman, Claudia L. (ed.). *Mormon Sisters.* Cambridge, Mass.: Emmeline Press Ltd. 1976.

Carter, Kate B. *Heart Throbs of the West.* Salt Lake City, Utah: Daughters of the Utah Pioneers. 1939–1950.

——. *Our Pioneer Heritage.* Salt Lake City, Utah: Daughters of the Utah Pioneers, 1958–1974.

Casterline, Gail Farr. "Ellis R. Shipp," in Burges-Olson, Vicky (ed.). *Sister Saints.* Provo, Utah: Brigham Young University Press. 1978.

Genealogical Society of The Church of Jesus Christ of Latter-day Saints, Salt Lake City, Utah. Milford Bard Shipp family group sheets, vital statistics of the Shipp family.

Noall, Claire. *Guardians of the Hearth.* Bountiful, Utah: Horizon Publishers, 1974.

Shipp, Ellis Reynolds. *The Early Autobiography and Diary of Ellis Reynolds Shipp.* Compiled and edited by Ellis Shipp Musser. Salt Lake City, Utah: Deseret News Press, 1962.

13

Medicine Woman

by JAN BARNHART and CAROL COHEA-O'HEARN

A native of Wisconsin, Franc Johnson Newcomb became a revered medicine woman among the Navajos of the far Southwest and was adopted into their tribe. A teacher and writer as well, she left many fine accounts of her life among the Indians.

N.S.Y.

Inside the semi-darkness of the thick-walled dome-shaped hogan, a fire burns in the middle of the floor. The only light comes from the fire, and a single shaft of bright sunshine streaming through the smoke hole in the roof. The Navajo medicine man sits in the place of honor. He is surrounded by pollen bags, prayer plumes and rattles. Finely ground colored sands are spread on a blanket near him. He carefully lets the sand fall through his fingers as he begins the sand painting. Then he starts waving a rattle. When the correct rhythm has been reached, the chant begins.

In the dim light, a woman is discernible. As the medicine man works his designs in the sand, she also draws characters. Her keen eyes note the shapes of his figures, and she copies them.

The woman is Franc Johnson Newcomb—Atsay Ashon to the Navajos. The name means Medicine Woman. The name was given to her after she first gained their confidence, then earned their respect.

Franc Newcomb was one of the first women to witness a Navajo healing ceremony and one of the earliest white women of record to be adopted into the Navajo tribe. A teacher, trading-post operator, recognized medicine woman and author, she used her skill as a writer not only to tell of her years on the Navajo reservation, but also to preserve and develop Navajo art and culture.

Franc Newcomb was born on March 30, 1887 in Tunnel City, Wisconsin. She was named after her father, Frank Johnson. Her mother was Priscilla (Tilly) Woodward Johnson. Johnson, an architect, was originally from Pennsylvania. The Woodwards were dairy farmers from the Cable, Wisconsin, area. Prior to her marriage, Priscilla had been a schoolteacher in nearby Tomah, Wisconsin.

Franc's father died of consumption when she was two. After his death, her mother and older sister and brother moved in with the Woodwards. Then, when she was twelve, tragedy struck again; her mother died of consumption, too. These deaths were later to influence her decision to come to the arid Southwest.

Raised on her grandmother's farm, Franc graduated from Tomah High School in 1904 at seventeen. She is listed on the graduation roll as Frances Johnson, an error—her birth certificate specifically spells out her name as Franc. Her part in the graduation ceremony was to speak on the representative art of the Egyptians. Even then her interests centered on art.

After a year at Wisconsin's Sparta Normal School, Franc obtained a teaching job in her home town of Tunnel City, where she taught for four years. She then taught for two years in the one-room Indian school at Keshena on the Menominee Indian Reservation in northern Wisconsin. There she learned of the possibility of teacher openings in the U.S. Civil Service. In the fall of 1911 she took and passed the civil service exam.

For some time, Franc had been troubled by a persistent cough. Fearing consumption, she believed a drier climate would be better for her health and readily accepted a teaching post on the Navajo Reservation at Fort Defiance, Arizona, an Indian boarding school, trading post and mission. Her teaching term began the fall of 1912 at a salary of $25 a month; she received free room and board. Her room was one of those in the dormitory; she ate her meals in the mess hall with the students.

Meanwhile, Arthur Newcomb, a small, slender, shy, young

man, was clerking at the Fort Defiance trading post. His salary was $10 a month, and he, too, received free room and board.

The Newcombs were from Ames, Iowa. Arthur was the youngest of the three sons of a jewelry maker and jewelry store owner. His oldest brother, Earle, was the first of the sons to come to the Fort Defiance area. He owned and operated the trading post at Crystal, Arizona. Arthur, a musician in an orchestra, had hopped off a westbound train for a brief visit with his brother. He never got back on the train; instead he ended up clerking at the Fort Defiance post.

With his father a jewelry store owner in Iowa and his brother a trading-post operator in Arizona, Arthur, too, wanted to have his own business. The opportunity came when Mike Kirk, an Indian goods wholesaler and buyer, offered him half interest in a trading post at the tip of Blue Mesa on the Navajo Reservation, halfway between Gallup and Farmington, New Mexico.

Franc and Arthur were married at the Oppenheim Dutch Reformed Mission Church. Their honeymoon was spent at the Pesh-do-clish trading post, on which Arthur had made a down payment with $400 Franc had saved. Arthur had earlier moved to the trading post to familiarize himself with the country, the people and the language.

"When my school year ended in June 1914, Arthur came to Fort Defiance where I had been teaching and we were married on June 30, going to Pesh-do-clish the same day," she once wrote.

If Franc was apprehensive, it was understandable. There was no direct means of communication between her home and Farmington and Gallup; the road was a mere horse trail; hired mule teams would bring supplies and mail to the store once a month; the nearest white neighbors were thirteen miles away.

"The Navajo Indians for the most part are scattered over sixteen million acres of land located in northwestern New Mexico, northeastern Arizona and southwestern Utah. It is an area of mountains, upland plains, high plateaus, fertile valleys, deep canyons and barren badlands," Franc said.

The newlyweds honeymooned in a two-room adobe structure: one room was the trading post, the other the living quarters. At one point, the previous owner had pasted blue calico to the walls and stuffed blue calico in the numerous cracks. When the frequent winds blew, the calico billowed into the room. Over all was a light coat of fine dust that had sifted between the cracks. Also hidden in the cracks was an army of tiny invaders: centipedes, tarantulas, bedbugs, wood ticks and more. Franc wasn't afraid of the snakes, but she hated those bugs.

In later years, Franc recalled her first reaction to that adobe. She wanted to burn it to the ground to get rid of the bugs. Out of self-defense, she became a "great Black Flag and kerosene user," her daughter, Lynette Wilson, said. Franc would routinely wipe the logs with a mixture of kerosene and linseed oil until the logs were polished and shiny.

With the help of Navajo neighbors, a bedroom was soon added to the adobe structure. Over the years, the adobe was remodeled numerous times until it included a rug showroom, an upstairs area, several wings, two bedrooms, a playroom, manager's house, guest house, studio, running water, a Delco battery system for electricity, and Franc's pride and joy—a refrigerator.

Originally, an ice house kept the food cold. It was built into the side of the mesa behind the store. The doors were made of heavy corrugated tin. The ice came from Toadlena, northwest of Pesh-do-clish. In the winter, horse-drawn wagons were used to haul the ice blocks down to the trading post. The ice lasted through the summer and into the fall.

Water was also hauled by a horse-drawn wagon in five- and ten-gallon drums. Well water at the store was too alkaline and unsuitable for drinking, but water from Fort Butte Springs, a few miles away, was almost pure.

At the Pesh-do-clish trading post, Franc met Hosteen Klah, the medicine man, stockman and weaver, who would play a significant role in her development as a sand painter.

Franc wrote:

When Arthur bought the Pesh-do-clish Trading Post and went there to learn the business in 1913, Klah was one of the first Indians with whom he became acquainted. Mr. Nelson, the former owner, stayed a few weeks to collect whatever outstanding debts he could, and then went to his farm on the San Juan River. . . . Klah came in the afternoons and spent many long evenings helping him [Arthur] with his study of the Navajo language. Klah was generally invited to stay for the evening meal, then the two would sit by the fireplace while Arthur wrote lists of nouns and phrases

which he would carry in his shirt pocket for days, until he was sure
he would not forget.

The first Navajo who came into our living room to greet the
new bride was Hosteen Klah. How he knew that a gift was in
order, I do not know, for it is not customary for Navajos to present gifts to the bride. But he brought me the most beautiful un-
tanned fox pelt I had ever seen then or since.

The Newcombs were new at the trading business and too deeply
in debt to carry a large amount of goods, but Klah was a loyal
customer and he brought his family and friends. The first time
Franc attended a healing ceremony was Klah's Yeibichai ceremony, considered his final graduation as unsurpassed medicine
man.

He had told me that the first large sand painting would be made
on the fifth day, starting early in the morning. Since I did not wish
to miss any part of this activity, we breakfasted by lamplight; and
as soon as the sun was up I was on my way to the ceremonial
lodge. As I pushed aside the door blanket and stepped over the
threshold into the cool dimness of the interior, I realized the room
was much larger than it had seemed from the outside.

The floor space was circular and about 18 feet in diameter, with
a fire pit toward the east about three feet from the door. Klah sat
in the place of honor at the southwest, surrounded by an amazing
number of pollen bags, prayer plumes and rattles, while a large assortment of medicine bundles was piled against the west wall.
Twelve or more chanters were seated or sprawled along the south
wall, while two messenger boys squatted near the door.

I handed Klah a polished abalone shell and a package of cigarettes, these being the customary ceremonial gifts and then passed
a package of cigarettes to the men.

Klah motioned me to the northwest "corner" where a couple of
saddle blankets had been folded for a seat. I carried a Navajo
shawl as I knew that Navajo women never exposed their ankles
and I was afraid I could not sit with my feet folded under me during the entire proceedings.

Someone questioned my presence in the lodge and was answered by Klah's nephew, but I understood very little Navajo at
that time, so sat as quietly as I could.

Franc spent the next three mornings in the lodge, watching the painter complete three more sand paintings. And, she explained, she did her best to memorize as many of the symbols as she could:

Since pencil, paper or camera was not allowed in the lodge, I had only my memory to depend on. But when the rites had ended and I had time to try putting these designs on paper, I found that my mental pictures were a jumble of rainbows, crossed logs, tall corn and medicine bags. In later years I trained myself to concentrate and if allowed to remain in a ceremonial hogan for a half-hour, I could reproduce the painting without error.

When Klah saw me at the hopeless task of drawing these first sand paintings, he asked if I would like to have him paint them for me. I was delighted and started looking for material of a quality that would last on which the paintings could be made.

The heavy wrapping paper we used for wrapping rugs for shipment through the mails was just the right sand color, of good weight and with a smooth texture to serve as the background. So from this I cut four 20-inch squares. I had a watercolor painting outfit and we obtained children's colored pencils from the store. Klah worked with the pencils and I with the paints. When two figures were alike, he drew one and I copied it for the other.

He made the intricate designs and I drew the rainbows and the plants. It took a couple of weeks of our spare time, but finally I had my first four sketches of Navajo sand paintings, which number grew to be almost five hundred in the next 20 years.

As Franc witnessed each new sand painting, she recorded the description of the symbols, the names of the figures and the powers they were thought to possess.

Franc made brown-paper patterns of the principal characters in the sand paintings so that if two or more of the same figures were required, they would be identical. She also made patterns of the principal animals, such as the bat. In that way, if a bat was required in another, later sand painting, she had a ready-made pattern to follow. She left nothing to chance; even straight lines were drawn with a thin four-inch-long glass ruler.

Franc also mixed her own colors in order that they would be

identical to those in the original sand painting. Blue was from cedar ashes, yellow from pollen, white from limestone or corn-meal, red from red sandstone.

By learning the meanings behind the sand-painting figures and their powers, Franc began to understand the Navajo religion and its link to faith healing. It's thought that she acquired her own rep-utation as a medicine woman during the flu epidemic of 1920. She felt her reputation was greatly enhanced by her use of the "safe" medicines—cough syrup, cod-liver oil and zinc ointment—which she received from the government doctor.

During February 1920, the weather was terrible, being mostly a series of wind-blown sleet storms turning to snow and ice. This month was known as the "Hunger Moon," when food supplies were running low and many Navajo families were rationing their store of corn and beans to make them last until spring and the sheep were much too thin to kill for mutton. There was always sickness at this time, but never like the present.

It has been estimated that one-tenth of the entire Navajo popu-lation died that winter, and I believe that estimate is far too low. After the epidemic had passed its peak, the agent at Shiprock sent out teams of men to bury the corpses and burn the death hogans. Three of our household did not catch the flu at this time. My Navajo maid, Louise Bicenti, Lynette and I were among the lucky few who seemed immune.

Franc was always willing to help her Navajo neighbors. When Klah brought home a small boy and five-month-old girl whose parents had both died, she took canned milk, baby bottles and nipples to Klah's sister and carefully explained to her how they should be sterilized.

Franc's induction into the tribe came after her own bout with the flu in 1920.

Klah came to talk to Arthur. He was very worried because I had been so ill and said it was because I had witnessed so many sand paintings and had been present when too many powerful prayers were recited. No one should do this until some ceremony had been held for him. We asked what ceremony he wished to hold and he answered, "Five days of the Yeibichai."

But this I flatly refused to endure. On four mornings during this ceremony the patient must take an emetic and I was so constructed that an emetic made me deathly ill. It was good therapy for a Navajo and I could see why any woman would be cured and never again admit that she was ill; but I was not a Navajo and this ceremony was not for me. He then suggested the three-day Apache Wind Chant; but this, too, had emetics, with the added discomfort of face-blackening and body-painting. I told him, "No!" I would rather have whatever illness might come than to have it prevented in such an unpleasant manner.

He was insistent that there must be a ceremony of some kind; and finally suggested the Hozhonji or Blessing Chant. It lasted only two nights and was mostly a series of chanted prayers, punctuated by pollen sprinkling and the drinking of little sips of herb infusion. In the forenoon there would be the emergence sand painting and the pollen trail. It was really a beautiful ceremony, but one not to be entered into as a lark. For one thing, I would be required to remain awake both nights, from sunset until dawn and the day between; and for another, I would be expected to memorize a prayer that took at least three quarters of an hour to recite in duo with the medicine man.

When it was learned that a ceremony had been held over Franc Newcomb, she was regarded as a member of the tribe. "Whenever I desired to witness a sand painting or a healing rite, on any part of the Reservation even among Indians I had never seen before, all I needed to say to gain entrance was, 'I have had a ceremony,'" she stated.

Day-to-day life in the middle of the vast, lonesome reservation was occasionally interrupted by socials and picnics with other trading-post families such as Lucy and George Bloomfield at Toadlena and Pearl and Ed Davies, who lived at Two Grey Hills or the missionaries, the Rev. and Mrs. Brinks and the Rev. and Mrs. Kobes. The families would converge at a prearranged trading post with potluck dinners. Before dinner, the men would sit and smoke cigars while the women prepared the food. After dinner there would be music and dancing. Arthur, who had played in an orchestra, would entertain on the cornet or saxophone, while Franc would accompany him on the violin or piano.

It is possible that during one of these gatherings in about 1916, the Newcombs and twelve other traders conceived the idea of a public ceremonial staged by the Indians to boost their trade and market their goods. This ceremonial would be held annually at Gallup, New Mexico, an important crossroads in the state and easily accessible to tourists. It became known as the Gallup Indian Ceremonial.

One of the visitors to an early Gallup Ceremonial was Mary Cabot Wheelwright, of Boston. During World War I, Mary Wheelwright was unable to travel in Europe and decided instead to visit the Southwest, the Navajo reservation and the Indian ceremonies. It was obvious to Franc that Mary wasn't interested on that first visit and that she would rather have been in Europe. But Mary's interest was captured, and she returned the following year. Gradually her stays became longer, extending one and two weeks, then several months at a time.

During one of these visits, she saw Franc's collection of sand paintings and ceremonial artifacts and realized the uniqueness of the collection. She once remarked to Franc that the collection should be in a museum on public display. The idea was the making of the Museum of Navajo Ceremonial Art in Santa Fe, New Mexico, now the Wheelwright Museum.

In 1927 Mary Wheelwright decided to make records of the hundreds of chants Klah used in his Yeibichai ceremony. Franc worked with her on the project. In 1931 Beaal Begay, Klah's chosen successor and protégé died. Beaal stood to inherit Klah's ceremonies and ceremonial artifacts, but his death left Klah without a successor.

When Mary came from the East in the autumn, she asked Klah what he thought would happen to his ceremony and all of his paraphernalia, and he said he did not know. Then she asked if he would be willing to have it stored in a place where everyone could see it and study its use if they wished. Klah was much pleased with this idea, for he had already recorded many of his songs for her and I had made copies of more than 50 of his sand paintings. All of this would be in one place, safely housed for study by future generations.

Plans were enthusiastically made for the museum.

At first Mary thought it might be located on the campus of the University of New Mexico in Albuquerque. She had the plans drawn up for the building, which was to be built of logs in an octagonal form with a domed roof. The university authorities, however, refused to allow a structure of this type erected on the campus since all the other buildings were of Pueblo design and it would not be in harmony with them.

Mary refused to alter the plans, so when Elizabeth White offered her some virgin land near the Museum of Anthropology in Santa Fe, she accepted this as the site of the Navajo Museum.

From this time on, Klah brought us articles he had hidden away for many years. There was his grandfather's long war bow with the puma-hide quiver which contained two or three iron-tipped arrows; there were ancient rattles and prayer plumes; and there were baskets, armbands and amulets. All of these we were to keep in storage until the museum was ready for them. But Klah did not part with any of the things he might be called upon to use when he held any one of his four ceremonies.

The museum was eventually built and Klah blessed it. He was also to be buried in it in 1937. Unfortunately, in 1968, during a break-in at the museum, two of his finely woven rugs, his medicine bundles and all of his paraphernalia were taken. Shortly after the burglary, Franc Newcomb's daughters, Lynette Wilson and Priscilla Thompson, requested the return of all her watercolor re-creations of sand paintings, 530 major or large ones and 360 smaller ones, as well as her collections of pottery and baskets. They are now housed at the University of New Mexico Maxwell Museum of Anthropology and available for researchers studying Navajo religion.

In May 1934, Arthur received a letter from New Mexico state officials, explaining an Indian exhibit was planned for New Mexico's entry at the Century of Progress Exposition in Chicago. Newcomb's assistance was requested to obtain Klah's presence. Klah's program was to include sand paintings and chanting. When Klah left for Chicago, he took with him for display Franc's book, *Navajo Sand Paintings*, which represented her first work as an author.

Navajo Sand Paintings was a collection of Franc's best sand paintings. The watercolor paintings were done on heavy brown museum paper. The holes to keep the pages bound had been made with a punch used for putting tags in sheep's ears; the Farmington newspaper had printed the cutlines and text; Franc had personally hand-lettered the cover and index pages. The whole was bound between covers of sheepskin.

The book was crudely constructed compared to its later editions, but it marked the first public appearance of Franc Newcomb, the author.

Her other works included *Navajo Neighbors; Hosteen Klah, Navajo Medicine Man and Sand Painter; Navajo Bird Tales; Navajo Folk Tales; Navajo Omens and Taboos; Sand Paintings of the Navajo Shooting Chant* (with Gladys A. Reichard); and *A Study of Navajo Symbolism* (with Mary C. Wheelwright).

Franc wrote in the introduction to *Navajo Tales:*

The Navajo tales were collected from various Navajo storytellers with no idea they would ever be presented to the public in book form. When my girls were small and while we were living in our trading post on the Navajo Reservation, I occasionally happened to overhear admonitions given them by the Navajo women who helped with the household tasks and the care of the children. I became aware that a wealth of folklore and folk saying common to every Navajo household was being instilled gradually into ours.

Franc established a residence in Albuquerque, New Mexico, in 1935 so that her daughters could attend high school and the university, and she launched her writing and lecturing career in earnest. She frequently lectured on Navajo history, legends and rites and wrote numerous articles on Navajo religion and her life on the reservation. Her work eventually earned her the Woman of the Year award from the National League of American Penwomen in 1964. In 1966, at the age of seventy-nine, she received the New Mexico Folklore Society Scroll of Honor.

On May 9, 1936, the Newcomb Trading Post, formerly Pesh-do-clish, burned to the ground. The fire, which began in the roof of the store, burned the living quarters, manager's house, guest house and all the furnishings. Though the trading post was rebuilt, Arthur never seemed to recover emotionally from the devastating fire; ten years later, on March 21, 1946, Newcomb died of cirrhosis of the liver.

After Arthur's death, Franc sold the trading post and made her permanent home in Albuquerque, where she became a patron of the Albuquerque Little Theater and New Mexico Museum, president of the Albuquerque Women's Club, involved in the establishment of the Christina Kent Day Nursery, on the board of directors of United Fund, instrumental in the establishment of the Albuquerque Boys Club, the Fraternal Order of Police Boys Camp and the Albuquerque Visiting Nurses Service. At one point she lobbied in Santa Fe for the right of women to have their own legal will written.

She was an avid bridge player and sports fan. Stories are told of her afternoon tea invitation to the entire University of New Mexico basketball team. Even more amazing was the team's acceptance.

She was also an avid reader and letter writer. A spinoff of her letter writing was her poetry about which little has been written though it figures prominently throughout her life. She was described once as a woman who never talked much about herself— yet her poetry paints a vivid portrait of her.

Franc used to compose her poetry mentally late at night in bed, when she couldn't sleep. During the day, she'd jot the thoughts down, sometimes reworking the words. She'd write her poetry on scraps of paper—on insurance notices, between the company letterhead and the opening salutation there was room for a short poem, she reasoned; and she used it.

On the back of the cardboard on which Belle Sharmer nylon stockings were folded, she began a poem with one of her favorite sayings: "I wish I had more time . . ."

On the back of another Belle Sharmer cardboard is "My Book of Life," a poem which shows she was not quite as brave as she often appeared to be: "I thought of smudgy pages/where the record was not clear;/and dreary lines of trouble/clouded over by doubt and fear."

The New Mexico winds and dust were frequent subjects, as in "The East Wind," in which she wrote: "The Wind from the East/Cares naught for me." In "Take Your Choice", she wrote: "Raging dust-storms now remind us,/If we wish to live we must/Wield our brooms with sternest purpose,/Or/Lie down and die and be buried in dust!!!"

Franc often had two or three poems a month published in such magazines as *Collier's, Saturday Evening Post* or *Ladies' Home Journal.*

Toward the end of her life, Franc was stricken with diabetes, cancer, for which she underwent a mastectomy, and crippling arthritis. Yet she continued to write as if driven by the knowledge of her own mortality. She once wrote: "And swiftly we pass twixt earth and sky,/the Wind, the dust, the leaf and I."

Franc's last effort was *Navajo Bird Tales*. The finished book was set for publication in August 1970. But by July she had been hospitalized and was daily growing weaker. By special request, an advance copy of the book was made available to her and airfreighted to Albuquerque. The book arrived at her bedside on July 23. Having lived to see her final book in print, she died on July 25, 1970.

———

Carol Cohea-O'Hearn is a professional writer and photo journalist with a decade of writing experience. She is a former newspaper reporter, magazine editor (New Mexico Stockman), *writer and currently a writer/researcher for a television news department. She has had historical and contemporary articles published in numerous magazines. She is presently working on a biographical history of women in New Mexico.*

Jan Barnhart is a library technical assistant at the University of New Mexico, responsible for the Coronado Room housing the New Mexican collection of the Special Collections Department. She has nearly a decade of work with New Mexico materials, has aided in the development of genealogical research tools, and has developed and presented lectures for classes and local organizations on various aspects of New Mexico history.

She is active politically, a Beta Sigma Phi, a member of various historical organizations, and is currently involved in the Women in New Mexico Project—a historical biography of New Mexico women.

BIBLIOGRAPHY

BOOKS

Mills, George. *Navajo Art and Culture*. Colorado Springs: Taylor Museum, 1959.

Newcomb, Franc Johnson. *Hosteen Klah: Navajo Medicine Man and Sand Painter*. Norman, Oklahoma: University of Oklahoma Press, 1964.

Newcomb, Franc Johnson. *Navajo Folk Tales*. Santa Fe, New Mexico: Museum of Navajo Ceremonial Art, 1967.

Newcomb, Franc Johnson. *Navajo Neighbors*. Norman, Oklahoma: University of Oklahoma Press, 1966.

NEWSPAPERS

Albuquerque Journal, April 13, 1969.
Albuquerque Tribune, April 21, 1969.
Santa Fe New Mexican, August 9, 1970.

MANUSCRIPTS

Women in New Mexico Archive (A.A.U.W.), University of New Mexico, General Library, Special Collections Department.

INTERVIEWS

Lynette Wilson, Albuquerque, New Mexico.

14

Horse Trader

by JOYCE ROACH

The early West also had its authentic two-gun girls. There was Sally Skull, Texan woman rancher and horse trader, who during the Civil War freighted cotton to Mexico to swap for supplies needed by the Confederacy.

N.S.Y.

At an early hour in the southwest region of Texas, when most frontier women, clad in nightgowns and wrappers, were rising to prepare the morning meal, Sally Skull was making ready for a trip across the border into Mexico. Inside her clothing she fastened a money belt. From her closet, the blue-eyed blonde could have selected rawhide bloomers and leather jacket, a long riding skirt and bonnet, or men's trousers—it all depended on her mood. A double holster was buckled low on her waist. A rifle and whip completed her ensemble.

Sally left her house on the Circle S ranch located near Banquette on the Agua Dulce Creek, and greeted her Mexican hands in their native Spanish. Redbuck, her horse, was restless under a fine silver-studded saddle. Sally shoved a rifle and whip in the saddle boot and called for her compañeros to make ready. All hit the trail for Mexico to buy and trade horses. Later there would be ranch work to do with both horses and cows.

Sally Skull's entry into the profession of ranching and horse trading occurred around age twenty-two. The actual facts of her life are briefly put, and these essentials appear to be true: She often rode astride, though sometimes sidesaddle; she wore men's clothing when working; she was a merciless killer when aroused, and it did not take much to arouse her; she admired Mexicans and the Mexican way of living; she drank and played poker expertly and possessed a vocabulary which would have scalded the hide off a dog. During the Civil War, when the Texas port was blockaded, Sally bossed freight wagons with supplies from East Texas to ports in Mexico. A Confederate marker dedicated to her stands at the intersection of U.S. Highway 183 and State Highway 202, two miles north of Refugio. The marker reads:

SALLY SCULL

Woman rancher, horse trader, champion "Cusser." Ranched NW of here. In Civil War Texas, Sally Scull (or Skull) freight wagons took cotton to Mexico to swap for guns, ammunition, medicine, coffee, shoes, clothing and other goods vital to the Confederacy. Dressed in trousers, Mrs. Scull bossed armed employees. Was sure shot with the rifle carried on her saddle or the two pistols strapped to her waist.

Of good family, she had children cared for in New Orleans school. Often visited them. Loved dancing. Yet during the war, did extremely hazardous "man's work." (1964)

Clearly, Sally was a woman with ideas whose time had not come. Women's liberation was a phrase she would never have recognized in her life time. That Sally was not typical of frontier females in the 1850s, however, did not appear to worry her much. She did not dress in the usual way or behave in the accepted pattern of domesticity. The frontier of Texas and the Mexican border area were dangerous places to live. Mexican bandits, renegades and Indians prowled the countryside and caused even grizzled frontiersmen to live carefully. Young women—or old ones, for that matter—did not travel about casually, if at all. Yet Sally thought nothing of crossing the border into Mexico, often unchaperoned and undismayed, pursuing her career as a horse trader. She asked no man's leave and needed no man's escort. How a Sally Skull came to be at all reflects the early, hard times in Texas and conditions peculiar to ranch country and ranch people who lived isolated lives and under rules made up by themselves as circumstances dictated.

Sally, known in childhood as Sarah Jane Newman, came to Texas about 1823 with her family from Pennsylvania when she was about six years old. Sally may have married for the first time at the age of thirteen. Sally's parents broke up the marriage, and the name of her first husband is lost to history. Sally first saw her second husband, Jesse Robinson, when he helped defend the family against an Indian attack in 1824. Jesse was twenty-three years old at the time, owned 1,100 acres and knew a lot about horses and horse racing. He later was a volunteer in the Army of the Republic of Texas and fought in the battle of San Jacinto. As a Texan, his credentials were outstanding.

Sally was still very young when she married Jesse, perhaps not more than fourteen. He was apparently a good deal older than she. They had three children: Alfred, Nancy and a baby who died in infancy. The couple was divorced around 1842. No one knows why; Sally may have been too high-spirited. She apparently lost no time in developing into a romping, stomping, pistol-toting, whip-popping virtuoso who ruled her kingdom alone.

Sally set herself up on a cattle and horse ranch in Nueces County, although no one knows how she came by the land and stock. Both the children may have stayed with their father after the divorce. In later life, Sally apparently had some contact with the children. In a letter to his wife in December of 1863, Alfred Robinson, Sally's son, mentions his mother: "I saw Mother at King's Ranch but had not time to speak to her but a few minutes." This was the famous King Ranch of today, known for the development of Santa Gertrudis cattle. Sally frequently stopped there for water; it was a popular watering hole between Brownsville and Corpus Christi.

Sally also saw her daughter and apparently did not get along with her. Their estrangement arose over a matter of dogs. The daughter, Nancy, kept several dogs whose presence she valued above humankind. One night when Sally went to visit, one of the dogs attacked her. Sally drew her pistol and shot and killed the animal. Nancy never forgave her mother, and Sally never visited her daughter again.

Like Chaucer's Wife of Bath, Sally may have had five husbands at the church door. Her second husband's interest in horses probably accounts for her entry into the horse trading business. She married again—some say as soon as two weeks after her divorce from Robinson, her second husband. In fact, she probably married three more times—once to a George Skull, who was also involved with horses in his work and by whose name Sally was ever after remembered. The name somehow seemed in keeping with Sally's reckless personality and wild ways. Watkins Doyle is mentioned as a fourth husband, and William Harsdoff as a fifth.

Aside from the scant facts, some of which are likely in error, there is much gossip. The gossip is every bit as interesting as the truth. Many stories have to do with Sally's guns. Ben Kinchlow, an old-timer, remembered seeing Sally put her finger through the trigger guard of a pistol, whirl it around, and then catch it and fire. And she could do it with either hand. On another occasion, a witness testified that Sally and an unidentified man faced each other and that the lady's gun spoke first. What the cause for gunplay was, nobody ever said, but the witness speculated that the victim was somebody who was better off dead. One family friend told that Sally's pistol was an old cap-and-ball six-shooter. The friend, Colonel Henry Perkins, reminisced in *Frontier Times* about a hog-killing expedition during which he observed Sally's marksmanship firsthand. Sally volunteered to capture a wild hog for Henry's mother and invited little Henry along. He climbed on double behind Sally declaring that the woman always rode side-saddle. After riding a distance down Agua Dulce Creek, Sally dismounted and found a bunch of wild hogs. When she came within shooting distance, Sally picked out a hog and felled it instantly with the first shot. Henry was impressed, but puzzled about how they were going to get the hog home. Sally solved that problem too. Tying a rope in the hog's mouth, she fastened the other end to her horse's tail and told Henry to climb on. After dragging the hog home, Sally proceeded to butcher the animal.

Henry Perkins further remembered that he longed to be an expert marksman and he chose not a man but rather Sally Skull to be his teacher. He said of her:

> She was one of the most courageous and fearless persons whom I ever met, kind hearted, true to her ideals, but very stern, and exhibited great strength of character. . . . People admired her yet they stood in awe of her, courting her favor rather than her displeasure. She was a woman with a wonder-

ful personality, and easily overcame obstacles with apparent ease.

Stories about Sally's methods of horse trading vary considerably depending on who is doing the remembering. Those who find fault with her behavior and dress tend to make her a notorious, even a villainous character. Sally's lifestyle was noticeably different, and it must have been easy to concoct stories about her. Dee Woods collected some of the tales for *Frontier Times*. It was said that Sally liked Mexican fiestas and that she danced and drank with her vaqueros. "Mustang Jane" may have been her nickname. Unpleasant jokes and stories circulated about her. One man suggested that Sally had married every nationality living in South Texas. Another replied that she had never married a Negro, but that the reason was that there were no black men living in the area at the time.

Rumors gathered around Sally and were disseminated by those who did not like her. One story told about how she shot one of her husbands during the Civil War. Another claimed she drowned a husband in a barrel of whiskey. Still another tale repeated by J. Frank Dobie in *Some Part of Myself,* told of Sally's going East with one of her husbands. When the husband was drowned in the San Antonio River, one of the Mexican hands asked if she wanted them to recover the body. Sally replied that she did not care about the body, but she would like to have the money belt her husband was wearing.

Sally Skull's name was often repeated in saloons. In addition to dancing and drinking, she is reputed to have gambled with all the leading men of the border, including John Wesley Hardin.

Mrs. Skull's friends leave a different impression of the woman's life. Sally's method of trading horses probably involved contacts in Mexico who knew she would come at fairly regular intervals. It is likely that Sally was a welcome guest in many of Mexico's haciendas. No doubt she was called upon to display her skill with whip and firearms. People along the way were sure to be impressed with her magnificent Redbuck, blanketed in bright colors, under a fine Mexican saddle trimmed in silver. It would have been no more than good business to dress flamboyantly, to be splendidly mounted, to enter fully into the life of fiesta or hacienda, and to give an account of herself in such a way as to show

how comfortably she fitted into and admired the Mexican way of life. Clearly, Sally was a woman to be trusted, and the large amount of money strapped to her waist must have been assurance that she would deal squarely.

Sally passed for the most part unmolested across the border during daylight and dark. Only once was there a rumor of any trouble. It was reported that Juan Cortina, a bandit and self-styled governor, put Sally in jail for a few days, but later released her. Border historians would be inclined to pay more attention to the report of Sally's confinement. Why did Cortina release her? Why didn't he kill her? Cortina was no ordinary, minor badman. He was more Texan than Mexican who had been raised on a ranch in Texas on land given to his family by a grant from the King of Spain. The Santa Rita Ranch was located a few miles up the Rio Grande from Brownsville. Cortina's mother lived as a cultured and refined widow whose lands and fortune were looked after and robbed by a German-American. Another, by the name of Still-man, was also instrumental in trying to take away the Cortina land, and Juan took up killing on a regular basis in order to pro-tect his property. Before it was over, Cortina was forced to flee across the border where he set himself up as a governor—but not before he captured two U.S. Army forts, two cities including Brownsville, $100,000 in gold, and drove off $500,000 in other people's livestock.

Cortina's hatred for Texans was deep and his bitterness was vented on all who passed his way. Why he allowed Sally Skull to cross his territory without serious incident is a matter for conjec-ture. It is possible that Juan and Sally knew each other well. Sally spent much of her time in and around Brownsville. She admired the Mexican lifestyle, spoke Spanish, hired only Mexicans to work for her, and always dealt squarely. This good relationship with her Mexican neighbors may have saved Sally's life and allowed her to go freely about her border business in Juan Cortina's territory.

Many stories circulated about Sally's vocabulary, which was re-spected almost as much as her guns. Once even a preacher had reason to be grateful for the Refugio woman's inspired exhorta-tions. Sally was hauling freight to Mexico when she encountered a two-horse buggy mired down in the road. The driver of the buggy, a preacher, tried to coax his team out of the mud by shaking his lines up and down on the animals' backs. The animals refused to pull. Sally watched for as long as she could stand it. Suddenly she rode forward and yelled: "Get out of here you god-damned-sons-a-bitches. Get the hell outta here!" The horses dragged the buggy and the startled preacher out of the way and proceeded hastily down the road. It was not long, however, before the preacher was stuck again. Not wasting any more time with his own feeble efforts, the preacher went back and got Sally. "Lady," he said. "Will you please speak to these horses again?"

Apparently, others remembered positive things about Sally. Crocks of butter delivered to a neighbor, material for a new dress for a little girl, defense of her Mexican hands, leading the way across a flooded river—all are a part of Sally's legend.

Some stories about Sally pertained to her positive attitude about her place in life and the rights she claimed. In his *Memoirs,* Judge W. L. Rea relates:

> I knew Sallie Scull by reputation and actually saw her one time when she came to Refugio. At that time she had two six-shooters hanging at the horn of her saddle, and she was riding astride. . . . She used to gamble with the men in the gambling houses here. . . . On one of her visits to this county she went to the Copano country and got up a herd of horses, and on her way back she met Jim Power, Jr., and Phil Power, who started to ride through her herd. She sharply told them, "Get around those horses; don't go through that herd," and they didn't. She never let anyone inspect her herds.

Only one fact of any consequence remains. Sally was last seen in 1866. She would have been only about forty-six years old at the time. The story circulated that she and Bill Harsdoff, her last husband, went to Mexico to trade. Bill was known as a hard character. He and Sally never did get along, and they were planning a divorce. They argued over a division of property and Sally informed him that he had no property coming to him. Supposedly, Bill ambushed and killed Sally with a shotgun, threw her body on a brush pile, and left the area.

That Sally Skull never achieved the national reputation of a Calamity Jane and that she remained only a border legend was probably her own fault. She was, to her own reckoning, a businesswoman. In spite of her reputation, based more on hearsay rather than facts, she must have ranged fairly close to home, busy at her work. There is no evidence that she deliberately sought notoriety either on a large or small scale. Hence she passed into the pages of folklore relatively unnoticed, more shadow than substance.

———————

Joyce Gibson Roach was raised in the rural community of Jacksboro, Texas, where she grew up hearing stories of frontier life. Later, after attending Texas Christian University from which she holds two degrees, her interests turned to writing about Western folklore. She has been president of the Texas Folklore Society, guest lecturer at universities and colleges on the subject of folklore and has published extensively in both scholarly and popular journals. Her book, The Cowgirls, *won the Western Writer's Spur award for the best book of nonfiction for 1977. Another book,* C.L. Sonnichsen: Folk Historian *will be published by Boise State Press in 1980. She has also contributed a chapter on ranch women for a book about cowboys soon to be published by the American Folklore Society.*

BIBLIOGRAPHY

BOOKS

Dobie, J. Frank. *Some Part of Myself*. Boston: Little, Brown, 1967.
Husen, Hobart. *A History of Refugio County*. Woodsboro, Texas: Rooke Foundation, 1955.

MAGAZINE ARTICLES

Perkins, Henry. "Sallie Skull." *Frontier Times*, November 1928.
Woods, Dee. "The Enigma of Juana Mesteña," *Frontier Times*, February 1966.

ARCHIVAL RESEARCH

Robinson, Jesse. File. Austin, Texas: State Library and Archives.

15

The Great Western

by NANCY HAMILTON

When her first husband enlisted for the Mexican War at Jefferson Barracks in Missouri, Sarah A. Bowman also joined as a laundress and cook. During the seven-day Mexican bombardment of Fort Brown, she prepared and served meals to the defenders at their guns. As the Americans advanced, Sarah, who had become known as "The Great Western," set up hotels catering to the military at Matamoros, Monterrey and Saltillo, then at El Paso. She later operated the first restaurant at Fort Yuma.

N.S.Y.

The first hotelkeeper of record in El Paso, Texas, had a commanding presence: something over six feet tall, powerful, intimidating to troublemakers, and equipped with an impressive war record. She was The Great Western: a remarkable woman who had dodged bullets while feeding the battling Americans at Fort Brown in the early days of the Mexican War, and who later carried casualties to safety—or at least nursed their wounds—at the Buena Vista battlefield. Her *nom de guerre* is believed to have been inspired by a huge steamer, the largest ship of its kind in the 1830s. Her true name is somewhat uncertain; though she always answered to Sarah, her surname appeared variously as Boginnis, Borginnis, Bourget, Bourdette, Bourjette or Bouget.

Born in Clay County, Missouri, in 1812, Sarah was married at the time troops were enlisting for the Mexican War. Her first husband joined a regiment at Jefferson Barracks near St. Louis. She quickly attached herself to the Army as a laundress and cook, signed up by Captain George Lincoln of Worcester, Massachusetts, who was to remain her friend until his death at Buena Vista. Brantz Mayer's 1848 history of the war said she was the wife of a man from the "far west" who joined the gallant Seventh. Three laundresses were allowed to draw rations in each company and were required to wash for the soldiers at a price set by a group of officers.

Sarah and her husband arrived at Corpus Christi, where General Zachary Taylor took his army in July 1845. A vast stretch of beach was dotted with neat rows of tents, almost as far as the eye could see. Although she was technically a laundress, her main work was keeping a mess for the officers, who still included Captain Lincoln. When Taylor moved his army south to the Rio Grande, she was among the few women who traveled overland with the troops; most of them, including Sarah's ailing husband, were sent by boat with the sick soldiers to Point Isabel. Sarah, however, felt duty-bound to the young men of her mess who, she said, "must have someone to take care of them on their toilsome march." She bought a cart and loaded it with luggage, cooking utensils and supplies. Mounting a donkey, she took whip in hand and gave a respectable imitation of a veteran teamster. Her boarders remained well fed.

Upon reaching the lagoon of Arroyo Colorado, near the Rio Grande, the Americans heard some elements of Mexican cavalry dashing around in the thick brush which hid them from sight. When General William Jenkins Worth began to test them with the Eighth Infantry, Sarah was among the first to cross the river in pursuit: "If the general would give me a stout pair of tongs [slang for trousers], I would wade the river and whip every scoundrel Mexican that dared show his face at the opposite side!"

The Seventh Infantry stayed behind at a new unfinished installation, Fort Texas, when General Taylor moved a force of about 600 to secure the supply depot at Point Isabel on May 1, 1846. Sarah was among 10 women and a defense unit of 50 men from the Seventh assigned to hold the earthen fort that Taylor had ordered built across the river from Matamoros. After the departure of the larger force, the Mexicans began a bombardment that was to last a week. They fired a battery of seven guns, eight-pounders. The usual stillness of the valley was punctuated by the thunder of cannon, the pealing of the Matamoros church bells, and the *vivas* of the townspeople cheering their soldiers. The Americans returned fire briefly until the enemy fire was silenced for a time during that first day of attack. The women were supposed to stay within the protection of storage magazines, sewing sandbags from the infantrymen's tents. Sarah refused to hide and, oblivious to gunfire, cooked breakfast in the open courtyard, serving it on time complete with hot coffee. Ranks were ignored as the men lined up for their fare. Sarah personally served the men who could not leave their guns. The shelling resumed and continued for hours. Throughout the day she continued to serve the men by producing a savory soup for dinner and asking no pay for it.

During the seven-day bombardment, Sarah was always at her post, preparing meals that were served on time and as tasty as she could manage with a dwindling supply of goods. On the second night of battle, she was among those writing letters to their loved ones. Her note to her husband at Point Isabel advised him that she fully expected the garrison to sustain itself and only regretted that he could not be with her. Her early request for a musket and ammunition had been turned down.

By May 8 ammunition was so low the men were ordered to fire only if the enemy came within 80 yards of the fort. Awaiting the inevitable final assault, the Americans were ready to give up when they heard the thunder of heavy artillery in the distance. Sarah's instinct had been correct: the battle would not be lost. Taylor's forces, having won the battles of Palo Alto and Resaca de la Palma, were coming to save the fort. The Mexicans, who had been moving in, retreated across the river. The wounded Major Brown died on May 9, and the fort was renamed in his honor. It later was to serve as a key to Texas defense lines along the border until the Civil War.

The formal declarations of war came after this battle. President Polk signed the U.S. bill on May 13; Mexico's was not proclaimed until July 1. Taylor took Matamoros on May 18 and began his advance up the Rio Grande on July 6. He occupied Camargo on July 14. While the Americans occupied Matamoros, The Great Western evidently set up the first in her series of hotels which were as memorable to the military as were her battle exploits.

It was at a June banquet in Matamoros that she was saluted as "the heroine of Fort Brown" and the "American Maid of Orleans." Lieutenant Braxton Bragg, later a general in the Confederate Army, was toastmaster for the occasion at which General Taylor was being honored. After many traditional toasts, he proposed one to Sarah, whereupon all the men jumped to their feet with loud cheers to honor her valor.

In September Taylor entered Monterrey; he took the city on September 24, after a four-day battle. The Great Western transferred her hospitality to that city temporarily by starting the American House. Monterrey was a popular town with the American soldiers, with a population of about 9,000. The military camp at Walnut Springs, some five miles from the town, was in a pleasant grove of trees with plenty of water available. Two mountains towered above the picturesque city, where the bishop's palace and the cathedral were popular with sightseers, but no more so than the American House. The occupation troops remained there until summer of 1848. Hotel prices ran $6.00 per week for room and board for one person, $5.00 for a horse. Samuel Chamberlain, whose book, *My Confessions,* details his war experiences, painted a watercolor of The Great Western, whom he identified as Sarah Borginnis, standing before a mirrored bar in Monterrey. She wore a long dress with bare shoulders revealing her more than ample bosom. (A Texan in the war reported: "You can imagine how tall she was, she could stand flatfooted and drop these little sugarplums right into my mouth, that way.") She had long dark hair, parted and brought back in curls that fell to her shoulders, large dark eyes, and wore as jewelry a cross at her neck and a bracelet on her left arm. In her right hand is something that appears to be a pistol. While Chamberlain's drawings tend to make all women look somewhat alike, Sarah dominated this picture; none of the ten other persons in the barroom could begin to attract the attention she commanded by her bearing. By this time Sarah's husband apparently had been killed in the Battle of Monterrey or in another confrontation soon afterward.

Saltillo was occupied without opposition on November 16, 1846. About twice as large as Monterrey, it also was a popular town with the American soldiers. The cathedral bells sounded in the narrow cobblestoned streets. The adobe homes with their barred windows looked like jails to the Americans, who camped outside the town. Their favorite diversions were village dances or visits to places of entertainment such as Sarah's new American House.

Dr. Frederick A. Wislizenus, a naturalist who was gathering data on northern Mexico, had chosen the unfortunate period of 1846–47 for his research. He arrived in Saltillo May 23, 1847, finding it a delightful town of fewer than twenty thousand on the slope of a hill overlooking a wide plain: "I stopped for some hours," he wrote, "in the hotel of the 'Great Western,' kept by the celebrated vivandiere, honored with that *nom de guerre,* and whose fearless behavior during the battle of Buena Vista was highly praised; she dressed many wounded soldiers on that day, and even carried them out of the thickest fight."

The two-day Battle of Buena Vista had begun on February 22, 1847. A Texan recalled that during the action, a regiment of Indiana volunteers was pursued by the Mexicans and some fled the seven miles north from Buena Vista to Saltillo, where they encountered The Great Western. She was, he said, six feet two, "a great nurse and would always get up at any time of night to get one something to eat—kept a sort of restaurant." One of the soldiers, so terrified of the Mexicans that he outran a jackrabbit getting to Saltillo, rushed to her establishment, described as "sort of headquarters for everybody," and came running in breathless, telling The Great Western that General Taylor had been defeated. "You damned son of a bitch!" she remonstrated. "There ain't Mexicans enough in Mexico to whip old Taylor. You just spread that report and I'll beat you to death."

Her great friend, Captain Lincoln, had been killed at Buena Vista. She paid $250 to the Kentucky Regiment for the fine white horse he was riding when he died. She attended to its needs herself, although she had a staff of Negro and Mexican servants.

Too many of her customers must have been returning to camp tipsy, for Sarah became the subject of Special Order No. 517, issued June 17, 1847 at Buena Vista headquarters and signed by Irvin McDowell, later Union commander at the First Battle of Bull Run. "By command of Brig. Gen. Wool," it read, "Mrs. Bouget having by permission of the General established a boarding house in the vicinity of the camp for the accommodation of officers, it is to be well understood that this permission is to be continued on condition that there shall not be a drop of liquor of any kind sold or kept at the establishment."

Fortunately for her thirsty clients, the war had nearly run its course. The Treaty of Guadalupe Hidalgo was signed in Mexico on February 2, 1848, and was ratified by the U.S. Senate on March 10.

With the fighting at an end, The Great Western collected her goods in three large Chihuahua wagons and headed northwest. She was on the road to Chihuahua when she encountered Major Lawrence P. Graham's squadron of Second Dragoons who had been ordered from Monterrey to California. She asked permission of Colonel Washington to join the expedition. He referred her to Major Rucker, who told her regulations required that she be married to one of the men in order to accompany the unit as a laundress.

Giving a snappy quasi-military salute, she replied, "All right, Major, I'll marry the whole Squadron and you thrown in but what I go along." Riding along the line, she called, "Who wants a wife with $15,000 and the biggest leg in Mexico! Come, my beauties, don't all speak at once—who is the lucky man?"

A fellow named Davis of Company E took her offer, saying, "I have no objections to making you my wife, if there is a clergyman here to tie the knot." His bride-to-be laughed. "Bring your blanket to my tent tonight and I will learn you to tie a knot that will satisfy you, I reckon!" And she was recorded on the company books as a laundress and drew rations. She was one of six women in the military group—two other wives, a servant girl, and the temporary mistress of Sam Chamberlain.

They had camped on a branch of the Rio Yaqui after leaving Chihuahua City when Sarah Borginnis Davis changed her mind about her choice of husband. In a group of New Mexico traders, she spotted a man whose size and strength were compatible with her own. Her first glimpse of him was while he was bathing, and she would not rest until she met him and told him of her "love" for his impressive proportions. He succumbed to her charms, and she ousted Davis from her tent in favor of the new Adonis.

A few months after this incident, The Great Western turned up in El Paso. She arrived without her "husband," since Major Lawrence P. Graham's squadron of Second Dragoons had been ordered to leave Mexico in July 1848 to head for California. Ap-

parently Sarah had become ill en route and stopped at Chihuahua
City to recover. By early 1849 she was able to move northward,
following the centuries-old trade route between Mexico City and
Santa Fe that led to the Pass of the North.

The town of Paso del Norte, which lay on the Mexican side of
the Rio Grande, the newly designated international boundary, had
about 4,000 residents. The lush river valley traced a startling
green line through the barren desert, cutting between thrusts of
limestone and granite mountains to form the pass. Since the first
Spaniards had gone north in the sixteenth century, the valley had
become an increasingly important network of farming villages.
The Pueblo uprising of 1680 in New Mexico had brought fleeing
Spaniards and Indians to the pass; some returned north, but many
stayed on in villages that are still there.

In the months after the Mexican War, the valley was taking on
a new character—but not entirely due to the terms of the peace
treaty. The movement West was beginning in earnest. Pioneer
travelers were trying to reach California; merchants were looking
for a better way to get from San Antonio to the West; soldiers
were being ordered to tiny new posts along the new boundary line
with Mexico, both to enforce the possession of the land and to
keep the Indians from molesting the settlers.

Paso del Norte (now Ciudad Juárez) and the smaller villages
on both sides of the river came into hard times. The residents
lacked military protection and were at the mercy of Indian raiders
who drove off their stock; they limited agriculture mainly to what
they could plant within running distance of their adobe buildings.
What little they were able to produce in the way of food was in
demand by the emigrants who came in an increasing tide, stopping
in the valley after the long journey across a nearly waterless
desert.

According to the travelers who remembered her, The Great
Western set up her hostelry on the American side of the river, opposite Paso del Norte. At that time, the settlement was a cluster of
adobe buildings on the ranch of Juan María Ponce de León, who
had large landholdings on both sides of the river. The buildings
were located in the heart of the present downtown district of El
Paso, along El Paso Street (then called the Alameda) which led
to the river crossing point where small boats ferried passengers to
the Mexican side.

Now that the river separated his landholdings under two flags, Ponce de León was uncertain about how long he could expect to keep his U.S. land—treaty promises notwithstanding. Benjamin Franklin Coons, a trader and merchant from St. Louis, solved his problem by offering to buy the ranch. Orders had been given by the War Department on November 7, 1848, to establish a military post at the location, and Coons may have figured on turning a profit in a short time. When the Army units reached the valley the following September, Coons was ready for them with several structures for lease, along with six acres of land. He began putting up more buildings for his own trade and business enterprises; among them a tavern, a warehouse, corrals and other adobes west of the post.

It is not known whether The Great Western had heard the Army was headed for the pass, but a location with soldiers acted as a natural magnet for her. She had gained plenty of experience during the war as a cook and hotel hostess at Matamoros, Monterrey and Saltillo. Some of her former patrons were among travelers to the valley while she was there.

The earliest report of her presence in El Paso came from John S. "Rip" Ford who, with Robert S. Neighbors, had been commissioned by merchants of San Antonio and Austin to determine a trade route to El Paso. Their journey in March and April of 1849 took them through what is now San Angelo, across the Pecos River at Horsehead Crossing, and along the southern pass of the Guadalupe Mountains. Their route, later dubbed the Upper Road, was a step toward improving the way West. Ford's description echoed somewhat the words of the soldiers who had known her during the war; Sarah's hourglass figure and impressive height were unforgettable. "On our side," he wrote, "an American woman, known as the Great Western, kept a hotel. She was very tall, large and well made. She had the reputation of being somewhat the roughest fighter on the Rio Grande; and was approached in a polite, if not humble manner by all of us, this writer in particular."

A member of Ford and Neighbors' party reported on his return to Austin that the El Paso area had "upward of four thousand emigrants with twelve hundred or fifteen hundred wagons. . . . Provisions were very scarce and dear, in fact not to be had in the neighborhood in sufficient quantities to supply the demand, and the Mexicans were beginning to be alarmed at the prospect of being eaten out." Even the ingenuity of The Great Western for meeting adversity must have been taxed to keep her boarders fed in such times.

Also in April, Lieutenant Henry Chase Whiting, a topographical engineer who had been exploring the San Antonio–El Paso route, made a journal entry about The Great Western. He and two friends planned to cross the river to Paso del Norte. As they set out the first person they met, passing in a dugout, was "the celebrated Great Western. Never was anyone more delighted at the sight of American officers than she appeared. Her masculine arms lifted us one after another off our feet."

Several of the emigrants wrote about meeting her. C. C. Cox, who arrived in the valley on June 27, 1849, said that Coons had recently purchased the property on the American side of the river, where he operated a large store. "Among the residents of this place is numbered 'The Great Western,' a female notorious in the late war," he noted. Lewis B. Harris, another Forty-niner, described her as standing six feet one inch tall, well proportioned, and having "treated us with much kindness."

Why did The Great Western leave El Paso? Possibly the problems of trying to operate a hotel became too great because of the flood of emigrants. Vagabonds were forcibly taking food and livestock from valley residents and causing disorder as food came into short supply. The Army's use of Coons's buildings may have displaced her from her hotel. Or she may have made up with her husband and followed his Company E of the Second Dragoons upriver to Socorro, New Mexico, where they were stationed in August 1849. Others speculate that she joined a group of Forty-niners and headed West.

The Great Western next turned up in Yuma, then known as Arizona City, as the first American woman settler and operator of the first restaurant. Her affection for the place was mixed; each time she left she returned, and most of her remaining years were spent at this town she once said was removed from Hell by just one thin sheet of sandpaper.

In the early 1850s Captain James Hobbs told of meeting her, "a very large Irish woman," and recalled that he had seen her earlier at Saltillo where he had gone with Colonel Alexander William Doniphan. "She was noted as a camp follower in the Mexican war," he said, "was liked universally for her kind motherly ways, and at the battle of Buena Vista busied herself in making cartridges for the army."

In about 1856, Jeff Ake encountered her at Patagonia, Arizona, where she kept a saloon: "They called her old Great Western. She packed two six-shooters, and they all said she shore could use 'em, that she had killed a couple of men in her time. She was a hell of a good woman."

Another war veteran, Lieutenant Sylvester Mowry, wrote home to Providence, Rhode Island, in 1855–56 from Fort Yuma that his young Mexican mistress lived with The Great Western but spent her nights with him:

The Great Western, you remember don't you, is the woman who distinguished herself so much at the Fort Brown bombardment just before the battles of Palo Alto and Resaca. She has been with the Army twenty years and was brought up here where she keeps the officers' mess. Among her other good qualities she is an admirable "pimp." She used to be a splendid looking woman and has done "*good service*" but is too old for that now.

Jeff Ake and his family were at Fort Yuma in 1861 when the captain warned them that they must be ready in three days if they wanted to travel with the protection of the army column. Their party, which did not get ready that soon, included several well-known residents of Yuma, among them The Great Western, whom his dad called "the greatest whore in the West." She sent her girls back to Mexico when she left town.

By 1860, even though her looks may have been fading, Sarah had taken another husband: Albert J. Bowman, a native of Germany. Fifteen years younger than she, he was an upholsterer. Despite her unsavory reputation, The Great Western had won the friendship of a priest in Yuma, Father Figueroa, who said she was a "good hearted woman, good soul, old lady of great experience who spoke the Spanish language fluently."

The Civil War did not take her away from Yuma for very long. By April 1862 she was back, according to a member of the California Column, George Henry Pettis, who saw her there.

She was fifty-four when she died on December 22, 1866, at the fort. She had a military funeral with Catholic rites and became the only woman buried in the post cemetery. Her grave was marked

"Sarah A. Bowman" when her body and others buried there were removed and reinterred at the Presidio National Cemetery in San Francisco. While legend has suggested that The Great Western was breveted a colonel and received an Army pension, her most diligent biographer, Edward S. Wallace, was unable to find evidence to that effect. Yet many a hero or heroine has been so honored for far less than the "good woman" achieved in battle.

When it comes to pioneer women of the West, the stereotype is a tiny lady in a calico dress and sunbonnet, surrounded by a flock of children, perhaps holding a rifle. The Great Western, who could literally sweep men off their feet, never fit this mold—hardly at six feet two!—and apparently never became a mother. She knew how to meet the hardships of desert life, six-shooter at the ready, but she was better known for her generous heart and loyalty to friends. Through all the references to her in diaries, letters and journals runs a theme that could have served as epitaph: "She was a good woman."

Alas, The Great Western was not the kind to be memorialized. She was too big, too rough, "not nice." Her coat of arms might have shown crossed serving spoons over a kettle at Fort Brown, or the steamship that inspired her nickname, determinedly plying the ocean when men thought it folly to move without sails. Any monument to her could not adequately express her brand of bravery in serving soldiers in battle, or her style of hospitality for them after the firing stopped.

––––––––––––

Nancy Hamilton, a longtime newspaper writer in El Paso, has spent twelve years in educational public relations and is an accredited member of the Public Relations Society of America. She is assistant director of the University of Texas at El Paso News Service, assistant editor of the university's quarterly magazine, NOVA, *editor of the El Paso Historical Society quarterly journal,* Password, *and a columnist for the Western Writers of America magazine,* The Roundup.

BIBLIOGRAPHY

Bieber, Ralph P. and Bender, A. B. *Exploring Southwestern Trails, 1846–1854*. Glendale: Arthur H. Clark Co., 1938.

Bloom, John Porter. "'Johnny Gringo' in Northern Mexico, 1846–1847." *Arizona and the West*, vol. 4 no. 3 (Autumn 1962).

Buchanan, A. Russell (ed.). "George Washington Traheur: Texan Cowboy Soldier from Mier to Buena Vista." *Southwestern Historical Quarterly*, LVIII (July 1954).

Chamberlain, Samuel Emery. *My Confession, Written and Illustrated*. New York: Harper, 1956.

Hail, Marshall. "New Research Throws Light on El Paso's First 'Anglo' Settler." *El Paso Herald-Post*, October 24, 1956.

Long, Grace. *The Anglo-American Occupation of the El Paso District*. Unpublished M.A. thesis. University of Texas, 1931.

Martin, Mabelle Eppard. "From Texas to California in 1849: Diary of C. C. Cox." *Southwestern Historical Quarterly*, XXIX (October 1925).

Mayer, Brantz. *History of the War Between Mexico and the United States with a Preliminary View of Its Origin*. New York: Wiley and Putnam, 1848.

McCall, George A. *New Mexico in 1850: A Military View*. Norman: University of Oklahoma Press, 1968.

O'Neil, James B. *They Die But Once: The Story of a Tejano*. New York: Knight Publications, 1935.

Sonnichsen, C. L. *Pass of the North*. El Paso: Texas Western Press, 1968.

Strickland, Rex W. *Six Who Came to El Paso*. El Paso: Texas Western Press, 1963.

Wallace, Edward S. *The Great Reconnaissance*. Boston: Little, Brown and Co., 1955.

Weems, John Edward. *To Conquer a Peace*. Garden City: Doubleday, 1974.

Wislizenus, Frederick A. *A Tour to Northern Mexico in 1846–1847*. Glorieta, N.M.: The Rio Grande Press, 1969.

16

Justice of the Peace

by MAE URBANEK

The earliest successful American crusader for women's rights was Esther Morris. At a tea party in her log cabin at South Pass City, Wyoming, in August 1869, she planted the seed that quickly ripened into a bill signed into law that December. It gave the women of her Territory full rights of franchise and made Wyoming the first in the Union to give women the vote. The following year, Esther was appointed the nation's first woman justice of the peace.

N.S.Y.

Esther Morris's tea party in her log-cabin home in South Pass City, Wyoming, started the women of the world on their successful struggle for the ballot and for equality in all financial fields. It was August 1869, and the men of Carter County were going to choose their representative to the first Wyoming Territorial Legislature. South Pass City, famous in trailblazing history, was at that time a booming gold-mining town of some 5,000 people.

Among the dozen or so invited guests at the tea party were the two candidates for the legislature. One of them later reported: "Mrs. Morris arose and stated the object of the meeting. She said, 'There are present two opposing candidates for the Legislature of our new territory, one of whom is sure to be elected and we desire here and now to receive from them a public pledge that whichever one is elected will introduce and work for the passage of an act conferring upon women of our new territory the right of suffrage.'" Both men pledged their support.

Colonel William H. Bright, Democrat, was elected and traveled to Cheyenne by stagecoach. Because of Esther Morris's request and his pledge to her, Colonel Bright sat in his hotel room the night before the opening of the legislature, and by the light of a kerosene lamp drafted a document that made world history: "That every woman of the age of twenty-one residing in this territory may at any election to be holden under the laws thereof, cast her vote. And her rights of the election franchise, and to hold office, shall be the same under the election law of the Territory as those of the electors."

At the session next morning, Colonel Bright was made president of the Territorial Council (Senate) and in due time read his revolutionary bill. Of the 104 bills presented in that historic session, the women's suffrage bill was the most controversial and far reaching. After a week of debate, the House passed it 7 to 4 and the Council 6 to 3. Territorial Governor John A. Campbell mulled it over in his mind for another five days before he finally signed it into law on December 10, 1869. That night the first women in the world to win equal suffrage were toasted at many Cheyenne parties. One lawmaker, half-joking, half-serious raised his glass and said, "To the lovely ladies: once our superiors, now our equals."

Women of Great Britain cabled congratulations: "To the women of Wyoming on the triumph you have won for all women by the emancipation of the women of your state from political serfdom."

King William of Prussia cabled congratulations to President Grant on this "evidence of progress, enlightenment and civil liberty in America."

From the 1869 session, Governor Campbell also signed three other bills protecting and upgrading the status of women. They could now own property in their own name, earn money and keep it for the first time in history, and could retain guardianship of her minor children if they were widowed. Women made up only one sixth of the population in this wilderness territory, but those women had endured the same hardships, shouldered responsibilities, and displayed the same strength and courage as their husbands in pioneering and settling this harsh new land. The legis-

lators recognized this, and they were also aware that Wyoming
needed to attract more women from the East and the Midwest.
They hoped that this bold new declaration of rights would appeal
to them.

It may have been more politics than chivalry that got women
the right to vote in Wyoming, but when Chief Justice John H.
Howe addressed the women in the first "mixed jury," he set the
standards for courtroom conduct and assured the women: "You
shall not be driven by sneers, jeers and insults from the temple of
justice, as your sisters have from some of the medical colleges of
the land. The strong hand of the law shall protect you. It will be a
sorry day if any man forgets courtesies due every American lady
and paid by every American gentleman by act or endeavor to
deter you from rights which the law has invested in you." Six
women were empaneled for that jury in March 1870, and they
added another page to the history of women's suffrage. They met
in the courtroom in Cheyenne and were led by Mrs. Martha Sy-
mons–Boise Atkinson, the first woman bailiff. Justice Howe later
commented that the eyes of the world were upon them in this pioneer effort of proving that women were capable of making decisions and protecting themselves from long standing injustices.

Meanwhile, back in South Pass City, Justice of the Peace P. S.
Barr promptly resigned, sarcastically saying that a woman could
better fill the office. To his amazement, the county commissioners
took the judge at his word. On Saint Valentine's Day 1870, they
appointed Esther Morris the world's first female justice of the
peace.

Esther Morris didn't really want the office, but she felt obliged
to prove this test of woman's ability in settling matters of justice
and holding office. She held court seated on a slab bench in her
log cabin and ordered all "shooting irons" be left outside. She
wore a calico dress with a green necktie and matching ribbons in
her hair. Around her shoulders was a worsted shawl to keep out
the chill of a Wyoming winter.

Her first case involved Mr. Barr, who wished he had not resigned and refused to give up his docket. Mrs. Morris ruled that
she herself was involved; therefore she had no jurisdiction. This
shrewd and wise decision made her popular with the audience that
had crowded into the log cabin "courtroom" to witness the actions
of a woman who dared take over a man's role in being justice of

the peace. Things hadn't been too peaceful in South Pass City of late. Indian trouble around the area had resulted in several people being killed and many more wounded. Governor Campbell had troops dispatched and rifles and ammunition were issued to civilians in South Pass City so they could defend themselves.

John Morris, local saloonkeeper and husband to the new justice, objected to her accepting the office and made a scene in the courtroom. Esther Morris fined him for contempt of court, and when he refused to pay his fine, she sent him to jail. "Justice first, then after that the law" was Esther's motto. When lawyers quarreled, she often said, "Behave yourselves, boys."

During her eight and a half months in office, Justice Morris rendered seventy legal decisions; not one of them was reversed in a higher court. She held court and conducted weddings, even marrying one scandalous couple that had been living together for two years without benefit of clergy or the law. She tried all kinds of cases, from claim jumping to assault. An attorney who practiced before her court testified: "To pettifoggers she showed no mercy, but her decisions were always just."

Mrs. Morris did not take office again. When she surrendered the docket of her court to her successor, she said, "Circumstances have transpired to make my position of Justice of the Peace a test of woman's ability to hold public office and I feel that my work has been satisfactory, although I have often regretted that I was not better qualified to fill the position. Like all pioneers, I have labored more in faith and hope."

Wyoming women picked up the challenge and went on to responsible positions in government. Mary G. Bellamy was the first to be elected to a state legislature and Nellie Tayloe Ross was the first woman governor. Since 1962 Thrya Thompson has served as Wyoming's Secretary of State, the first woman in the nation to be elected to that position.

Esther McQuigg Morris was born at Spencer, New York, in 1814. Orphaned at the age of eleven, she earned her living doing housework for a neighbor. At an early age she started a millinery shop and satisfied her love of the beautiful and original by decorating hats. Later, a flower garden on the bleak hillsides of rough and rugged South Pass was to add that bit of beauty in her life. Always aware of people's needs, and human rights, Esther worked as ardently in the antislavery movement as she was later to work for women's suffrage.

In 1841 she married Artemus Slack, a railroad man, and by him had one son. Slack had property in Illinois, and after his early death, Esther went there to settle his estate. She became keenly aware then that women had no rights—even to their deceased husband's property, or to their own children. Incensed, she vowed to devote her life to fighting for women's rights. In 1845 she married John Morris, a storekeeper in Illinois. Some twenty years later, Esther and her three sons followed John to the Wyoming goldfields at South Pass City, where he had set up a business as saloonkeeper.

Esther Morris was a large, plainspoken woman with a confident bearing, ready wit and great human sympathy. She had a cheerful disposition and made friends quickly. A good nurse, she became an important member of the community where "law and order" and medical help were three stagecoach days away. Around her log cabin was the flower garden, a colorful note in a dusty mining town.

William Bright and his young bride were friends of John and Esther, and they often discussed politics as the four of them sat around a fireplace in the Morris cabin. Bright believed that women were better qualified to vote than the recently emancipated Negro men. He willingly took up Esther's tea-party challenge and wrote the bill that was to become a law and earn for Wyoming the title of "Equality State."

South Pass City did not prove to be the bonanza so many prospectors hoped it would be, so the miners drifted on to other boom towns. The Morris family moved to Laramie in 1872 and later to Cheyenne, where John died in 1876.

When Susan B. Anthony, president of the American Suffrage Association, visited Cheyenne in the early 1890s, Esther Morris presided at the public meeting given in her honor. The fight for women's rights went on across the nation, with the Western states always in the lead. In 1892, when she was seventy-eight years old, Esther Morris was elected a delegate to the National Republican Convention in Cleveland, Ohio. It was an exciting moment for her when she could officially cast Wyoming's votes for Benjamin Harrison.

Esther spent a serene and happy old age among friends and relatives. When she died on April 2, 1902, her son published the following eulogy: "Her quest for truth in the world is ended. Her mission in life has been fulfilled. The work she did for the elevation of womankind will be told in the years to come, when the purpose will be better understood."

The log cabin at South Pass City has since been restored. A stone cairn reads: "Home and office site of Esther Hobart Morris, first woman Justice of the Peace in the world. February 14, 1870. Author with W. H. Bright of the first equal suffrage law, December 10, 1869."

Following Wyoming's example, the rest of the states, one by one, adopted equal suffrage laws. In 1920 the Nineteenth Amendment to the Constitution of the United States made women's suffrage nationwide. Esther Morris had sparked the movement at a tea party in South Pass City, Wyoming, fifty-one years before.

In 1955 the Wyoming legislature chose Esther Hobart Morris as the person whose statue should fill the Wyoming niche in Statuary Hall in the Capitol Building, Washington, D.C. This nine-foot bronze statue in lasting tribute to Esther Morris, "Mother of Equal Rights," was carved by sculptor Dr. Avard Fairbanks and unveiled on March 15, 1960.

Through all descriptions of Esther Morris runs the hint of steel. She was a person who took charge. Without being in any way unfeminine, she was one of the West's indomitable women.

———————

Mae Urbanek was born in Denver, Colorado, grew up on a western North Dakota farm, and presently lives in Wyoming. She now has ten published books about Wyoming: two novels, Almost Up Devil's Tower *and* Second Man; *two biographies:* Chief Washakie *and* Memoirs of Andrew McMaster; Songs of the Sage, *Wyoming poetry;* Uncovered Wagon, *homestead tales;* Know Wyoming, *a bibliography of literature about the state;* Wyoming Place Names *and* Ghost Trails of Wyoming, *historical; and* Wyoming Wonderland, *a history.*

BIBLIOGRAPHY

American Guide Series, WPA. *Wyoming*. New York: Oxford University Press, 1941.

Beach, Cora M. *Women of Wyoming*. Casper, Wyo.: S. E. Boyer & Company, 1927.

Bragg, Bill. *Wyoming's Wealth*. Basin, Wyo.: Big Horn Books, 1976.

Linford, Velma. *Wyoming, Frontier State*. Denver: Old West Publishing Company, 1947.

Whittenburg, Clarice. *Wyoming's People*. Denver: Old West Publishing Company, 1958.

Williams, Beryl M. *This Is Wyoming . . . Listen*. Basin, Wyo.: Big Horn Books, 1977.

Newspaper articles. Wyoming Historical Department, Cheyenne, Wyoming.

17

Reformer

by PAMELA HERR

Rising above an unhappy, blighted childhood in New York State, Eliza Farnham set out upon a remarkable career. In 1849, a widow with two young sons, she sailed around the Horn to California where she developed a run-down ranch into a paying concern, taught school and became an ardent crusader for much-needed prison reform and for women's suffrage.

N.S.Y.

"She has nerves enough to explore alone the seven circles of Dante's Hell," a friend said of Eliza Farnham, a thirty-four-year-old widow who had become the object of gossip and whispered innuendo from New York to the gold-rush port of San Francisco. Author, lecturer, prison reformer, and ardent advocate of the superiority of the female sex, Eliza Farnham was a spirited and unconventional woman who created controversy wherever she went.

Her notoriety began one cold February day in 1849, the first year of the California gold rush, when she issued a remarkable circular in New York City. Beneath a sketch of a sailing vessel labeled "Ship Angelique," bold letters proclaimed: "CALIFORNIA ASSOCIATION OF AMERICAN WOMEN." Scanning the curious broadside, New Yorkers learned that Eliza Farnham's husband had died in California the previous September, and she planned to go there to settle his affairs. At the same time, "having a desire to accomplish some greater good" by her journey, she announced an extraordinary emigration scheme.

"Among the many privations and deteriorating influences to which the thousands who are flocking thither will be subjected, one of the greatest is the absence of woman, with all her kindly cares and powers." Since the presence of women "would be one of the surest checks upon many of the evils" of the gold rush, she proposed to organize a group of one hundred or more "intelligent, virtuous and efficient women" to emigrate to California. Requirements for participation were stringent: only women twenty-five or over were eligible, and each applicant was required to submit "testimonials of education, character, capacity, &c." from her clergyman or other town dignitary, as well as pay $250 for her passage. "A spacious vessel," the packet ship *Angelique,* had been chartered for the voyage and would set forth on the six-month, 13,000-mile journey around Cape Horn about April 12.

Eliza Farnham's unusual proposal was endorsed by a prominent group of reformers, whose names appeared at the bottom of the circular. Among them were newspaperman Horace Greeley, poet-editor William Cullen Bryant, the charismatic preacher Henry Ward Beecher and writer Catharine M. Sedgwick.

Soon after the broadside appeared, Catharine Sedgwick confided her opinion of Eliza Farnham in a letter to a friend. "She is, of all women created , . . the fittest for the enterprise. She has the physical strength and endurance, sound sense and philanthropy, earnestness, and a coolness that would say 'I know!' if an angel were sent to tell her the secrets of the upper world."

Despite such support, Eliza's plan met with smirks and knowing smiles, rumor and cruel gossip. Lurking behind the laughter and talk was the suspicion that grave, bookish Eliza was a procuress, and her earnest enterprise no more than an elaborate prostitution scheme. Eliza—whose intelligent, deep-set eyes behind wire-rimmed spectacles and dark hair arranged in prim ringlets hardly suggested such a vocation—was dumbfounded by the sniggering public reaction, the complete misunderstanding, of what she sincerely felt was "one of the best endeavors" of her life.

Nevertheless, during the next few weeks, as New Yorkers speculated about the strange proposal, Eliza busied herself recruiting volunteers for the voyage. Horace Greeley's *New York Daily*

Tribune kept its readers informed of her activities, while giving the plan a flowery boost:

Mrs. E. W. Farnham has just returned to the city after visiting the Eastern States for the purpose of making up her company of migrating ladies who having no husbands to engage their attention here, are desirous of going on an errand of mercy to the golden land. . . . the enterprise in which Mrs. Farnham is engaged is one which evinces much moral courage. Her reward will be found in the blessings which her countrymen will invoke for her when the vessel in which the association is to sail shall arrive in California with her precious cargo. May favoring gales attend the good ship *Angelique*.

Eliza Farnham's Far Western countrymen didn't bother to wait for the ship's arrival before they began to bless her. In a region where there were at least twenty men for every woman, it mattered little what kind of "migrating ladies" would arrive on the *Angelique*. One forty-niner's journal expressed the general enthusiasm: "June 10, 1849: Went to church 3 times to day. a few ladies present. does my eye good to see a woman once more. hope Mrs. Farnham will bring 10,000."

Despite the *Tribune*'s endorsement and the zeal of California's bachelors, the gossip continued, and gradually it wore down even the determined Eliza. Deeply humiliated, she fell seriously ill. Though she reported that more than two hundred women replied to her proposal, she ultimately lacked the strength—or the heart—to carry it through.

San Franciscans were especially disappointed. When they learned that the scheme had collapsed, one observer reported: "I verily believe there was more drunkenness, more gambling, more fighting, and more of everything that was bad that night, than ever before occurred in San Francisco within any similar space of time."

When Eliza herself finally sailed for California in the early summer of 1849, she was accompanied only by her two young sons and three "migrating ladies." Though her plan had failed, she set her face westward, determined to make a new life for herself and her children, alone in a strange land.

Eliza had been on her own almost from the beginning. Born on November 17, 1815, in Rensselaerville, New York, she was only five when her mother died and she was sent to live with a domineering aunt and alcoholic uncle on their western New York farm. "Dark and neglected looking," she was given little love or schooling. Nevertheless, she snatched moments between chores to read Voltaire and Thomas Paine, and she developed strength and independence in the blighted environment. At twenty she made her first trip West. Traveling by stagecoach and steamboat, she joined a married sister in frontier Illinois, where she exulted in the freedom of prairie life and the spaciousness of the landscape. A year later, in 1836, she married Thomas Jefferson Farnham, a New England lawyer who had also caught the westering fever.

Eliza kept house in a two-room cottage and rode the prairie on a roan pony her husband had given her. In 1838 she bore her first child, a son. But tragedy struck. Her sister died when yellow fever swept the region the following year, and soon after her baby succumbed, too. "The little coffin . . . seemed to carry my very heart into the earth with it," she mourned. As Eliza weathered her loss, her husband set out for Oregon as the leader of one of the first groups of pioneers to make the long overland trek. Heading west, the men carried a banner that Eliza had made and embroidered with a motto. "Oregon or Death" it read.

Only Thomas Farnham and a few others completed the journey to the Pacific. When her husband returned the following year, he had tales of adventure in Oregon, Hawaii, California and Mexico to tell his young wife. But Eliza, too, had stories to relate. During her year alone, equipped with two trunks and a rifle, she had traveled through much of Illinois by stagecoach and farm wagon, observing people and scenes for a book she hoped to write one day.

Despite Eliza's growing love for the West, the Farnhams returned East and settled in New York State, where Thomas produced *Life and Adventures in California* and Eliza two more sons. But she was writing as well. In 1843 she published her first thoughts on the superiority of women—developing an unusual theory that elevated women above men but paradoxically denied them the political rights many nineteenth-century women were beginning to demand. A woman's superiority was moral and spiritual, Eliza argued, and her main job was motherhood. The more mundane tasks of life—soldiering, pioneering, inventing, even voting—were best left to the lesser sex, freeing woman for her higher purpose.

Three years later, in *Life in Prairie Land,* a lively personal account of her years in Illinois, Eliza again pondered woman's role, particularly as the civilizer in a frontier society. It was a theme that would continue to preoccupy her for the rest of her life; a more immediate and sensational result was her California emigration scheme.

Meanwhile Eliza had also been writing about prison reform. She was given the chance to try out some of her innovative ideas when a new, liberal prison board appointed her matron of the Sing Sing women's prison, in Ossining, New York.

"A very great reform has been instituted at Sing Sing, the rule of love," one journal reported after Eliza's arrival. Serious, soft-spoken, and fearless, twenty-seven-year-old Eliza ended the cruel beatings and fire-and-brimstone religiosity that were standard for the time, and turned the prison into a school. The women were supplied with books and taught to read, a piano was installed, crafts introduced, potted plants placed in the windows, and maps and pictures hung on the walls. Even the harsh silence system, which prevented prisoners from speaking to one another, was abolished.

But Eliza's reforms were extremely controversial. She often tangled with the prison chaplain, who was especially outraged when she neglected grim, fire-and-brimstone religious tracts and instead read popular novels like *Oliver Twist* aloud to the prisoners. Meanwhile, an all-male inspection team, deeply suspicious of her newfangled reforms, reported that discipline was lax and, even worse in their eyes, had "nothing *masculine*" about it. Eliza's revolutionary experiment lasted four years before a new and more conservative prison board purged her and other reformers from the system.

While Eliza was experimenting with the rule of love at Sing Sing, her own marriage was crumbling. Though she scarcely mentioned her restless, adventure-loving husband in her writings, men on his 1839 Western expedition had complained of his "low, intriguing disposition." Whatever the circumstances, Thomas Farnham went West again in 1847 and settled permanently in California. By then Eliza, absorbed in prison work and writing, had made a life of her own.

But in September 1848, Thomas Farnham died of a fever in San Francisco, leaving Eliza several tracts of California land, including a 200-acre ranch at Santa Cruz, a remote settlement 60 miles down the coast from San Francisco.

Though Eliza had by then found work at the well-known Perkins Institute for the Blind in Boston, she resolved to go West and claim the land. But the sheer adventure of the experience was the real lure. In *Life in Prairie Land,* Eliza had described her exhilaration while writing that book: "I have lived again in the land of my heart. I have seen the grasses wave, and felt the winds . . . and exulted in something of the old sense of freedom which these conferred upon me." In wild, unsettled California, she hoped to find that freedom once more.

But as Eliza began her journey, controversy dogged her heels. Her prison reforms had met with outraged protest, her emigration scheme had created a storm of gossip, and now, on board ship, she encountered more trouble.

It began when the captain announced that he would not make a scheduled stop for fresh water. Incensed, Eliza immediately drafted a petition demanding the stop. The water on board, which had been stored for months in the ship's vats, had a slimy, foul taste. When the captain read the petition, which energetic Eliza had persuaded all but one of the passengers to sign, he grew livid with rage. Angrily, he made the stop, but at the same time swore revenge against the brazen female meddler who had challenged his authority.

In Valparaiso, Chile, he paid her back. Using a pretext, he persuaded her to go ashore, then headed the ship out to sea. Stunned, Eliza watched its grey sails and black hull disappear into the distance—carrying her two sons—five-year-old Eddie and nine-year-old Charlie, on to California without her. "I did not faint," she recalled, "for I am strong and resolute by nature." Still, it was a nightmare to be stranded in a foreign land with nothing but the clothes on her back. Fortunately, the sympathetic English consul gave her money and clothes, and she found lodgings with a kindly couple. A long, anxious month passed before she was able to catch another ship for San Francisco.

Forty-seven days later, Eliza paced the ship's wet deck as it waited, trapped in heavy fogs, outside the Golden Gate. At last it entered the great ship-clogged harbor and dropped anchor at North Beach in a heavy rain. Eliza could see little of the famous gold-rush port as she and the other passengers, steadied by husky sailors in top boots, waded ashore through the crashing surf.

She found her boys still on the other ship, cared for by a friend on board. But Eddie was weak and feverish, and this increased Eliza's anger at the vengeful captain. Unwilling to accept an injustice without a fight, she decided to stay in the city long enough to begin what proved to be a fruitless lawsuit against the captain.

From the start, Eliza despised San Francisco. It was not only the fog, rain and incessant winds that "meet you face to face and search you like an officer of the customs," but even more the wild, reckless abandon of a city raging with gold-rush fever. Walking the muddy, unpaved streets, she saw brilliantly lit gambling houses and gaudy saloons, jammed with men at all hours of the day and night. Great bags of gold dust stood open on the gaming tables, and the music blared through the laughter and talk. Even at the crowded, jerry-built boardinghouse where she and the children stayed, the drinking and gambling and raucous noise went on just beyond the flimsy calico cloth walls of her room. Worst of all, there were so few women in the city that wherever she went, men stared. "Doorways filled instantly," she reported, "little islands in the street were thronged with men who seemed to gather in a moment, and who remained immovable" until she passed.

It was a relief to give up the lawsuit and take the steamer down the coast to the little port of Santa Cruz in late February 1850. The sky was a deep, cloudless blue and the air soft and warm as Eliza and her boys were deposited on the beach, "landed like bales of goods through the surf, partly in boats and partly in the arms of seamen." They set off eagerly to find the ranch, some two miles away. Half-running through the lush, dew-drenched clover and grass, with the boys trotting beside her, she reached her new home at last.

Staring in dismay, Eliza saw that it was little more than a shack —a small, windowless cabin with dilapidated log-slab walls. Venturing inside, she found a dirt floor and a few sticks of furniture: a rough table, a few old benches, some crude plates and bowls. The walls and flimsy roof were black with soot from the open fire on the floor where cooking had been done.

As the boys scampered off to explore a willow-lined creek just twenty feet from the door, Eliza climbed a nearby hill to survey her domain. Despite the disappointment of the house, she found it

beautiful. Around her rose green hills, where herds of wild cattle
grazed in the thick grass. Behind was a deep ravine, filled with
towering red-barked trees, and beyond, the densely forested slopes
of the Coast Range. Looking toward the ocean, she saw a sunny
valley with a few scattered ranches and an old red-tiled mission.
In the distance gleamed the blue-green waters of Monterey Bay.
As she gazed around her in wonder, the sound of the surf seemed
like distant music.

But her brief peace was shattered as the boys ran up, hungry
for lunch. Rummaging among their satchels, she found them some
bread, then sat down inside her sooty, ramshackle hut, tired and
depressed. But slowly her strength returned as in her imagination
she cleaned and patched the blackened walls, laid out a new wood
floor, built cupboards and closets and curtained off a space for a
bedroom. She had once made a home out of a crude pioneer cottage in Illinois. Now she would do it again.

The first months at Rancho La Libertad, as Eliza called her
new home, required all her energy and resourcefulness. Camping
out in a large tent loaned by a neighboring rancher, she patched
the log-slab walls of the cabin, then cut windows and glazed them
with thin cloth. She even managed to set up a stove purchased in
San Francisco, though seemingly vital parts had been lost in the
surf while it was being unloaded. Soon Eliza and the boys had
moved into the renovated shack, sleeping in a bedroom improvised with a curtain, while the rest of the cramped cabin served as
kitchen, sitting room, study and storage space.

By March, with the help of a hired man, Eliza was ready to
farm. But her troubles began almost immediately. The man hurt
his hand while plowing, and Eliza could find no one to take his
place. Since most able-bodied men had gone to the mines, "invalids and drunken sailors were the staple of the laboring community." Moreover, wages were exorbitant in a land where gold
could be picked out of the ground. "I wished, then, for the power
to be man and woman both, to add to my vocations of dairymaid,
housekeeper, nurse, and physician, that of plowman," Eliza wrote.
Everyone pitched in, including nine-year-old Charlie, and the seed
was at last put into the ground.

But her problems continued. Much of the seed was bad and
never sprouted; wild cattle constantly foraged in her planted
fields; and in one disastrous two-week period, grasshoppers de-

stroyed half her crops. That year Eliza planted her fields four times before she harvested her first crop.

She also found that even the most basic household staples were hard to come by in remote Santa Cruz. "Either the beef or the tea, or the sugar, or salt, or molasses, or flour, or butter, was out, or the cow strayed away, or something that we had sent for in time to save ourselves from want, was lost in the surf or stolen from the beach."

By the Fourth of July, however, Eliza was able to celebrate her own independence by marking the ground for the new house she planned to build. Lumber had already been hauled by wagon from a sawmill in the mountains, and for months she had constructed the house in her head. Now as the boys watched, wide-eyed, she took out a stick and scratched out a long front section, with a spacious porch running its entire length, and then drew in a wing at the east end. It would be an ample two-storied house, she explained, with spires and gabled windows. Here would be the parlor, there the dining room, through there, the bedrooms—and beyond, in that quiet, sunny spot, her own room, where she could study and write.

Eliza intended to do much of the building herself. Her first job was the "tenanting of the joists and studding for the lower story. . . . I succeeded so well," she exulted, "that during its progress I laughed, whenever I paused for a few moments to rest, at the idea of proposing to pay a man $14 or $16 per day for doing what I found my own hands so dexterous in."

But her long, full dress constantly hampered her work, and after the second day, she changed into a pair of "bloomers" concocted from an old gymnastics suit. At first she felt so self-conscious in her "Albanian trousers" that she scurried to hide or change whenever strangers approached the site. Later she learned to brave the shocked looks of local folk, considering it "a great victory" when she could face the public in pants.

Despite the progress on her house, Eliza was desperately lonely. The endless physical work of running the ranch and building a new home absorbed all her energy; she found she thought only of potatoes, bricks and shingles. She no longer heard the sound of the surf or gazed at the great hills that surrounded her ranch. She complained in a letter to friends in the East: "I have been harder at work . . . than any Southern slave—books, pen, thinking, talking—all as utterly given up as if I were an [Eskimo] woman in her ice hut." Confined to a remote valley, overburdened with work and worries about the future of the ranch, with few to share her feelings and no outlets for her earnest reformist tendencies except occasional doctoring, she felt useless and unwanted. "The necessities to be served here are physical: washing linen, cleansing houses, cooking, nursing," she wrote. There was little need for a controversial reformer with advanced ideas and an iconoclastic spirit.

But as if in answer to her distress, a friend from the East arrived in the fall for a long stay. "A woman of genius," Eliza described her, "yet . . . practical, musical, witty, independent, affectionate," Georgiana Bruce was a young Englishwoman whose childhood, like Eliza's, had been painful and unhappy. Her father had died just before her birth, and she had grown up in a morose, penny-pinching household. "It is a bad beginning to be born of grief," she said. "It narrows the chest and makes the blood less buoyant and hopeful." Like Eliza, Georgiana was never a proper Victorian girl. A tomboy, she wanted "forbidden knowledge" and "purposely let the sawdust out" of her doll. Later, working as a governess, she made her way to America and eventually to Brook Farm, the famous Transcendentalist cooperative colony in Massachusetts.

Eliza, introduced to Georgiana at Horace Greeley's home in 1844, had hired her as an assistant matron at Sing Sing. As adventurous as Eliza, Georgiana had now come to California, hoping to find work as a nurse or teacher. Meanwhile, she would stay at Rancho La Libertad and help Eliza with the farm work. Together they would make the land bloom.

As winter rains threatened, the two women raced to finish "the Mansion," as they now called the new house. Santa Cruz residents were soon agog to see *two* bloomered women atop the house, nailing shingles and talking energetically as they worked. Georgiana, fresh from the East, was full of news, and their sophisticated conversation amazed the local folk: abolition, phrenology, prison reform, homeopathic medicine, the new water cure (which Georgiana had tried), spiritual knockings, women's rights (Georgiana, unlike Eliza, was an ardent suffragist), Swedenborgianism—all the fads and fashions, causes, cults, and crusades of mid-nineteenth-century America.

The new house was finished just before Christmas. Settled at last in spacious quarters, Georgiana and Eliza made optimistic plans for the farm season ahead. From January through the spring, the two worked daily in the fields. Together they repaired fences and dug ditches for irrigation, took turns at the plow, and planted potatoes, wheat, vegetables and fruit trees.

The days were mild and the sun warm on their backs as they dug and planted and weeded. White seagulls circled overhead, and blackbirds wheeled and called. In the distance they sometimes glimpsed a solitary buzzard, cruising idly, resting on giant wings.

Despite their best efforts, the farm did not pay that year. Potatoes were their downfall. The year before, when food production could not keep pace with the demand from forty-niners, the price of potatoes had skyrocketed. Recognizing a good thing, every farmer in the region—including Eliza—had planted potatoes. The market was soon glutted. Prices dropped, and many farmers, unable to sell their crop, were forced to plow it under.

But there were other problems as well. Eliza's hired man proved incompetent, and his successor was a "half fool, half knave," at least in Georgiana's blunt judgment. Looking back on the experience, she felt that Eliza, though a woman of brilliant and inventive mind, lacked common sense and a head for business. "I have grown old fretting about [her] troubles and perplexities," she confided to her journal some time after she left the farm. "She was so ignorant of business, so careless, so easily imposed on, and at the same time so determined to get so much under way at once that she was constantly in debt or in hot water some how."

Eliza's difficulties were compounded when she remarried some two years after her arrival in Santa Cruz. Her new husband was an Irishman from San Francisco named William Alexander Fitzpatrick, whom Georgiana branded in her journal, "the greatest blackguard in the country." According to Georgiana, he struck and mistreated Eliza, and their life together became a series of stormy partings and reconciliations. Tragically, Eliza's own son Eddie, who had never been strong, died during this tense time, as did a new baby daughter.

Meanwhile, Georgiana had married a wealthy tanner and moved into a large new house in town. There she would live for the rest of her long life, bearing five children and becoming Santa Cruz's most formidable matriarch.

Though Eliza's personal life was in shambles, California was thriving. As the new state grew and prospered, she was able to find more congenial work. She inspected the state prison at San Quentin and issued a report on her findings; she served as principal of the first Santa Cruz public school; she toured the state, lecturing on topics ranging from spiritualism to women's rights. In 1856, the year she divorced William Fitzpatrick, her vivid account of her California experiences, *California In-doors and Out,* was published. Again, a central thread was the role of women in a pioneer society. "None but the pure and strong-hearted of my sex should come alone to this land," she concluded.

Eliza's life in gold-rush-era California, with its gambling and greed and reckless abandon, along with her unhappy marriage to the notorious Mr. Fitzpatrick, had only strengthened her belief in women's superiority. Her theory was no doubt rooted in her childhood, in the loss of her own mother when she was only five. Deprived of that love, Eliza developed a philosophical system in which motherhood was the highest human role—even though it contradicted her own adventurous temperament.

Carrying her theme East, she spoke at the 1858 National Woman's Rights Convention in New York City. Sharing the platform with such well-known suffragists as Susan B. Anthony, Lucy Stone, Lucretia Mott, and Elizabeth Cady Stanton, Eliza created a stir in the crowded hall with a long speech on the superiority of women. While man might be the pioneer of civilization, she looked to the dawning of a "higher era" when woman would assume "her true position in harmony with her superior organism, her delicacy of structure, her beauty of person, her great powers of endurance, and thus prove herself not only man's equal in influence and power, but his superior in many of the nobler virtues." Through maternity, Eliza firmly concluded, women were a power "second only to God himself."

Eliza was now in her forties, and she was suddenly blooming. Georgiana had noted that as a young woman Eliza "just escaped being handsome." But as Eliza grew older, her friend noticed that "the expression of every feature was softened" and she had become beautiful.

Eliza had never resolved the contradiction between her reverence for the maternal virtues and her own bold and spirited character. But as Charlie, her only surviving child, grew to manhood, her motherly duties ended. She began to feel a "secret joy" in this new phase, in the inner growth that seemed possible once motherhood was behind her.

Her life was now filled with useful work. She traveled frequently, lecturing, writing, working for the causes that moved her most deeply. As the Civil War began, she served as women's matron at the new state insane asylum at Stockton, California, where she continued the rule of love that had been so revolutionary at Sing Sing. When the war intensified, she traveled to Washington, D.C., to petition Congress to end slavery through a constitutional amendment. During these years, she also began to gather her thoughts on women into what would become a major two-volume treatise: *Woman and Her Era,* published in 1864 and dedicated to Georgiana Bruce. She also completed two other books: *Eliza Woodson,* a fictionalized account of her bitter childhood, and *The Ideal Attained,* a novel based on her California experiences.

In the winter of 1863, Eliza answered a desperate call for nurses to care for soldiers wounded at the Battle of Gettysburg. Working among the sick and maimed, she fell ill herself. She never recovered. Less than a year later, at age fifty, she died of tuberculosis in New York City.

A forthright, unconventional, and immensely earnest woman, Eliza Farnham seemed a strange, eccentric figure to most nineteenth-century Americans. Her adventurous spirit led her West, first to pioneer Illinois, then to California at the height of the gold rush. But she traveled to new frontiers in her imagination as well—daring to believe that prisoners and the mentally ill should be treated with love; that slavery should be abolished; that woman's role in society deserved serious thought and concern. In her youthful book on prairie life, she had described a certain type of American whose "boldness and love of adventure" could find "no proper field but the wild frontier." Such individuals, she believed, moved in advance of civilization. Heading always "toward the setting sun," they recognized that only there could they find the freedom they sought.

Though she did not realize it at the time, Eliza Farnham was describing herself.

Pamela Herr is a California writer specializing in Western history and biography. Born in New England and raised mainly in California, she graduated from a high school located in the Himalayan Mountains of India. She has a B.A. in English from Harvard/Radcliffe and an M.A. from George Washington University.

She has worked as an editor of social studies and language arts textbooks, and for three years as managing editor of The American West, *a magazine of Western history, where several of her articles have been published. She is currently working on a full-length biography of Jessie Benton Frémont, another adventurous nineteenth-century woman who, like Eliza Farnham, arrived in California during the gold rush.*

BIBLIOGRAPHY

BOOKS

Burhans, Samuel. *Burhans Genealogy.* New York: privately printed, 1894.

Camp, William Martin. *San Francisco: Port of Gold.* Garden City, New York: Doubleday, 1947.

Coy, Owen Cochran. *Gold Days.* Los Angeles: Powell, 1929.

Davies, John D. *Phrenology, Fad and Science.* New Haven: Yale University Press, 1955.

Dewey, Mary E., ed. *Life and Letters of Catharine M. Sedgwick.* New York: Harper and Brothers, 1871.

Farnham, Eliza W. *California, In-doors and Out.* New York: Dix, Edwards, 1856; reprinted Nieuwkoop, Netherlands: B. De Graaf, 1972.

——. *Life in Prairie Land.* New York: Harper and Brothers, 1846; reprinted Nieuwkoop, Netherlands: B. De Graaf, 1972.

——. *Woman and Her Era* (2 vols.). New York: Davis, 1864.

Harrison, E. S. *History of Santa Cruz.* San Francisco: Pacific Press, 1892.

Kirby, Georgiana Bruce. *Years of Experience: An Autobiographical Narrative.* New York: AMS Press, 1971.

Koch, Margaret. *Santa Cruz County: Parade of the Past*. Fresno, California: Valley Publishers, 1973.

Lewis, W. David. "Eliza Wood Burhans Farnham," *Notable American Women 1607–1950, A Biographical Dictionary*. Cambridge, Massachusetts: Harvard University Press, 1971.

——. *From Newgate to Dannemora: The Rise of the Penitentiary in New York, 1796–1848*. Ithaca, New York: Cornell University Press, 1965.

Stanton, Elizabeth Cady, Anthony, Susan B., and Gage, Matilda J., eds. *History of Woman Suffrage*. Rochester, New York: Charles Mann, 1887.

Woodward, Helen Beal. *The Bold Women*. New York: Farrar, Straus and Young, 1953.

MAGAZINES

Higginson, Thomas Wentworth. Review of *Woman and Her Era* and *Eliza Woodson*, *Atlantic Monthly*, September 1864.

Stern, Madeleine B. "Two Letters from the Sophisticates of Santa Cruz," *The Book Club of California Quarterly News-Letter* 33, Summer 1968.

MANUSCRIPTS

Kirby, Georgiana Bruce. Unpublished journal, 1852–53 (25 pp.). Copy at California Historical Society, San Francisco.

18

From Rags to Riches

by ROBERTA CHENEY

*An illegitimate child of the Ohio coal country, May Arkwright
Hutton was a natural leader. Her courage and persistence took her
from rags to riches, from Idaho mining-camp cook to millionaire
owner of a silver and lead mine, militant suffragist and noted phi-
lanthropist.*

N.S.Y.

It was a tough-looking bunch, those young men in their twenties
and thirties gathered around the kitchen table in Hutton's two-
room house at an Idaho mining camp. The year was 1889 and the
men were grimy from hand digging on their claim. They didn't
look like potential millionaires, but they were.

May, huge of frame, big-boned and big-bosomed, barged over
from the stove, coffeepot in hand, "Me and Al'll make it twenty-
five apiece. That'll make another $50."

Each month the ever-hopeful and persistent group of some
seven or eight "investors" met to raise enough money to buy
powder for blasting. "I—I got $10 left over from my board and
room," stammered Gus Paulsen, "and I can put in more work this
month."

"Dad" Reeves added up the total: $185. That would buy half a
dozen cases of powder, and work on the "poor man's mine" could
go on. In a moment of confidence, they had named it "The Her-

cules." Their claim on a barren mountainside near Wallace had
been worked on Sundays and after hours for six years by these
men, among them the grocer, a schoolteacher, the milkman, and
Al, engineer on the train that daily hauled rich ore from the
nearby Hecla Mine. May fed them and bolstered their waning
spirits with her exuberance, strength and blueberry pies. She had
come to the Panhandle mining camp six years before with a fierce
determination, not only to make her way in this rugged man's
world but to become rich—with luck, maybe very rich. As a boardinghouse cook, she had established her independence and a reputation not only for good food, but also for a shrewd business
sense.

May learned early in life that next best to being wanted was to
be needed, and people from all walks of life came to need her: the
blind grandfather who offered the only family security she had
during childhood; the hungry, discouraged prospectors; the gentle,
soft-spoken husband; powerful labor union organizers; young girls
in trouble, and finally politicians at the national level.

Born in Ohio in 1860, the illegitimate child of an irresponsible
father and a mother who seems to have disappeared soon after her
birth, May lived much of the time with the grandfather who was
interested in every new economic and political theory that appeared and discussed all the "isms" with her as well as with his
cronies in the village square. Together the old man and the little
girl listened to soapbox orators and met politicians who came by,
and thus added some kind of knowledge to what May acquired
from the meager three years she spent in school. One day budding
politician William McKinley placed a patronizing hand on her
head and expressed the hope that when this lassie grew up, she
would be able to vote. McKinley spent the night at the Arkwright
home and praised the doughnuts the ten-year-old girl had made—
perhaps the first recognition of the cooking skill that was to take
May into the realm of independence, popularity and power. A
century later, James Montgomery was to write a biography of her:
Liberated Woman: A Life of May Arkwright Hutton.

As a young woman, May worked in a boardinghouse and became keenly aware of the hopeless plight of the underpaid, overworked coal miners in that area. She was determined that her life
would not be ground down like theirs, that riches must lie some-

where ahead for someone courageous enough to look for them. A Northern Pacific Railroad advertisement caught her eye:

Nuggets weighing $50, $100, $200 of free gold for the picking up; it fairly glistens.

The railroad was ready for passengers, settlers, and freight in the Idaho Panhandle. May was ready to go. In 1878 she persuaded forty men from the Ohio mines to join her in the trip West to this land of promise. May had had a brief brush with matrimony, but after less than a year of marriage, her husband Bert Munn left and took the couple's savings. Later she heard that he had drowned; righteous neighbors said it was a judgment on him, but May thought it was because he couldn't swim.

With one wicker basket as luggage, May left the train at Rathburn, Idaho, and engaged a steamboat to take her and the forty men across Lake Coeur d'Alene. She was headed for Eagle City up the north fork of the Coeur d'Alene River. Overwhelmed by the beauty of the mountain lake and the river, her heart lifted. She "belonged," and surely here she could make good. First she would get a job cooking and then, somehow, someday, she would get rich. The last few miles of the journey were by horseback, and her oft-quoted assessment of her arrival summed it up: "I came West at the age of twenty-three and went into the boardinghouse business in the Coeur d'Alene district which I reached on the hurricane deck of a cayuse pony."

Jim Wardner, entrepreneur of the Coeur d'Alene mining district, had been on the train with May; he offered to open up a food counter in the room behind his saloon. May had a job and she felt at home. The work was hard—she was on her feet fourteen hours a day while the men worked only ten hours in the mines—but $20 bills began to accumulate in her wallet, and with them her sense of independence and success. "The only other women in the camp were not big and homely; they were painted and pretty," wrote her biographer, but May saw the emptiness in their eyes and had great compassion for them. In her loneliness, the boardinghouse cook enjoyed the only other feminine companionship available.

Fate played into May's hand when the railroad extended its narrow-gauge line into Kellogg. Ready to move on and to have a boardinghouse of her own, May found out where the tracks were to be and set up her own restaurant at Wardner Junction. She says she bought a cow, a broom, a bucket, a cookstove, a piece of land and a two-room shack. In the front room she put a big table and a stove. Payday at the mines was Saturday, so at the evening meal on that day, she walked around the table making a pouch of her kitchen apron and collected board money. Standard price was $6.50 a week; sometimes grateful miners put in more, but May saw to it that the fee was never less. She earned that money and she needed it.

Along with the miners at the boardinghouse came some railroad men; among them was Levi W. Hutton, called "Al" by his co-workers. Immediately he was on common ground with May because as an orphan, he, too, had been shuttled about, unwanted and poor. They had both struck out on their own, made good, and needed each other. What May lacked in looks, she made up for in a good head and, best of all, a good heart. She was fat—225 pounds worth—and her personality was powerful. She was outspoken and opinionated. Al was quiet, sober and hardworking, but sure enough of himself not to be threatened by May's voluminous rough exterior and inner strength.

The wedding was to be a quiet and simple affair, she wrote to her half-brothers and sister back in Ohio. She was a cook and Al a $150-a-month railroad engineer, but May demanded three things for her wedding: a parson, a wedding gown in the latest Spokane fashion, and a table full of fine food for all the guests. The marriage took place in Wardner Junction on November 17, 1887; newspapers reported that the bride wore a gown of light blue plush, cut princess style with a close-set line of pearl buttons down the front. And a large bustle! Guests arrived on foot, on horseback, in buggies, by rail and even in the cab of a locomotive. Presents from ex-boarders were stacked high. May cooked the food, but when it was all prepared, she exchanged her kitchen apron for her blue plush dress, and conducted the party with all the fanfare she loved. For that day, plain rawboned May was the prima donna.

The Huttons moved to Wallace, a new town up the south fork of the Coeur d'Alene River. They bought a two-room house on the hillside and May settled into the life of a housewife . . . well, almost. Her marriage gave her new status, but even as Mrs. Levi Hutton, she couldn't quite fit in. "Her looks were against her; she was huge, homely, strident, uncouth and given to strong language. Her clothes were kaleidoscopic. The costumes in which she walked the streets, and the gowns in which she appeared bare-necked and bosomy at evening affairs, shocked wives and daughters of mine owners," wrote Montgomery. Spoken of as "that woman," sometimes "that awful woman," May didn't make the social register even of a primitive mining town.

That concerned her very little; she was really interested in the working man's problems, and she came to see organized labor as the answer. The Huttons' two-room house above the tracks became a rendezvous for representatives who were trying to get unions established in all the mines. Blueberry pies and sympathy made her popular with them. The early years with her grandfather had instilled several "isms" in her mind, and she was fiercely in favor of the working man and against mine owners and big corporations.

Quiet Al did not share her militancy, but he was unwittingly drawn into center stage of the disastrous Rocky Mountain Revolution. Wages at the Wallace mines were $3.00 a day; at a nearby unionized mine, the muckers were getting $3.50. Negotiations failed, tempers flared, labor became arrogant, management greedy. Union miners refused to work; owners brought in scab laborers. In retaliation, a group of miners climbed the mountain behind the Frisco mill, put sticks of dynamite under the mill and blew it into kindling wood. Of the 40 men in the mill at the time, 3 were killed. The rest scattered, but were shot and pounced upon by the 400 union men. That was the story according to the news release; May had a different version which she acclaimed loudly and was later to put into a book.

The "Troubles of 1892" were only the beginning of the labor problems in northern Idaho, and May was in the thick of it. The caldron bubbled for the next seven years.

Al, the Day brothers, Paulsen, Reeves, and any other "investors" they could recruit continued to work the Hercules claim. They brought down ore samples and spread them out on the table at the Huttons'. Occasionally a fleck of silver showed up and encouraged them. There were offers from the big mining companies to buy them out, but May, with her distrust of big corporations and her determination to strike it rich, felt this mine was their best chance. Come hell or high water, they would stick with it.

By 1899 the big Bunker Hill and Sullivan Mine had become everything that labor hated. The company claimed it was not making a profit and closed shop. They laid off all the miners and then reopened with imported non-union men. May's great compassion for the working man did not extend to scabs. She felt they were tools in the hands of corporations, not honest working men. She came to know local and national labor leaders and championed their cause in speeches and letters to the editors of Idaho and Spokane papers.

The smoldering labor fire burst into flames on April 29. Al Hutton, as peaceful as his wife was belligerent, was plunged headlong into the fray. At an early morning meeting, the union men had voted by a slim margin to proceed with a plan to punish the mine owners and establish their standing as a force demanding fair treatment and wages. The men left the union hall to get their firearms. They met half an hour later at the railroad station, each wearing a white handkerchief as an armband to identify members.

Two extra cars were put on the train to accommodate the mass of "passengers." Al, in his engineer's cab, was trying to assess the situation when he felt a gun in his ribs. "Get this thing going!" ordered the gunman. Al drove the train slowly along the mountain tracks. "Stop at the Frisco powder house," he was commanded as the non-paying passenger load filled every seat, aisle, and boxcar. When the train ground to a halt, some of the men rushed to the powder house, broke open the locks and began loading giant boxes of dynamite into boxcars with the men. A second stop added another 3,000 pounds of powder. With this potentially explosive load, Al inched the heavy locomotive through the canyons, stopping often along the way to pick up more men.

At Wallace, twenty armed men surrounded the locomotive and instructed Al to take the train down to Wardner on the Oregon Railway and Navigation Company tracks. Al hesitated. That roadbed was too light for his heavy locomotive, and he ran the risk of a head-on collision with an oncoming train. A Winchester 45-90 jabbed into his back; he no longer had a choice. With a load of nearly one thousand men and thousands of pounds of powder, Al slowly pulled the throttle and started his train over the unfamiliar tracks. "The Dynamite Express" covered the 12 tedious miles to Wardner, a tribute to Al's years of engineering experience and his cool head.

The men piled off the cars; the first contingent of skilled riflemen was dispatched to roust out the guards at the concentrator. Then the "regulars"—men with rifles or sidearms—moved up the hill. The mine guards had long since taken to the tall timber, but the prearranged signal of "one gunshot means the regulars are to come on" was unknown to many of them. When that shot was fired, excited miners just started shooting. Chaos reigned. Before the leaders could get things in order, one of their own men had been killed. By this time, all scabs had cleared the plant. The 3,000 pounds of powder was ignited. In three earthshaking blasts, it blew the huge mine concentrator to smithereens.

Governor Steunenberg (called Governor Stepanfetchit by May in her letters to the press and in the book she was to write) wired President McKinley for troops to quell the riot. The Idaho militia had been called to the Philippines, so no state troops were available. Brigadier General H. C. Merriam, followed by some 700 troops, got off the train, lined up his men in front of the coaches and ordered the arrest of every miner carrying a union card. Between 600 and 700 miners were hustled into boxcars and taken to a giant hay barn near Wardner. This "bull pen" became the target for dramatic press releases. May was furious. Not only was this a violation of human rights, but among those arrested was her beloved Al. The general claimed he was an accomplice. May stormed the "bull pen," the press and officialdom. When the air was finally cleared, the troops gone, and the men freed, May made her decisive move.

After her marriage, May had worked off and on at her boardinghouse business; at one time she had managed the dining room of Wallace's best hotel. But, by and large, she had time on her hands, and she used it. She had read every book she could borrow. She studied and she wrote letters to the press and to people in power, and notes to herself of her thoughts and opinions. Now the time had come. May was ready to write a book; the dramatic subject was at hand. She was angry with the press and felt that "the true story" of the Rocky Mountain Revolution should be written. May called her book, *The Coeur d'Alenes: A Tale of the Modern Inquisition in Idaho*. It was written, published and promoted by May Arkwright Hutton in 1900.

"Names have been slightly modified to avoid being considered personal, but it goes without saying, that those living in the district affected will have little trouble in seeing through the mantle which thinly shrouds the identity of some of the characters and corporations mentioned," she wrote in the introduction.

The names were indeed "thinly veiled." Dr. Hugh France, the company doctor, she called Dr. Huge Fraud; Brigadier General Merriam, she called General Bulldozium, along with Governor Stepanfetchit, and the Mushroom Mining Men's Association. May pulled no punches in castigating the mine owners, the state officials and the U. S. Army, though she proclaims in the Preliminary Remarks that the "writer being neither miner nor mine owner is in a neutral position and able to give a true and impartial account of the events . . . during a residence of 14 years in the state . . . the characters and incidents are real ones."

With the "true" incidents, May exercised a "novelist's privilege" and adds a romantic love story about an Indian maiden, "a poor and humble child, but rich in virtue and grace, Louise grew to womanhood like a lily amid thorns. . . . Her most important work was among the medicine men who by their diabolical acts imposed upon the simple and ignorant. Louise was endowed with a courage above her sex . . . to this valiant woman of the wilderness . . . is due credit of overcoming dangerous superstitions so profoundly rooted in the Coeur d'Alene Indians."

The reader is constantly confused about what parts of May's book are factual and what are fiction. Is the Indian maiden a "thinly veiled" and romantic version of May's own life? The book is weighted down with so much propaganda that the slender thread of the novel barely hangs together. A great deal of early-day mining history is related, but it is colored and slanted with May's opinions. Little gems of fact shine through. The tribe of Indians from which the mining area, the lake, and the river take their name, she says, was named by the French fur traders because these Indians had cruel hearts, sharp as an awl. Thus the name, Coeur d'Alene, translated from the French into awl hearts.

There was also the story of the first bank in the Coeur d'Alenes: It was a small iron box brought into Murray on a toboggan, drawn by a bulldog over the Belknap Trail from the Northern Pacific station. Billy Hawkins of the Ainsworth First National Bank of Portland, Oregon, brought in the box containing $40,000 in gold. The bank furniture consisted of the strongbox, one bank ledger, and the bulldog for a guard. Mr. Hawkins set up business in one corner of a saloon, and what the bank lacked in paraphernalia, it made up in profits. The banker trebled his capital in a few months.

May's book would rise from its fancy cover to haunt her in years to come, but for the present she reveled in the limelight of being an author. Her best sale was at a Miners Union convention. However, people across the state and in other states too were anxious to read the controversial exposé of the big corporation "slave drivers." No one knows exactly how many copies were printed. One biographer says 6,000; in one letter, May casually refers to "an edition of 25,000." At any rate, it became a best seller in the Pacific Northwest. May was ecstatic; at last she had carved for herself a little niche in the literary world she so much admired.

Work went on at the Hercules Mine. One corporation offered the owners $6 million for their claim. May figured that if Big Business thought the mine was worth that, someday it should yield many times that amount. She was adamant that they resist the temptation of what she considered marginal wealth. She had come West to get really rich, and she still intended to do it.

It was June of 1901 when Gus Paulsen broke through to an ore of silver and lead that, when tested, proved to be the most concentrated of any so far produced in the Coeur d'Alenes. For eight years, the little group of nonprofessional miners had drilled their way through nearly 2,000 feet of solid rock, believing that it could happen . . . and at long last it did. Suddenly the "investors" were no longer poor; they were very rich. For a time the Hercules produced 6 per cent of all lead mined in the United States.

The mine was active for twenty-four years and employed up to 800 people at a time. It produced over $100 million worth of ore and elevated 18 everyday working people into multimillionaires.

The Huttons' first dividend payment was $750. In future years, the dividends were to be as high as $500,000. They moved from the two-room shack on a Wallace hillside to a corner lot and an elegant house within the city. May acquired a hired girl, but not a cook. When guests came, there was a white damask cloth, silver and sparkling crystal on the table, but it was May herself who emerged from the kitchen to greet them, "her expansive person bisected by strings of a voluminous kitchen apron." She loved to cook and saw no reason to stop. In this Wallace home, the Hut-

tons entertained the great and the near great. Crusaders for any
cause were favorites with May.

"The politically sensitive who came to Wallace and Spokane
needed somebody to function as interpreter and catalyst for that
inland sea of strange and different values, that intermountain pla-
teau known as the Inland Empire. . . . May was square in the
middle of its economic, political, and cultural life. It was an important political unit that few held the key to," Montgomery wrote
in explaining why the politically ambitious people of that day
found their way to the Hutton door. Teddy Roosevelt, Clarence
Darrow, William Borah and William Jennings Bryan became her
friends and listened to her. "They were far too experienced, far
too wise to misread this big, plain, rough spoken, overdressed
working woman. Friendships were established that would last and
would deliver clout to the suffrage movement so important to
May."

In spite of an obvious lack of training in social skills and niceties of "culture," May moved into the circle of the wealthy with a
fair amount of ease. There were the inevitable snubs from local
"society," but May was too busy to let it bother her. She had new
worlds to conquer; the women's suffrage movement was now her
prime concern. She supported church bazaars and community
charities; she put $5 gold pieces in the plate at "silver tea" fund-
raising parties. May still lived by her own counsel, and now her
wealth gave her power.

May was a millionaire and a mine owner moving into a
different level of society, with a need to change her image from the
labor union promoter. Thousands of copies of her book castigating mine owners and corporations as well as government officials
had been sold in the Northwest. She realized how damaging they
could be to her now, and how vulnerable her newly acquired
wealth made her. Quietly she withdrew all copies that were on
consignment to book dealers. She traced down every one she
could find through friends and book dealers who had sold books
and bought them back at the original price. Dealers who had been
selling them to her for $5.00 suddenly realized the potential for
profit and upped the price to $25. May paid it. The remaining
copies are now collector's items.

It wasn't that May was turning her back on the laboring men;
she continued to support their projects, but there was enough li-

belous material in that book to cause her serious trouble. When the book was published, no one thought of suing her because she had no money. Now they might, and shrewd May endeavored to forestall that possibility. Fortunately, it was before the day of libel-suit popularity and no one bothered.

With no children of her own, May took on her Ohio relatives. Her father's four legitimate offspring had always looked askance at this independent, often shocking offshoot of the family tree. Now they welcomed her with open arms. She visited them occasionally and gave out money judiciously where she felt it was needed. May even sought out and finally located her mother and, in the end, paid her funeral expenses. Independent and successful though she was, May must have felt a real need for family and roots.

Al was an ardent lodge man; his Masonic ties were especially strong, and the Masonic Lodge in the early West was influential and powerful. It was May's best social contact, too; she dressed in her finest gowns and proudly accompanied her husband to the banquets and balls. Al, in his modest business suit, and May, resplendent in bright ruffles and flounces, were the center of attention at many affairs.

For an Elks' convention in Wallace, May parodied one of her favorite poems and read it at the banquet. There were many stanzas, as was her wont, but the last one was:

> And though the forest now is dead
> And muddied each pure rill,
> The Elk of this our later day
> Still often drink their fill.

May loved poetry; she studied it and read it aloud at any possible occasion. She admired poets, and poetesses even more, and once was able to "capture" Ella Wheeler Wilcox for a tea and reception in her Wallace, Idaho home. May wrote reams of verse and some made it to print in the local papers. She became an avid student of Shakespeare and an ardent supporter of all drama and musical events. May Arkwright Hutton knew that she had a lot to learn about the niceties of life, about the English language, and culture if she were to fit into this new world of wealth. She picked up that challenge as she had all others in her life and worked on it.

But the theater, the poetry, and the lodge social affairs were only the frills in May's life. Politics and women's suffrage became her prime concerns. The Idaho legislators finally gave women the right to vote, and May decided it was time a woman ran for the legislature.

Her ingratiating approach to county delegates was, "You know, that being a woman, I don't stand the ghost of a chance in the Democratic convention to get the nomination, but do give me your vote on the first ballot—just to let folks know a woman counts for something in Shoshone County. Afterward, switch to anybody you please." Politics was a whole new ball game now; the Democrats needed those feminine votes, and they needed Mrs. Hutton's support. Obliging delegates went along with May's request and found —to their own astonishment—that she was nominated. May wasn't surprised. In the ensuing campaign, she "gave away cigars, hustled" and almost got elected.

Gradually the wealthy people of the Coeur d'Alenes moved to Spokane. Most of the Huttons' friends who had struck it rich already had business interests and palatial homes in that city. Al wanted to diversify his interests; May was ready to broaden her scope. They moved in 1907. Al immediately began work on the Hutton Block, a four-story business building on one of Spokane's busiest corners. Later three additional stories were put on to make it one of Spokane's tallest buildings. Al furnished a fine office for himself on the first floor and managed his ever-increasing properties and investments from there. One large section of the fourth floor was reserved for their own living quarters. Apartments were a new idea in Spokane; May liked the novelty of it and set out to make it as luxurious as "anything West of the Rockies." "No cost will be spared," she told reporters, who found good copy in this homely, fat, but extremely wealthy woman who was willing to talk anytime and willing to be quoted. "When I go to Chicago to buy furniture," she told them, "I will be staying at the home of my friend Clarence Darrow." May added that she also planned to shop in Cleveland, Boston, Baltimore and Philadelphia, and visit relatives along the way.

May got the apartment in order and immediately tackled the problem of women's suffrage in the state of Washington. The battle had been won in Idaho, but the Washington legislators still held out. May had made her own mark in Idaho, but in this new town, she was somewhat of a stranger; though a colorful person like May could never be quite a stranger since she had lived only 90 miles away. Gossip and news of her soon crossed the state border. Spokane, just emerging from rugged mining-camp status, had its high society, and May was aware that she would never be totally accepted. Conformity was not May's game, anyway. There were social injustices to be righted; there were people who needed her.

May found a children's home and started mothering the little ones who lived there. Al was interested, too. He had been an orphan and had great compassion for unwanted children. May was not content with supporting the home; she wanted to know why these children were there. Who were they? "May sniffed out the trail like a she-bear roaring through the woods looking for her young," wrote Montgomery. "The path through the urban forest led back from the orphanage to dance halls, cheap hotels and brothels, hired girls' rooms on the big ranches, and maids' quarters in the fancy homes on the fashionable first terrace." From these places May followed the trail to the Florence Crittenden Home for unwed mothers. Very soon she was on the board of directors.

May related easily to the young girls and to their babies. Fifty years before any social service agency or university school of social work came up with the idea, May understood the needs of the whole person. The girls should not be dismissed from the home without a job or a plan for their future life. Babies shouldn't be trundled off to orphanages. May knew there were plenty of lonely hardworking ranchers and miners who needed a wife. A baby would be a bonus. May had no intention of running a casual matrimonial bureau; she carefully screened every one. When she was convinced that things were right, she sponsored a wedding in her own apartment, complete with trousseau, minister, refreshments and presents.

May contributed generously to the children's home, and helped lift the mortgage on the Women's Club Cottage; she invested in a shoestore and gave away more shoes than the clerks sold. She cooked turkeys in her own kitchen and delivered them to needy families.

May's happiest recreation was the theater. She attended every road show, vaudeville, grand opera and Shakespearean play that came to Spokane. She sat in the most expensive box. The story is told that David Warwick, starring in *The Music Master* missed his lines when, glancing upwards at a tragic moment, he caught sight of the mountainous lady in a baby-blue gown, black lace mantilla, and remarkable pink-and-blue plumed headgear, who hung over the box rail sobbing audibly.

Beginning in 1850, bills were intermittently passed and rescinded giving the vote to women. When Washington was admitted to the Union as a state, suffrage was voted down. May picked up the torch, joined Susan B. Anthony and live-wire Oregon editor and suffragist, Abigail Scott Duniway and toured the state. She spearheaded the Spokane and eastern Washington campaign, but clashed with Emma Smith DeVoe, a paid national organizer from Chicago, who concentrated on Seattle and western Washington. DeVoe was cultured, well educated and committed to a program of winning the vote for women through education. May agreed on the goals, but her proposals for action were more immediate and dynamic. The two sections of the state were and are still divided geographically, economically and culturally. The two suffrage leaders were divided by philosophy as well as geography. May continued to support the movement with speeches and money and ignored the snubs. She wrote up reports for the Spokane press and rallied supporters in eastern Washington. Finally the legislators approved suffrage, but it had to be submitted to the voters, and it was Mrs. DeVoe who was appointed chairman to canvass the state. May and the Spokane area lost that round.

The Washington Equal Suffrage Association was to meet in Seattle just before the national organization met. May organized campaign contests and contributions to lead the large delegation from Spokane. She withheld all dues and names of delegates until the eve of the convention. The "Suffrage Special" train stopped in Spokane, where a colorful reception awaited the ladies. May and her fifty delegates boarded the train and left amid fanfare and cheers.

At the convention hall in Seattle, May presented her "credentials": 400 paid-up members in the Spokane area and 50 delegates ready to vote. The delegation was denied admission to the convention. May objected and asked why. The chairman of the credentials committee said that her methods of getting members were "reprehensible" and it was unethical to withhold dues and membership lists until two days before the convention was to begin.

Pandemonium ensued; Mrs. DeVoe alternately wrung her hands in despair and wielded the gavel. They called the police; two men came. The officers took one look at the mass of moving millinery and heard the babel of angry voices. They retired immediately to the comparative safety of the city streets.

Undaunted even by this setback, May rented a hall across the street from the convention center and led her eastern Washington delegation to organize a "rump" convention with herself as chairman.

When the National American Woman Suffrage Association actually convened two days later, both the eastern and western Washington factions demanded seats. In this dilemma, the national officers decided to seat both groups but allow neither to vote, so little could be accomplished except some questionable publicity.

May Arkwright Hutton was a power to be reckoned with. Though the Seattle trip backfired, May simply changed her tack and plunged on. She returned to Spokane and organized an independent Washington Political Equality League with headquarters in the Hutton block and herself as president. She continued to put her money and her energy into "the cause" hosting a dinner for 200 Chamber of Commerce men, giving speeches, and writing releases for the newspapers.

May knew that publicity was her best weapon, but she also realized that the job was more than she could handle alone and "that reporters were often smiling at her verbal lapses." To help her with publicity, she hired Minnie J. Raynolds of Denver. With this professional writer on deck, the Spokane papers were bombarded with news of the suffrage movement, both on the local and national level. May was still good copy; her sensational utterances often made it into print, and not only those about political issues. Sometimes it was fashions that raised her ire. About the new "tube" skirt, May was quoted as saying: "This risky gown foisted upon women by men designers should be boycotted. Women should refuse to buy the audacious, venturesome, undress contraptions which prevent . . . taking a forward stride literally and figuratively." Certainly May could not fit into a "tube" skirt herself, and anyway she still preferred ruffles and flounces. No amount of advice from her dressmaker could change that.

Not content with newspaper coverage, May sought other means of publicity. In one parade she rode on a float personifying Woman. With her were two animals from the zoo: one in chains and the other just looking stupid. Her emblazoned sign read: "Criminals and idiots can't vote; neither can women." She toured the state, spoke at schools, ran essay contests and planted trees.

Washington state passed its Equal Suffrage Act in the fall of 1910. With that goal accomplished, the suffrage organizations disbanded but not May's Washington Political Equality League. She rallied the members into a nonpartisan group with new worlds to conquer.

May was appointed to the Spokane Charities Commission. She sat in on meetings and listened to reports and requests for money. "Then as a self-appointed committee of one, she stormed into each institution, beat down excuses, flung open closed doors and raised a tremendous dust," reported a Spokane historian. There was no puttering around; May made a straightaway attack on the conditions she found. Her reports directly to the press raised havoc in city hall. The city jail needed a matron, she declared, and the ladies of Spokane offered to take turns serving. May said they needed a trained professional and that the city councilmen could find the money for a salary if they tried. They did. May barged through the county poor farm and other institutions and demanded action.

Each morning May sallied forth in their chauffeur-driven bright red Thomas Flyer. Only the rich could afford a car in 1907, and the Huttons took great pride in their machine. Al drove all over the Inland Empire when state highways were two parallel tracks with weeds growing between. May decorated the car and rode in the Portland Rose Festival. The Flyer was later replaced by a Chalmers, and then a Pierce-Arrow.

Through her contact with national leaders and her suffrage campaign, May Arkwright Hutton had become a person of political importance. Uncouth though she still appeared, politicians knew her to be wise and fearless. She broke completely with her old friend Teddy Roosevelt when he denied the suffrage movement by saying that "a decent woman's name should appear in the newspapers but twice—once when she marries and when she dies."

He soon found that "Hell hath no fury" like May Arkwright Hutton scorned.

May had been a Democrat all her life, championing the cause of the working class. In 1912, when the state of Washington had finally seen fit to allow women at the party convention, May supported William Jennings Bryan, whom she saw as the most progressive of all candidates. The old-line Democrats were annoyed with May, but they knew they had to reckon with her because all those feminine votes were crucial to any election. May made accusations of political intrigue, challenged the convention expenses and reported seeing one man stuffing the ballot box.

Four women delegates attended the 1912 convention in Walla Walla, Washington. May had a carefully prepared speech ready to deliver but the state convention leaders gave her no opportunity to read it. Her favorite candidate, Bryan, lost to "Champ" Clark, but May won an appointment to the National Democratic Convention in Baltimore. She said that she wanted the state of Washington to have the honor of sending the first woman delegate to a national convention, and there was no doubt in anyone's mind about what woman she felt should go.

May wrote later that Al's one admonition to her before she left for Baltimore was "Just don't make an unholy show of yourself." Outside the convention hall, May spoke freely and at length to other delegates and to reporters. Inside the convention hall, she was only given a chance to say: "Washington casts fourteen votes for Clark," and she really didn't want to say that because he was not her choice for the nomination. Socially her life was full as she again met the many politicians who had been her guests in Wallace and Spokane. The convention dragged on. May was finally released to vote for Bryan, but in the end had to switch to Bryan's own substitute candidate, Woodrow Wilson.

May returned to Spokane more tired than she had ever been. She worked on her scrapbooks. Over the years she had filled seven of them: clippings from newspapers, letters from important people and sometimes cartoons or jokes that had caught her fancy. An eighth scrapbook was added after her death and contains the newspaper stories from across the nation at the time of her death.

May and Al had a secret dream. They wanted to establish a home for unwanted children, but it was not to be an institution with one big building. Instead, the Huttons visualized a place in the country where little cottages with "mothers and fathers" would create a real home atmosphere for children. There were to be animals to love and care for and responsibilities for each child. Al bought a tract of land near Spokane, but the home was not to become a reality until several years after May's death. In her will she left all her money to Al with this final humanitarian project in mind, but her Ohio relatives descended upon the courts and contested the will. In order to get on with the building, Al bought them off with a gift of $175,000. The Hutton Settlement opened in 1920, and "Daddy" Hutton was almost a daily visitor. It was the great absorbing love of his last years, and to date more than two thousand lonely children have found in this quiet place a sense of belonging and individual worth.

Al had another dream: he wanted to build a beautiful home for May and he did. The mansion on Seventeenth Avenue in Spokane with its stately pillars had picture windows that looked out on the mountains. It was on a streetcar line, so their less affluent friends as well as their wealthy ones could come to their home. Two years after the Baltimore convention, the Huttons moved into the spacious hill-terrace home. May employed several "helpers." She never allowed them to be called "servants"; that was a demeaning term, and she didn't like it.

Next, May took up the crusade for peace. Europe was on the brink of war, and her own country could easily get involved. She spent hours at her desk, writing as always, though in a gentler tone. May's health was failing, and she could no longer be the militant crusader that she once was. But she was a recognized and influential woman whose words had weight.

May had scoffed at doctors who recommended fewer cherry pies and pork roasts and told them in strong language what she thought of that prescription. But now, at fifty-two, diabetes plagued her and she realized that she could no longer cope with the problem alone. She began to listen to the doctors; she tried every remedy she heard of "from Sassafras tea to Christian Science."

Combining her long time love of theater and her new campaign for peace, May sponsored theater programs, patriotic songs and even wrote "The Song of a Soldier Boy," which was set to music and featured in the theater which Al had recently bought.

As a last public gesture, May sat in a wheelchair and welcomed one thousand members of a Washington State Federation of

Women's Clubs to a reception on the spacious lawn of her home. With all the others, she signed a petition of Women for Peace to be presented to the President.

That day in 1915 when the Methodist minister conducted funeral services in the great drawing room with plate-glass windows overlooking the city, there were young girls with babies, rough miners, derelicts and famous people crowding into the house or standing reverently on the lawn. At the cemetery, the woman who followed May as chairman of the Democratic Club released a white dove of peace to fly away into the blue.

It was Drama to the last. May would have loved it.

Roberta Carkeek Cheney is the author of Names on the Face of Montana *and is Montana chairman for the National Place Names Society. Recently released from Naturegraph Press is her latest book,* The Big Missouri Winter Count. *Cheney is also co-author of four books:* Music Saddles, and Flapjacks, This Is Wyoming . . . Listen, Your Personal Writers Workshop, *and the Heritage Award winning* Hans Kleiber, Artist of the Big Horn Mountains.

In Western Writers of America, she has served as national president, awards chairman, contest judge, convention co-chairman, and executive board member. She is also a member of Wyoming Writers, of The National League of American Pen Women, and the Last Chance Gulch Corral of Westerners.

BIBLIOGRAPHY

Bankson, Russell and Harrison, Lester. *Beneath These Mountains.* New York: Vantage Press, 1966.

Fargo, Lucile F. *Spokane Story*. Minneapolis: The Northwestern Press, 1957.

Holbrook, Stewart H. *The Rocky Mountain Revolution.* New York: Henry Holt and Company, 1956.

Hutton, May Arkwright. *The Coeur d'Alenes: A Tale of the Modern Inquisition in Idaho.* Denver: Published by the author, 1900.

Montgomery, James W. *Liberated Woman: A Life of May Arkwright Hutton.* Spokane: Gingko House Publishers, 1974.

May's scrapbooks and the published and unpublished accounts by Lucile Fargo as well as histories of the Spokane and Wallace area made it possible for James W. Montgomery to write a fine, perceptive biography of this remarkable woman. *Liberated Woman: A Life of May Arkwright Hutton* preserves for all time a delightful picture of the woman who rose from camp cook to wealth and political power. With it is the history of her environment which both molded her life and was molded by her. The writer of this anthology chapter gives full credit to Mr. Montgomery and Ms. Fargo for most of the information about May.

The University of Montana Library had a photostatic copy made of one of the few extant copies of May's own book and made it available to the author.

Index

New Avon/Discus Titles

CATASTROPHE THEORY
Alexander Woodcock & Monte Davis   48397 $2.75

This vanguard book explains the catastrophe theory—a revolutionary new way of predicting sudden change—to laymen, explores the controversy surrounding it, and gives fascinating examples of how it can be used to understand problems in psychology, biology, politics, economics and history that affect everyone.

PRICK UP YOUR EARS
John Lahr   48629 $3.50

From diaries, drafts of plays, unpublished novels, and the recollections of those who knew Joe Orton—one of Britain's most promising playwrights of the 60's—John Lahr constructs a sensitive portrait of a man who was just beginning to taste the fruits of success when he was killed. 16 pages of photographs.

THE EXECUTION OF CHARLES HORMAN
Thomas Hauser   49098 $2.75

A young American in Chile accidentally stumbles onto the evidence of covert U.S. involvement in the overthrow of the Allende government—and is afterwards murdered. This is the chilling account of Charles Horman's last days—and of his family's determination to learn the truth about his death. "Reads like the scenario of a Hitchcock thriller."   *Los Angeles Times*

ECCENTRIC SPACES
Robert Harbison   49122 $2.50

Robert Harbison examines the interplay between our imaginations and the spaces we create for ourselves: gardens, rooms, buildings, streets, museums, maps as well as fictional topographies and architectures. "He has written the ultimate guidebook, for one can not only visit real cities, but imaginary ones." *The Baltimore Sun*

COCAINE: The Mystique and The Reality
J. Phillips & R. D. Wynne, Ph.D.   48678 $3.50

The most comprehensive work ever published on every aspect of cocaine. It examines in depth the history, pharmacology, trafficking, and socio-psychological effect of its use and abuse. It also captures the romance, excitement, and absurdity of the drug, tracing its role in the literature of Doyle, Stevenson, Sayers, and others; Hollywood movies; cultures from the Incas to the Nazis; and music from Harlem jazzmen to today's rockers. Avon Original

WILLA CATHER: A Critical Biography
E.K. Brown, Completed by Leon Edel   49676 $2.95
This biography traces Willa Cather's life as it was
illuminated by her art—from her life-long fascination
with Nebraska and the Southwest, where she found
the beauty and raw power that inspired O PIONEERS!
and MY ANTONIA, to the compelling religious experiences that influenced THE PROFESSOR'S HOUSE and
DEATH COMES FOR THE ARCHBISHOP. "All readers
of Willa Cather will rejoice in it."   *Chicago Tribune*

ERNEST HEMINGWAY: A Life Story
Carlos Baker   50039 $4.95
A major literary sensation and a national bestseller, this
is an eloquent, unflinching biography by Carlos Baker,
the foremost authority on Hemingway's life and work.
Illustrated with rare photographs. "This is the true
Hemingway."   *The Atlantic Monthly*

WOMEN AND SPORTS
Janice Kaplan   50260 $2.50
Packed with inspiration and information for the new
female athlete, this comprehensive guide covers all aspects of women in sports today—nutrition, competition,
psychology, physiology, the choice of sport, economics
and sex. "Immensely helpful."   *Publishers Weekly*

THE LIFE IN THE STUDIO
Nancy Hale   75721 $2.75
Eminent author Nancy Hale traces her childhood and
growth as writer in this intimate and insightful examina-
tion of the lives of her parents, both recognized artists.
"We are immersed in and captured by this private
world of artists."   *New York Times Book Review*

THE HUMAN USE OF HUMAN BEINGS
Norbert Wiener   50682 $2.95
A landmark in social and scientific upheaval, this is the
classic study of cybernetics, the science which explores
the unique set of communications existing between
man and his machines.

FUTURES: The Anti-Inflation Investment
Michael Geczi   75713 $2.95
Michael Geczi, Markets and Investments Editor of
Business Week, reveals in jargon-free language how
to safely make money in the most mercurial financial
arena in the world. Avon Original

Available wherever paperbacks are sold, or directly from the
publisher. Include 50¢ per copy for postage and handling:
allow 6–8 weeks for delivery. Avon Books, Mail Order Dept.,
224 West 57th St., N.Y., N.Y. 10019.

New Discus II 6-81 (2-A)

New Avon/Discus Titles III

NEW YORK'S OTHER THEATRE—
A Guide to Off Off Broadway
Mindy N. Levine with the Off Off
Broadway Alliance (OOBA)   77909 . . . $4.50

For out-of-towners or native New Yorkers, this first comprehensive guide provides all the essential information
for New York's other theatre—where to go, how to get
there, what type of production to expect, and even where
to eat nearby!

ADOPTION: *The Grafted Tree*
Laurie Wishard and William R. Wishard
                                    55640 . . . $3.50

This is a guide for everyone involved in an adoption, from
parents giving up their child, to adoptive parents, to adop-
tees searching for their "real" parents. "Concise, clear,
well-organized. . . . Essential reading for persons involved
in the adoption process." *Library Journal*

LIFE WITH PICASSO
Francoise Gilot and Carlton Lake   55475 . . . $4.50

LIFE WITH PICASSO is a revealing picture of the most
famous artist of the twentieth century, written by the
woman who was his mistress for ten years, and the mother of two of his children. With 32 pages of photographs.
"A completely fascinating volume, one of the most illum-
inating we have had on the mind and spirit of Picasso."
Irving Stone, *Los Angeles Times*

Available wherever paperbacks are sold, or directly from the
publisher. Include 50¢ per copy for postage and handling;
allow 6-8 weeks for delivery. Avon Books, Mail Order Dept.,
224 West 57th St., N.Y., N.Y. 10019.

Discus V (8-81)